The Alphabet of the Trees

The Alphabet of the Trees

A Guide to Nature Writing

Edited by
Christian McEwen
&
Mark Statman

Teachers & Writers Collaborative

New York

The Alphabet of the Trees: A Guide to Nature Writing

Library of Congress Cataloging-in-Publication Data

The alphabet of the trees : a guide to nature writing / edited by Christian McEwen and Mark Statman.
    p.cm.
  Includes bibliographic references (p.).
  ISBN 0-915924-63-3 (alk. paper)
    1. English language--Rhetoric--Study and teaching. 2. Natural history--Authorship--Study and teaching. 3. Natural history literature--Study and teaching. 4. Nature in literature--Study and teaching. I. McEwen, Christian, 1956- II. Statman, Mark, 1958-

PE1479.N28 A45 2000
808'.042'071--dc21

                                    00-041761

Teachers & Writers Collaborative
5 Union Square West
New York, NY 10003-3306

Cover art: *True Facts from Nature No 10 (Northern Leaves for Cy)* and an untitled painting of a leaf by Rory McEwen

Cover and page design: Christopher Edgar

Printed by Philmark Lithographics, New York, N.Y.

Acknowledgments

Many thanks to Romana McEwen for permission to reproduce six works by Rory McEwen. The painting on the front cover, *True Facts from Nature No 10 (Northern Leaves for Cy)*, is from *Rory McEwen: The Botanical Paintings* (Edinburgh and London: Royal Botanic Garden/Serpentine Gallery, 1988). The leaf on the back cover and the four leaves reproduced on pages x, 6, 238, and 312 are from Kenneth Koch and Rory McEwen's *From the Air* (London: Taranman, 1979).

Our thanks to Chris Edgar, for his editorial wisdom and for shouldering so many of our burdens; to Ron Padgett and Jordan Davis, for their spirited editing; to Moheb Soliman, for his work on the bibliography; to Nancy Shapiro, for her ongoing leadership and support; and to all the contributors for their fine writing (and willingness to revise it).

Christian McEwen's Acknowledgments
Many thanks to Kate Stevens, John Hofmann, Pru Grand, and Dot and John Fisher-Smith, who fed and sheltered me during an enormously tumultuous year. Thanks too to Ann Stokes at Welcome Hill and to the Macdowell Colony for their support. Love as always to Randy Kehler, Edite Cunha, Susan Davis, Simon Korner, and Maia for their patience, and to my mother, Bridgid McEwen, for remembering me in her prayers. Special thanks, too, to the following family and friends: Anabel Bartlett, Barbara Bash, Hosie Baskin, Lisa Baskin, Sarah Bauhan, Sarah Buttenhauser, Meg Davis, Anna Dembska, Chris Edgar, Robert Finch, Bea Gates, Janice Gould, Don Guttenplan, Andrea Hawks, Parker Huber, Terry Iacuzzo, Kim Jessor, Marion Kelner, Helene Kendler, Clare Walker Leslie, Maria Margaronis, Isabella McEwen, John McEwen, Barbara Mor, Pat Musick, Aina Niemela, Ron Padgett, Elaine Parker, Roz Parr, Susie Patlove, Ellen Pohle, Mary Clare Powell, Sarah Rabkin, Sue Riley, Jim Rosen, Joy Seidler, Yvonne Shanahan, Kathy Shorr, Michelle Spark, Alton Wasson, and my inimitable collaborator, Mark Statman.

Mark Statman's Acknowledgments
My thanks to Christian McEwen, whose idea this all was; to Kenneth and Karen Koch, to Suds and Mary Ann Elwood, and to Katie Porter, who bring me to the country, the river, the sea; and to my wife Katherine and son Jesse, for art, gardens, and baseball.

The work of Teachers & Writers Collaborative is made possible in part by grants from the New York City Department of Cultural Affairs and the National Endowment for the Arts, and with public funds from the New York State Council on the Arts, a State Agency. Teachers & Writers Collaborative is also grateful for support from the following foundations and corporations: Arts & Business Council, Axe-Houghton Foundation, Barneys New York (in memory of Jairrod Windham), Bell Atlantic Foundation, Bronx Borough President and City Council, The Bydale Foundation,

The Louis Calder Foundation, The Cerimon Fund, Chase Manhattan Bank, Con Edison, Ravenel B. Curry III Foundation, Duban Accountancy, E.H.A. Foundation, Herman Goldman Foundation, gURL.com, Heckscher Foundation for Children, Thomas Phillip Johnson and Jane Moore Johnson Foundation, The Janet Stone Jones Foundation, M & O Foundation, Manhattan Neighborhood Network, NBC, New York Community Trust (Van Lier Fund), New York Department of Cultural Affairs (DCA) Cultural Challenge, New York Times Company Foundation, Henry Nias Foundation, The Open Society Institute, Oppenheimer Family Foundation, Queens Borough President and City Council, Joshua Ringel Memorial Fund, Maurice R. Robinson Fund, Helena Rubinstein Foundation, The Scherman Foundation, and the Lila Wallace-Reader's Digest Fund. T&W's 30th-Anniversary Endowed Residencies are supported by Marvin Hoffman and Rosellen Brown, the New World Foundation, Steven Schrader, Alison Wylegala (in memory of Sergio Guerrero), and an anonymous donor.

Table of Contents

THE WEB OF LIFE

Preface

The poetry of earth is never dead.

—John Keats

*I can't even enjoy a blade of grass unless
I know there's a subway handy.*

—Frank O'Hara

In his essay in this book, Matthew Sharpe poses the question "What is nature?" to his students. Sharpe's students, like most, are pretty good at coming up with answers. They can identify different parts of nature: trees, grass, bees, eagles, sharks, apes, deserts, and so forth. They're familiar, too, with natural disasters: air and water pollution, the destruction of the rainforest, the hole in the ozone, and global warming. They can see beyond the sentimental idealization of nature as something always good, always pure, always Mother. They know that animals eat other animals, and understand that this is simply nature's way. And of course, they're also well aware of nature's own spectacular destructiveness, from volcanoes and hurricanes to tornadoes and tidal waves.

The problem most students seem to have is that they see nature as "Other." Nature is a tourist destination, a place on a map, something saved by buying and selling crunchy candy. They rarely understand that they themselves might actually be part of it. This became especially clear in one fourth grade classroom when a student wrote a beautiful prose poem called "The Nature around You is Family." The title alone generated an extremely interesting discussion. How could one even begin to consider bugs and plants as related to oneself? Many children would respond this way, no matter where they lived. But for urban students, thinking about nature is even more problematic. They're not used to understanding a city as an actual geographical place, or as being in any way "natural."

Such ignorance and alienation are not surprising. They have deep roots in Western culture. Nature, we read in *The Bible*, is something people are supposed to dominate:

> Then God said, "Let us make man in our image, after our likeness; and let him have dominion over the fish of the sea and over the birds of the air, and over the cattle, and over all the earth and over every creeping thing that creeps upon the earth...."

—*Genesis 1:26*

Technology also separates us from nature. With air conditioning and central heating, we're less subject to the changing seasons. Because of advances in science, we can now fly higher than any bird, go deeper in the ocean than any fish, move on land faster than any animal. It is hard for us to share the assumptions of the Inuit poem "Magic Words," in which human beings and animals are seen as equal and interchangeable:

In the very earliest time
when people and animals lived on earth
a person could become an animal if he wanted to
and an animal could become a human being.
Sometimes they were people
and sometimes they were animals
and there was no difference . . .

And yet that sense of there being no essential difference is at the cutting edge of nature writing today. Jack Collom, for example, sees nature writing as so broad a category that it practically transcends genre, and prefers to use the term "Ecology Literature." In similar vein, Gary Snyder goes back to the ancient Greek in rendering ecology as "Earth House Hold" (the title of one of his early books). Human beings and animals, rocks and stones and trees, are all part of the larger natural community, all part of one living, breathing planet.

Such an attitude is, of course, a world away from the the usual ideas of education. Many classroom teachers approach nature in one of two ways: either they emphasize the importance of scientifically proven fact (as in, "please study the life cycle of the boll-weevil") or they return to the comfortable sentiments that Ann Zwinger describes in her essay here as "sighing over how exquisitely dew drops bespangle a spider web at dawn." Often, they simply do not know how many other models are available. Practical considerations may also make it hard for them to bring observation and imagination together, or to move beyond the conventional emphasis on "Good Usage and Good Writing."

This book is an attempt to inspire teachers to move beond the more usual approaches, and at the same time to give them access to the many terrific resources that are available. The lessons described here are intended to be practical, to teach students to be attentive both to what they experience and to what they create. Put simply, by exploring the connections between observation and imagination, we learn a lot about writing. To quote Snyder:

Ordinary Good Writing is like a garden that is producing exactly what you want, by virtue of lots of weeding and cultivating. What you get is what you plant, like a row of beans. But really good writing is both inside and outside the garden fence. It can be a few beans, but also some wild poppies, vetches, mariposa lilies, ceanothus, and some juncos and yellow jackets thrown in. . . . Its connection to the wildness of language and imagination helps give it power.

The Alphabet of the Trees begins with Snyder's insightful essay "Language Goes Two Ways," from which the paragraph above is taken. We have divided the remainder of the book into five sections.

The essays of the book's first section, "Questioning Nature," challenge the reader to consider what nature is, how we view it and understand it, and how we feel both connected to it and estranged from it. Matthew Sharpe's and Susan

Karwoska's essays raise questions about the difference between stereotypes about nature and how we actually see it, particularly in an urban environment. Joseph Bruchac stresses the importance of asking students to be meditative and observant; he reminds us that "we were meant to listen." Sam Swope uses Wallace Stevens's "Thirteen Ways of Looking at a Blackbird" to help his students see outside their classrooms in new, multiple perspectives. Eleanor Bader's "Thinking Green: Writing the Advocacy Essay" anticipates times when a fiercer, more politicized response might be necessary. Kim Stafford's "Wild Child Words" reflects on the "importance—and the delight—of the adult scribe with the child observer."

The next section, "Close Looking," focuses on observation itself. The authors describe how their students go out into the field, go *to* nature and look at what is there. Their essays then elaborate upon the ways in which direct observation can lead to various forms of writing: from field journals to poetry, prose, and essays. John Tallmadge's "A Matter of Scale: Searching for Wilderness in the City" takes the reader on an eye-opening walk through an urban neighborhood. "A Pen and Paper and Breath of Air" by Mary Oliver gives us an inside look at a poet's field journal/notebook. Barbara Bash's "Birds in the City: A Field Sketchbook" is a visual narrative by a talented nature artist. Sarah Rabkin's essay "A Great Excuse to Stare" tells how she and her writing students learned from their interactions with a gifted drawing teacher. Clare Walker Leslie and Charles Roth discuss nature journals, showing how they can encompass many disciplines and styles of learning. Christian McEwen demonstrates how writing exercises based on the five senses can sharpen students' powers of observation and imagination. Suzanne Marshall takes her students outdoors, where they learn to see local flora and fauna with fresh eyes. Holly Masturzo's "With my Artist's Eyes I See" describes a writing exercise based on estrangement from nature that leads students to write imaginative poems. For Ann Zwinger's college students, seeing takes place first in the field, then in the classroom and the library, culminating in essays that reveal "the natural world as an inspiration and guide to good writing." Carolyn Duckworth's "Buffalo Journal" reminds us that the experience of observing and writing can spur another kind of awareness: of the connections between people, animals, and place.

The authors of the essays in the next section ("Into the Classroom") have invented writing exercises that take nature as a starting point; in this case, however, teachers doesn't need to leave the classroom. Most use models from literature. Mary Edwards Wertsch looks to Pablo Neruda's mysterious *Book of Questions* to inspire her students. Michael Morse describes how Wallace Stevens's "A Rabbit as King of the Ghosts" led his students to question the "relative nature of nature" and to experience a new kind of "discovery, growth, and change" by writing persona poems. A sense of perspective and personification is also important in Penny Harter's "A Delicate Web: Writing about Animals," which uses a number of different literary models, including John Haines and James Wright.

William J. Higginson enlightens us about the awareness of the seasons found in haiku, and discusses how haiku can be expanded using traditional Japanese forms of linked verse. Cynde Gregory asks her students to think about gardens while appealing to their sense of humor, and so guides them into writing. Jordan Clary examines nature imagery in *Beowulf* and other Old and Middle English poems, and discovers surprising connections with contemporary American cowboy poetry. Jack Collom's comprehensive "Ecosystem of Writing Ideas" offers a range of writers and writing ideas almost as diverse as nature itself—giving many practical nature-based poetry assignments along the way.

The diversity and interconnectedness of the natural world are the focus of the last section, "The Web of Life." Terry Hermsen opens with an essay that invokes the four elements, and asks his students to examine where earth, water, air, and fire exist in their own lives. For Margot Fortunato Galt, "Ecological concerns have no borders, and one of the greatest challenges facing us is finding ways to respect differences in our attitude toward nature and yet protect the natural world." Her two interlocking poetry exercises aim at helping students achieve such an understanding. Janine Pommy Vega also explores perspective and persona: she asks her students to choose something in nature with which they can identify, and then to write from that thing's point of view. Barry Gilmore's "The Naming of Things" also examines identity and diversity in inventive ways, including a playful exercise in which students write pieces that combine scientific (Latin) names with their common English counterparts. Finally, Carol Peck's "Prayers to the Earth" describes an exercise that has students explore the Native American understanding of "The Web of Life," and then re-consider their own.

The Alphabet of the Trees is intended as a practical handbook, an introduction to nature writing, nature poetry, and field work as well as a guide to some basic teaching strategies. As editors, we have done our best to make room for the juncos and yellow jackets as well as the more pragmatic vegetables. We do not doubt that teachers will be helped by the many useful ideas to be found here. As for their students—for whom nature is so often something "Other"—we believe the opportunity simply to listen, to observe, to write, and to draw will be especially valuable. "What thou lovest well remains / the rest is dross," Ezra Pound wrote in *The Pisan Cantos,* "What thou lov'st well shall not be reft from thee." Our world today is in recognizable jeopardy. If the up-and-coming generation is to help pitch in and save it, that effort will be grounded not in the shallow, scattered sound-bytes provided by the public media, but in the kinds of local knowledge and imaginative identification that are celebrated here.

—Christian McEwen and Mark Statman

For the Green Man, P. H., with love and thanks.
(C. McE.)

For Anne Porter
("The autumn crocus / Around the tool shed door.")
(M.S.)

The alphabet of
the trees

is fading in the
song of the leaves

the crossing
bars of the thin

letters that spelled
winter

and the cold
have been illumined

with
pointed green

by the rain and sun—
The strict simple

principles of
straight branches

are being modified
by pinched-out

ifs of color, devout
conditions
the smiles of love—

—From "The Botticellean Trees" by
William Carlos Williams

Gary Snyder

Language Goes Two Ways

LANGUAGE HAS BEEN popularly described, in the Occident, as that by which humans bring order to the "chaos of the world." In this view, human intelligence flowers through the supposedly unique faculty of language, and with it imposes a net of categories on an untidy universe. The more objective and rational the language, it is thought, the more accurate this exercise in giving order to the world will be. Language is considered by some to be a flawed mathematics, and the idea that mathematics might even supplant language has been flirted with. This idea still colors the commonplace thinking of many engineer types and possibly some mathematicians and scientists.

But the world—ordered according to its own inscrutable mode (indeed a sort of chaos)—is so complex and vast on both macro and micro scales that it remains forever unpredictable. The weather, for hoary example. And take the very mind that ponders these thoughts: in spite of years of personhood, we remain unpredictable even to our own selves.

Often we wouldn't be able to guess what our next thought will be. But that clearly does not mean we are living in hopeless confusion; it only means that we live in a realm in which many patterns remain mysterious or inaccessible to us.

Yet we can affirm that the natural world (which includes human languages) is mannerly, shapely, coherent, and patterned *according to its own devices*. Each of the four thousand or so languages of the world models reality in its own way, with patterns and syntaxes that were not devised by anyone. Languages were not the intellectual inventions of archaic schoolteachers, but are naturally evolved wild systems whose complexity eludes the descriptive attempts of the rational mind.

"Wild" alludes to a process of self-organization that generates systems and organisms, all of which are within the constraints of—and constitute components of—larger systems that again are wild, such as major ecosystems or the water cycle in the biosphere. Wildness can be said to be the essential nature of nature. As reflected in consciousness, it can be seen as a kind of open awareness—full of imagination but also the source of alert survival intelligence. The workings of the human mind at its very richest reflect this self-organizing wildness. So language does not impose order on a chaotic universe, but reflects its own wildness back.

In doing so it goes two ways: it enables us to have a small window onto an independently existing world, but it also shapes—via its very structures and vocabularies—how we see that world. It may be argued that what language does to our seeing of reality is restrictive, narrowing, limiting, and possibly misleading. "The menu is not the meal." But rather than dismiss language from a spiritual position, speaking vaguely of Unsayable Truths, we must instead turn right back *to* language. The way to see *with* language, to be free with it and to find it a vehicle of self-transcending insight, is to know both mind and language extremely well and to play with their many possibilities without any special attachment. In doing this, a language yields up surprises and angles that amaze us and that can lead back to unmediated direct experience.

Natural Language, with its self-generated grammars and vocabularies constructed through the confusion of social history, expresses itself in the vernacular. Daily usage has many striking, clear, specific usages and figures of speech that come through (traditionally) in riddles, proverbs, stories, and such—and nowadays in jokes, raps, wildly fluid slang, and constant experiment with playful expressions (the dozens, the snaps). Children on the playground chant rhymes and enjoy fooling with language. Maybe some people are born with a talent for language, just as some people are born with a talent for math or music. And some natural geniuses go beyond being street singers, mythographers, and raconteurs to become the fully engaged poets and writers of multicultural America.

The world is constantly in flux and totally mixed and compounded. Nothing is really new. Creativity itself is a matter of seeing afresh what is already there and reading its implications and omens. (Stephen Owen's *Traditional Chinese Poetry and Poetics: Omen of the World* speaks to this point.) There are poems, novels, and paintings that roll onward through history, perennially redefining our places in the cosmos, that were initiated by such seeing. But creativity is not a unique, singular, godlike act of "making something." It is born of being deeply immersed in what is—and then seeing the overlooked connections, tensions, resonances, shadows, reversals, retellings. What comes forth is "new." This way of thinking about language is a world away from the usual ideas of education, however.

The standards of "Good Language Usage" until recently were based on the speech of people of power and position, whose language was that of the capital (London or Washington), and these standards were tied to the recognition of the social and economic advantages that accrue to their use. Another kind of standard involves a technical sort of writing that is dedicated to clarity and organization and is rightly perceived as an essential element in the tool kit of a person hoping for success in the modern world. This last sort of writing is intrinsically boring, but it has the usefulness of a tractor that will go straight and steady up one row and down another. Like a tractor, it is expected to produce a yield: scholarly essays and dissertations, grant proposals, charges or countercharges in legalistic disputes, final reports, long-range scenarios, strategic plans.

Truly Excellent Writing, however, comes to those who have learned, mastered, and passed through conventional Good Usage and Good Writing, and then loop back to the enjoyment and unencumbered playfulness of Natural Language. Ordinary Good Writing is like a garden that is producing exactly what you want, by virtue of lots of weeding and cultivating. What you get is what you plant, like a row of beans. But really good writing is both inside and outside the garden fence. It can be a few beans, but also some wild poppies, vetches, mariposa lilies, ceanothus, and some juncos and yellow jackets thrown in. It is more diverse, more interesting, more unpredictable, and engages with a much broader, deeper kind of intelligence. Its connection to the wildness of language and imagination helps give it power.

This is what Thoreau meant by the term "Tawny Grammar," as he wrote (in the essay "Walking") of "this vast, savage, howling mother of ours, Nature, lying all around, with such beauty, and such affection for her children, as the leopard; and yet we are so early weaned from her breast to society. . . . The Spaniards have a good term to express this wild and dusky knowledge, *Gramatica parda,* tawny grammar, a kind of mother-wit derived from that same leopard to which I have referred." The grammar not only of language, but of culture and civilization itself, comes from this vast mother of ours, nature. "Savage, howling" is another way of describing "graceful dancer" and "fine writer." (A linguist friend once commented, "Language is like a Mother Nature of feeling: it's so powerfully ordered there's room to be ninety-nine percent wild.")

We can and must teach our young people to master the expected standard writing procedures, in preparation for the demands of multinational economies and of information overload. They will need these skills not only to advance in our postindustrial precollapse world, but also to critique and transform it. Those young learners with charming naive writing talents may suffer from the destructive effect of this discipline, because they will be brought to doubt their own ear and wit. They need to be assured that their unique personal visions will survive. They can take a deep breath and leap into the current formalities and rules, learn the game, and still come home to the language of heart and 'hood. We must continually remind people that language and its powers are far vaster than the territory deemed "proper usage" at any given time and place, and that there have always been geniuses of language who have created without formal education. Homer was a singer-storyteller, not a writer.

So, the more familiar view of language is:

1. Language is uniquely human and primarily cultural.
2. Intelligence is framed and developed by language.
3. The world is chaotic, but language organizes and civilizes it.
4. The more cultivated the language—the more educated and precise and clear—the better it will tame the unruly world of nature and feeling.
5. Good writing is "civilized" language.

But one can turn this around to say:

1. Language is basically biological; it becomes semicultural as it is learned and practiced.
2. Intelligence is framed and developed by all kinds of interactions with the world, including human communication, both linguistic and nonlinguistic; thus, language plays a strong—but not the only—role in the refinement of thinking.
3. The world (and mind) is orderly in its own fashion, and linguistic order reflects and condenses that order.
4. The more completely the world is allowed to come forward and instruct us (without the interference of ego and opinion), the better we can see our place in the interconnected world of nature.
5. Good writing is "wild" language.

The twelfth-century Zen Buddhist philosopher Dōgen put it this way: "To advance your own experience onto the world of phenomena is delusion. When the world of phenomena comes forth and experiences itself, it is enlightenment." To see a wren in a bush, call it "wren," and go on walking is to have (self-importantly) seen nothing. To see a bird and stop, watch, feel, forget yourself for a moment, be in the bushy shadows, maybe then feel "wren"—that is to have joined in a larger moment with the world.

In the same way, when we are in the act of playful writing, the mind's eye is roaming, seeing sights and scenes, reliving events, hearing and dreaming at the same time. The mind may be reliving a past moment entirely in this moment, so that it is hard to say if the mind is in the past or in some other present. We move mentally as in a great landscape, and return from it with a few bones, nuts, or drupes, which we keep as language. We write to deeply heard but distant rhythms, out of a fruitful darkness, out of a moment without judgment or object. Language is a part of our body and woven into the seeing, feeling, touching, and dreaming of the whole mind as much as it comes from some localized "language center." Full of the senses, as

Sabrina fair
   Listen where thou art sitting
Under the glassy, cool translucent wave,
   In twisted braids of lilies knitting
The loose train of thy amber-dropping hair;
   Listen for dear honor's sake,

> Goddess of the silver lake,
>   Listen and save.

—*John Milton,* Comus

Chill clarity, fluid goddess, silvery waves, and silvery flowers.

The faintly visible traces of the world are to be trusted. We do not need to organize so-called chaos. Discipline and freedom are not opposed to each other. We are made free by the training that enables us to master necessity, and we are made disciplined by our free choice to undertake mastery. We go beyond being a "master" of a situation by becoming a friend of "necessity" and thus—as Camus would have put it—neither victim nor executioner. Just a person playing in the field of the world.

Bibliography

Owen, Stephen. *Traditional Chinese Poetry and Poetics: Omen of the World.* Madison: University of Wisconson, 1985.

QUESTIONING NATURE

My heart in hiding
Stirred for a bird,—the achieve of, the mastery of the thing!

—From "The Windhover" by Gerard Manley Hopkins

Matthew Sharpe

Urban Nature Writing

for James Hairston, Betsy Pratt, and Joe Ubiles

"WHAT IS NATURE?" I asked a group of thirty or so seventh graders early one November morning. The air outside the classroom window was frosty, and the deciduous trees on West 48th Street in Manhattan were just about done giving up their leaves for the year. I added that I myself was not a scientist or science teacher, but I did have some ideas about nature, which I wanted them to join me in grappling with. Several hands popped up.

"Nature," said one girl, "is anything that's natural."

"Okay," I said, "so what's natural?"

"Anything that isn't man-made," a boy said. The rest of the class seemed to like that answer pretty well.

Someone said, "A tree is nature," and someone else said, "Yeah, but not if it's planted and watered by a person. Like Central Park is not really nature. It's like nature because it has trees and grass and flowers and everything, but all that stuff was put there by somebody, so it's not *really* nature."

This discussion began a ninety-minute lesson on urban nature writing that I taught as part of a twelve-week journal writing course for middle school students at the Professional Performing Arts School (PPAS) in Manhattan. The theme of the course was New York City. I met once a week with three classes— one sixth, one seventh, and one eighth grade—and every assignment I gave them had something to do with city life. I told the students that at the end of the twelve weeks, I would gather their writing together in a book that would constitute a guide to New York City from their own point of view, a document of what it's like to be a twelve- or thirteen- or fourteen-year-old living in one of the world's great metropolises at the end of the twentieth century. And I told them that I thought such a document would not be complete without a section on nature.

I don't think there's a special genre of writing called "urban nature writing" or even "nature writing" in the way that there is, say, a genre called "mystery writing." As far as I'm concerned, nature writing is any kind of writing on the subject of nature. So I didn't want to begin the lesson by teaching the students a particular technique of writing, but rather by asking them to observe and think about their immediate surroundings. I figured they could spend the first forty-five-minute class period thinking and talking, and the second one writing.

After some lively dissension and debate on the topic of whether Central Park was nature or not, I asked the seventh graders in what category they would put a building like the one we were in. "Definitely not nature," was the consensus.

I said, "What about a bird's nest?"

"Oh that's nature," someone said.

I said, "Well a bird's nest is not man-made, but it is bird-made. I mean, a bird makes a bird's nest—which is a kind of bird building—with the most advanced technology available to birdkind, right? So why does a bird's nest get to be nature while a brick-and-mortar school building doesn't?"

"Okay," a girl said, "if you want to talk about like a human nest or something then maybe a log cabin would be nature, but *not* a skyscraper. A school, I don't know."

Again the class was divided. Some felt that humans are entitled by the laws of nature to make shelter for themselves no matter what the shelter is made of, while others felt that a towering steel-and-concrete building was too far removed from the basic animal impulse of shelter-making to count as natural. What I was trying to suggest is that one could think about an urban center like New York City as a kind of teeming ecosystem; that cities, in other words, might be a natural habitat for humans and other urban-dwelling organisms.

"Okay, I have another question," I said. "If something isn't natural, what is it? What's the opposite of natural?"

"Artificial," one girl said.

I said, "What's an example of something that's artificial?"

"Polyester!"

"What *is* polyester?"

"Plastic."

"And what's plastic made of?"

"Isn't it made of oil?"

"And where does oil come from?"

"Dinosaur fossils!"

"Dinosaur fossils, hmm," I said, giving myself over to the role of Socratic investigator, aka pain-in-the-neck teacher. "Aren't dinosaur fossils natural?"

"Yeah," a student said, "but what they do to them when they make them into some ugly polyester leisure suit is definitely *not* natural." This shut me up for the time being.

Then one tall, elegant, and vocal girl named Rachel made an interesting leap of thought. If log cabins and skyscrapers and possibly even polyester are things that are natural because they are nature plus human ingenuity, then human ingenuity must also be natural. "Like when I was younger, me and my brother used to take all the remote controls in the house and use them as pretend telephones. I would hold the clicker for the VCR up to my ear and make like I was dialing a number and then I would go "br-r-r-r-ring, br-r-r-r-ring," and my brother would pick up the clicker for the TV and put it to his ear and we would pretend like we were having a phone conversation. So we were doing something that was part of nature because when children pretend, that's nature."

What Rachel said reminded me of an essay by the anthropologist Gregory Bateson in which he discusses the way that non-human mammals play with one another. Bateson says that these animals, when they bite each other in play, must have a way of signaling to one another that the bite is a fake bite, not a real one; otherwise they'd be fighting and not playing. I told the class this and added, "That means dogs have such a thing as 'make believe,' too, so even if you're one of those people who says nature is anything that's not man-made, you'd have to admit that pretending is natural."

"See what I'm saying?" Rachel asked.

"So maybe," I continued, "we can say that at least some of the ways humans change the world are natural, whether the change is physical—like using technology to turn some trees and mud into a log cabin—or mental—like using your imagination to turn a VCR clicker into a telephone."

*   *   *

The discussion in the sixth grade class I taught that day followed a different trajectory. The first twenty minutes were devoted to the differences between city and country, and what in each was natural or unnatural. A charming and opinionated boy named Massimo, for example, made a strong argument for buying "natural" toys for Christmas—that is, toys made one at a time from wood and cloth by trained craftspeople, as opposed to toys made of metal or plastic by electronic equipment on an assembly line. Then the sixth grade humanities teacher, Betsy Pratt, politely raised her hand and said, "There's one kind of nature that nobody has mentioned so far: human nature." The talk turned quickly to things people do to their own bodies. Most of the sixth graders were willing to concede that clothing and makeup and hair dye—though perhaps not green hair dye—are natural, while all of them were quite adamant that cosmetic surgery is crazy and gross and most emphatically unnatural. As I had done with the seventh graders, I encouraged these kids to consider as natural some of the things that didn't obviously conform to their ideas of nature—skyscrapers, for instance. But they found a place where they drew an absolute line between nature and non-nature. When people do something that is against nature by being destructive to nature, then what they are doing is clearly and unequivocally unnatural. The discussion that began with facelifts and tummy tucks moved from doing bad things to your own body toward doing bad things to the bodies of other people and other creatures, i.e., hurting the environment. In fact, the sixth, seventh, and eighth grade classes all agreed on this point: human carelessness with—and disrespect for—nature isn't natural. As one girl said, "Maybe a factory is natural because it's like an ant colony or something, but then if the people dump garbage and chemicals into the river that kill the fish, that's not natural."

I realize that by asking my students to consider the meaning of nature this way, I was running the risk of making nature mean so many different things that it would end up meaning nothing at all. But this was a risk I was willing to take, in order to encourage them to pay attention to the world around them, and to pay attention to the way they think about the world and the conclusions they draw about it.

The last thing I said was, "For the next seven days, look around the city, and whatever you notice that you think is natural, observe it as carefully as possible, because next week you'll be writing very thorough descriptions of nature."

*   *   *

A week later, I began the next session by handing out copies of the first paragraph of an essay by Joseph Mitchell called "The Rivermen." I asked one of the students to read it aloud to the class. (As I usually do, I asked the other students to circle any words they didn't know while they were being read to.) Joseph Mitchell was a southerner and a journalist who eventually made his home in New York City. In the middle part of this century he was a regular contributor to *The New Yorker* and developed an approach to nonfiction writing that combined the fact-gathering techniques of a reporter with the lyrical sensibility and ear for dialogue of a novelist. He was also an avid and delighted observer of urban nature, as this passage demonstrates:

> I often feel drawn to the Hudson River, and I have spent a lot of time through the years poking around the part of it that flows past the city. I never get tired of looking at it. It hypnotizes me. I like to look at it in midsummer, when it is warm and dirty and drowsy, and I like to look at it in January, when it is carrying ice. I like to look at it when it is stirred up, when a northeast wind is blowing and a strong tide is running—a new-moon tide or a full-moon tide—and I like to look at it when it is slack. It is exciting to me on weekdays, when it is crowded with ocean craft, harbor craft, and river craft, but it is the river itself that draws me, and not the shipping, and I guess I like it best on Sundays, when there are lulls that sometimes last as long as half an hour, during which, all the way from the Battery to the George Washington Bridge, nothing moves upon it, not even a ferry, not even a tug, and it becomes as hushed and dark and secret and remote and unreal as a river in a dream. Once, in the course of such a lull, on a Sunday morning in April, 1950, I saw a sea sturgeon rise out of the water. I was on the New Jersey side of the river that morning, sitting in the sun on an Erie Railroad coal dock. I knew that every spring a few sturgeon still come in from the sea and go up the river to spawn, as hundreds of thousands of them once did, and I had heard tugboatmen talk about them, but this was the first one I had ever seen. It was six or seven feet long, a big, full-grown sturgeon. It rose twice, and cleared the water both times, and I plainly saw its bristly snout and its shiny little eyes and its white belly and its glistening, greenish-yellow, bony-plated, crocodilian back and sides, and it was a spooky sight.

After we went over vocabulary, I invited my students to mention anything they noticed about the paragraph. "How old is he?" one girl in the sixth grade class asked.

"Well, he's dead now, but I think he was middle-aged when he wrote this. Why?"

"Because he seems like a kid."

"How so?"

"He gets so excited about the river."

"Where in this paragraph do you see his excitement?"

"He keeps saying 'I like to look at it' over and over, like he's a little kid or something."

I asked which of the five senses Mitchell invoked in this passage. One student said sight, noting the amazing description of the sturgeon. Another said hearing, because Mitchell hears the tugboatmen talking about the sturgeon. Yet a third said touch, because Mitchell described the river as "warm."

"Any metaphors or similes in here?" I asked. Someone suggested the word *drowsy* was a metaphor because water can't really be drowsy, only a person or animal can, which meant Joseph Mitchell was comparing the river to a person or animal without using *like* or *as*. I added that Mitchell used a simile when he described the river as being "unreal as a river in a dream."

Then I gave them their writing assignment: "Being as specific and passionate as you can, write a short description of something natural that's in New York City. Remember that people who read this might never have seen or heard or smelled or tasted or touched the thing you're describing, so help them out by appealing to any or all of their five senses. Also remember that similes and metaphors can help a reader to understand the thing you're writing about by helping them to understand *your* feelings about it, plus they can make a piece of writing more fun to read since they usually convey something about the personality of the writer." I asked one student in each class to repeat the assignment back to me so I could make sure that everyone understood. Then I fielded questions, many of which had to do with whether it was okay to write about a particular thing that wasn't what people usually thought of as nature. "Is sleep nature?" asked a sixth grade girl named Swan.

"What do you think?"

"I think so."

"I think so too." (See her description below.)

Five minutes into the intended writing time, a seventh grader named Chaz wasn't writing anything. I asked him what was going on. "I can't think of anything to write," he said. I asked him if he'd had any memorable encounters with nature.

Chaz, a burgeoning comedian and raconteur, began to describe his philosophical differences with his mother: "She won't even kill a cockroach because it's a living creature like herself. But then one time I was in the bathroom and there was this red lizard on the floor. Even I didn't want to kill that." He then explained how he gently swept the creature into a dustpan and put it outside the bathroom window, pantomiming his own fear and comically exaggerating the details of the story. I often find that kids who are having writer's block need little more than a few moments of personal attention from the teacher and a question or two about what's on their minds.

Following are a few pieces of writing produced by the kids at PPAS, together with my brief comments.

My Favorite Tree

My favorite tree is right in front of my apartment building in Manhattan. In spring, tiny buds open up fast, the first on my street, and sway carelessly, with a lazy feeling, in the cool, swift breeze. It looks prettiest then, unlike in summer. In the summer, the tree changes. It stands upright and still, as though it were glued into the ground. Often times, the tree stands there in the hot summers looking like it lacks water and air. As fall comes, the colors begin to change, and it starts to sway in the breeze again. For the last week of November, the tree looks like it is blazing with fire. The tree loses its leaves with every swipe the wind takes. By Thanksgiving, the first tree to have its leaves would be the first to lose them. The tree looks lonely without its leaves, so bare.

—*Izumi Miyahara, seventh grade*

I like how Izumi is alert not only to the physical details of the tree in front of her building, but to how those details change over time. She uses similes and metaphors to convey not only the way the tree looks, but also her own emotional connection to it. And she leaves us with the powerful image of the lonely, bare tree, reminding us that nature is not always a pleasant, regenerative force, but can sometimes be harsh and unsparing.

Sleeping

Sleeping is one of the best things I love to do (next to swimming). What I like about sleeping is . . . that it smells like fresh roses, it feels like I'm cool and I am in heaven, it looks like I'm in a garden with roses all around me, it sounds like children laughing all around me, it hurts when something bad happens in my dream, and it helps when I have good dreams.

Once I wake up it is very different from my dream. It smells like my sister's bad breath in the next bed, it looks like I'm sick and in bed, it sounds like my sister snoring, it hurts me that I'm not in Wonderland, and it helps me that I'm with my family.

—*Swan Echeadia, sixth grade*

The two things I like most about Swan's piece are the odd originality of the subject—given that this was a nature writing assignment—and the variety of sensory imagery, especially the smells. I also like the way she organized the piece, with one paragraph on sleeping followed by a contrasting paragraph on waking. But I do think her way of describing the different sensations of sleeping and waking was a little programmatic: if she had told the story of her dream rather than just making a list of things she smelled, saw, and heard, we readers would have a more complete picture of her dreamworld.

My Backyard

In my backyard I have an old, shattered, worn-down porch. When I stand up there and look down I see my cemented backyard, old and gray. I see the swings that hang down from the porch with the blue ropes just like this ink. They have white bottoms to sit on, like this page. One of them has a hard bottom and the other one has a hard bottom but flexible and rubber. Behind the cemented ground is my garden with all different kinds of plants, including the roots of my rosebush that hovers over the wood fence that separates my backyard from my neighbors', as if it is going to eat it. The thorns are short, thick, and SHARP. Next to the rosebush is the grapevine, which seems to be dancing, going in all directions, instead of eating the fence. Then there's the path that leads to the front of the house. . . .

On the other side of the garden is a patch of some kind of plant that grows short and green, with little white flowers in the middle. Next to the path is a pile of old, old logs that I used to pretend the pioneers collected to burn for firewood. And then there are the steps back up to the porch.

—*Emily Parson, sixth grade*

I like the big stones of Central Park. They thrust out of the ground like great jaws of a beast. I like the way you can climb up them, and stand on a ledge with the sun beaming on you, and you feel like a god. I like the way you can climb up their jagged rock and slide. I like the bike road that slithers down the side of the river, where I can stroll up the misty brownish water where it glops on top of the small, sandy shore full of soggy wood logs from the devoured dock that the water had eaten up. It smells. It smells like sea water—salty. You can also smell boat fuel from small motorboats. I love that smell, and the calming sight.

—*Charlotte Blythe, sixth grade*

*　　*　　*

In my ninety-minute lesson, I was mainly interested in getting kids to be attentive first to their surroundings, and then to the language they use to describe those surroundings. Since this was a journal-writing course, a descriptive passage of prose suited my purposes. But there's no rule that says you can't write a poem in your journal. So the next time I teach urban nature writing, I plan to ask my students to write a poem instead of a piece of nonfiction. As a model poem, I'll use "Millinery District," by Charles Reznikoff:

The clouds, piled in rows like merchandise,
become dark; lights are lit in the lofts;

the milliners, tacking bright flowers on straw shapes,
say, glancing out of the windows,
It is going to snow;
and soon they hear the snow scratching the panes. By night
it is high on the sills.
The snow fills up the footprints
in the streets, the ruts of wagons and motor trucks.
Except for the whir of the car
brushing the tracks clear of snow,
the streets are hushed.
At closing time, the girls breathe deeply
the clean air of the streets
sweet after the smell of merchandise.

One of the things this poem is about is how people who live in cities have their own unique way of experiencing a natural event like snow. Like the opening paragraph of "The Rivermen," "Millinery District" is abundant in sensory information. How do city workers know it's snowing? They "*hear* the snow scratching against the panes." How do they measure how much it has snowed? By how high the snow has piled up on the windowsills, and by how quickly the snow has filled up footprints and the tracks of wheels, and by how it muffles the usual sounds of the city. I like that opening simile, in which clouds resemble merchandise, and the way that the poem's last line seems to assert that if all you do is compare nature to merchandise, you're not being fair to nature.

My writing assignment would be:

1. Describe a very particular kind of weather (a snowstorm, a thunderstorm, a hailstorm, the first warm day of spring, the first cold day of autumn, a summer day of unbearable heat and humidity, etc.).
2. Describe how people in a very particular part of the city notice the weather and react to it.
3. Include, as Reznikoff does, at least one simile that compares something usually considered natural to something usually thought of as artificial ("the chunks of hail were as big as footballs").

Since I would be asking the students to write poems based on memories, I'd have them close their eyes for a moment before they started to write. I'd do this to help them remember details about what happened on the day of the dramatic weather event in question. Where were they? Who was there with them? What did the sky look like? Smell like? Sound like? Did anybody make any memorable remarks? How did they feel? They could then use these remembered facts as raw material for the poem.

*   *   *

I offer these few ideas—on how to lead a discussion on nature in an urban classroom and on how to give an urban nature writing assignment—simply as examples of one approach to a huge topic. I am not, as I said, a scientist or a science teacher. But a language arts teacher certainly could join forces with a science teacher to teach nature writing. A lesson on the Joseph Mitchell passage about the Hudson River could be combined with a lesson in marine biology, and a lesson on the Charles Reznikoff poem about snow in the millinery district could be combined with a lesson in meteorology. The nice thing about nature writing is that it links creative writing with science, and offers students an imaginative way to make a personal investment in scientific facts.

Bibliography

Bateson, Gregory. "A Theory of Play and Fantasy." From *Steps to an Ecology of Mind*. Chicago: University of Chicago Press, 2000.

Mitchell, Joseph. "The Rivermen." From *Up in the Old Hotel*. New York: Random House, 1993.

Reznikoff, Charles. "Millinery District." From *Writing New York: A Literary Anthology*. Edited by Philip Lopate. New York: The Library of America, 1998.

Susan Karwoska

White Clouds and the BQE

Using Children's Literature to Explore the Theme of Nature in the City

WHEN SPRING COMES to the neighborhood around the Brooklyn Navy Yard, it is not the spring described in most children's books. There are no fields of flowers, forests of green. The most obvious things in view remain unchanged: the elevated Brooklyn-Queens Expressway (known as the BQE) muscling its way through the middle of everything, the half-abandoned Brooklyn Navy Yard with its crumbling stone buildings covered in vines, the tall brick apartment towers next to a parking lot. These things dominate the view out the classroom windows at the elementary school where I worked for twelve weeks with a class of first, second, and third graders and their teachers. And yet the spring does come, of course, creeping in and changing everything, even those things that remain the same.

How do children in an urban environment experience and respond to these changes? What does nature mean to them? These were the questions I set out to survey during my spring residency at the school. I wanted to find out what these city kids knew about the world of nature, but I also wanted to explore with them, to open up their—and my—awareness of how these two worlds come together.

What I found is that the children who live in this neighborhood observe nature from a perspective that is not often reflected in children's literature about the natural world. In many children's books, outside is where you go to be by yourself, to get away from people. Being in the natural world is depicted as a contemplative experience. For my students the opposite is most often true. If they want to be alone, they stay inside. To be outside is to be social, watching the world go by from their stoops or playing in the park with friends. The presence of nature in the city, whether by accident or by design, serves to draw people together. It is also intertwined with the built environment: a park with trees and grass and benches and a basketball court, or peregrine falcons building a nest in a tower of the Brooklyn Bridge, high above the East River that borders the neighborhood. But the natural world can also be scary and strange for city kids.

"What is nature?" I asked the students on my first day there, a warm day in early February. "Nature? Ick, *disgusting!*" said a girl, a bright and outspoken first grader. "What do you mean?" I asked her. "Cockroaches!" she answered emphatically. "But what else?" I asked the students. Trees, they said, and grass, rocks, clouds, rats, parks. Within minutes our list had grown quite large, and it wasn't all "disgusting." But I wanted more details, so I asked them to look out the window and to record any signs of spring they see. Each week, at the beginning of class, we started the same way. Some of what they wrote was not particular to the city. They saw "flowers blue-ing" and "the sun making the grass grow." "You feel cool when you are in the shade," one girl wrote. Another boy said he saw "a rising in the sky." But most of what they wrote down showed an awareness of the natural world that was grounded in the changing rhythms of city life:

"It's spring because you can smell food."
"I see colors. I see streets. I see taxis."
"I see people in T-shirts."
"I see people working on buildings."
"I hear the cars going."
"I swim in the pool."
"Kids are coming outside."
"I see white clouds and the BQE."

Over the course of the next twelve weeks I asked my students to observe, to dream about, to imagine, and to remember the presence of nature in their city lives. Together, and with their teachers' help, we explored the intersection of these two different worlds. To generate ideas for their writing we did many exercises and projects together. We read myths, stories, and poems; went outside on a warm and windy spring day; examined objects from nature in the classroom; planted seeds and watched them sprout; collaborated on group poems; studied the view out the window; read about the animal inhabitants of New York City; observed the coming of spring to their neighborhood; and drew pictures. The students answered my initial questions with insight, honesty, creativity, and sometimes startling vision. Here are three of the class writing projects we did during our time together.

Looking Closely

We had spent the previous week's class taking in the big view out the window, so I wanted to spend some time during our next meeting studying just one thing up close. To prepare, I went for a walk in my Brooklyn neighborhood and filled a basket with objects from nature, some picked up from the sidewalk or snipped off a tree or plant, others purchased at the corner store: buttonballs from a sycamore tree, walnuts, a sprig of thyme, rocks, shells, a pussywillow branch, pine cones, forsythia branches, a mango, a kiwi, an artichoke, a pineapple.

The two books I chose to read to the kids that day were about looking closely and seeing with fresh vision. Both books—*Snow* by Uri Shulevitz and *Snowflake Bentley* by Jacqueline Briggs Martin—have snow as their subject, and as it turned out it was snowing lightly off and on all day, an early spring surprise. It gave the city a dreamy and excited kind of feeling, which is just what the two books evoke. The Shulevitz book starts by describing a city in winter: "The skies are gray. The rooftops are gray. The whole city is gray. Then, one snowflake." A little boy sees the snowflake. "It's snowing," he says, but the adults around him tell him, "It's nothing," "It'll melt," and other such things to discourage his excitement. But miraculously the snow doesn't melt, and instead covers the whole gray city—to the top of the buildings!—in a blanket of white. ("Now that's going a little too far," said one of the boys in my class, with delight.) As the boy dances along the snowy city streets, he passes a sign for Mother Goose Books and invites the characters there to come join him, which, with a smile and a bow, they do.

Snowflake Bentley is a good companion book to *Snow*. It tells the true story of a boy, Wilson Bentley, "who loved snow more than anything else in the world." The story takes place in rural Vermont, far from the city, but the passion for observation it describes is perfect for this exercise. The boy, Bentley, wants to find a way to preserve and study snowflakes and dedicates his life to this task. At first he tries to draw the flakes, but they always melt before he can finish. At the age of seventeen he acquires a special camera with a microscope attached, and, after over a year of effort, manages to get his first picture of a snowflake. As the years go by he continues to work in obscurity, making more and more prints. He finds that no two snowflakes are ever alike and takes great pleasure in capturing their fleeting beauty. He lives to see a book of his prints published, then dies weeks later from pneumonia contracted during a long hike in a snowstorm. The book pays homage to the tenacity and passion for beauty that guide Bentley and is itself a kind of poem to looking closely.

After we read the books I talk with the kids about all the different ways that snow and snowflakes are described. In *Snow*, "Snowflakes keep coming and coming and coming, circling and swirling, spinning and twirling, dancing, playing, there, and there, floating, floating through the air, falling, falling everywhere." Bentley thinks that snowflakes are "as beautiful as butterflies, or apple blossoms."

I take out the basket of things I've brought and set it on a desk in front of the class. They have been eyeing it—and wanting to touch the things—and can hardly wait to find out what we are going to do. I pull out the pineapple, hold it up, and—using an idea from Kenneth Koch's book, *Rose, Where Did You Get That Red?*—read to them from Wallace Stevens's poem "Someone Puts a Pineapple Together" to show the many ways Stevens describes a pineapple. They enjoy this a lot, though they ask for explanations of several of the lines.

Next I pull a beautiful deep purple eggplant from the basket and place it where everyone can see it. Many of the kids do not know what it is, but I tell them this doesn't matter. Reminding them to keep in mind everything we have just learned about ways to look more closely at things, I ask them to describe it to me in as many different ways as they can while I write their words on the board. Some of the kids want to describe the pineapple in their own words as well. This is what they come up with:

Eggplant

Gray, purple, burgundy, black
Shiny
It's wearing a hat.
A short, fat, juicy, ugly jellybean.
It grows on a plant.
It's from Ohio.
A fat man who says "Hey dude!"
Smells like a cucumber.
Feels like a tomato.
Gooey.

Pineapple

Pointy.
Green leaves coming out of the top.
Looks like it came from Hawaii.
Yellow inside, green outside.
It has circles on it.
Juicy.
A fat woman with a hairdo.

After this exercise I go around with my basket and let each kid pick out one of the objects in it. I ask the students to spread out around the room to keep their objects out of plain view as much as possible. After they have finished, I tell them, I will read each piece aloud and the other students will guess what it is that the author has described. They like being secretive, and this has the added benefit of quieting some of the more rambunctious kids, allowing them to concentrate on the task at hand. I give everybody a piece of paper with a list of questions on it, and ask them all to describe what they've chosen in at least five lines, using the questions as a way to think about what to say. These are some of the questions I give them:

• What color is it, exactly?
• Does it have a smell?
• What does the shape look like?
• If this thing were a person, what kind of a person would it be?

- How does it feel?
- What do you think it would taste like?
- Is it heavy or light?
- Where did it come from?
- Could you eat it?
- Does it remind you of anything?
- Where do you think you could find it?
- Is something going to happen to the thing or will it always stay the same?
- If you had to make up a name for this thing, what would it be?
- If it suddenly could talk, what would its voice sound like?

They write for a while, some kids spying to see what others have ("He's *peeking*, Ms. K.!"), some totally absorbed in their writing. After they have finished, I collect their papers together and then arrange all the chosen objects on a table at the front of the room. As I read each description, I ask the kids (but not the author!) to guess which object is being described. They like this part very much, and love hearing their own descriptions read and seeing the other kids guess. The kids come up with some great images. One girl says a clamshell smells "like foot powder" and would taste like "an old egg." One boy says an artichoke would "sound like a frog," and another boy writes that a sprig of thyme looks "like a skinny person with lots of arms."

Mango

Juicy.
Red, yellow, green, orange.
Egg shape.
Fat, juicy, soft, smooth, squashy.
Juicy sweet.
Light.
It came from Jamaica.
I could eat it.
It has a bump.
It grew on a farm.
It spoils.
If it had a name it would be Naquan and it would say, "Hey dude!"

—*Daquan Batts*

Artichoke

A fat, juicy person.
It's heavy, a little bit.
It comes from the ground.
It feels rough.
It has a smell.

It looks like a circle.
If it could talk it would sound like a frog.

—Joshua Murray

Thyme

Can I eat it? No.
Green and brown.
Leafy.
It looks like a string, like a skinny person with lots of arms.
It smells like a perfume.
Its voice sounds just like mine.

—Devonald Williams

Clamshell from the Ocean

It smells like foot powder!
If it were a person it would be a man.
It feels like a chair.
It would taste like an old egg.
It is not light.
It came from Ohio.
I cannot eat it.
I could find it in the sea.

—Tanonya Floyd

Pineapple

It's green and it has hair.
The hair is green and it's yellow inside.
It smells sweet.
It would have a sweet voice.
It is hard.
It is brown at the bottom.
It's so delicious!
It's long and short.
It will taste like sweet juice.

—Monae Ollivierre

Putting the Picture Together

In Sally Derby's book *My Steps*, a girl describes the passing of her days and of the seasons from the vantage point of her stoop. She talks about playing in the water from the fire hydrant, eating popsicles in the hot sun, lying on the cool cement or under the shade of a blanket-tent, sweeping leaves in the fall and shoveling snow in the winter. I like this book because it shows an awareness of the seasons that is filtered through the lens of city life: there are neighbors and strangers passing by, cars and buses going down the street, and sometimes there is broken glass on the steps that must be swept up. The seasons assert their presence in ways that are probably familiar to the kids I teach. In the fall the leaves make wet prints on the cement. In the spring the steps are "shady, cool and hard and smooth." I ask my students to think about how they see the seasons from their stoop, or from the front of their building, or on their morning walk to school.

Subway Sparrow by Leyla Torres also juxtaposes the natural world with the city in an interesting way. The story takes place in Brooklyn and is about four people—a young girl and a basketball-carrying teenager, both of whom speak English; a Spanish-speaking man in a fedora; and a Polish-speaking woman—and the way they respond when a sparrow flies into their subway car. When the story opens, each person is depicted sitting in his or her own world in a way that will be familiar to any rider of subways. The girl finds the bird first. As she tries to catch it, the others are drawn into the action, responding in their own languages, but being understood by the others nonetheless. After a number of attempts the Polish woman throws her scarf over the bird and the young girl picks it up. At the next station, all four exit the car with the bird and ride the escalator up to set it free. Then, in their own languages, they all say goodbye.

Both of these books carry the message that the presence of nature in the city is something that brings people together. Responding to the natural world makes us more human, more connected to each other, they tell us. I want my students to describe to me the nature that is a part of *their* lives, that surrounds *them*, and to use these descriptions as a point of connection for them. To do this we are going to make a picture-poem that brings all of their individual work together. I hold up a collection of cutout oak tag in the shapes and colors of flowers, the sun, stars, clouds, rain, grass, trees, the sky, and the moon—a collection of the celestial and the terrestrial familiar to any city kid. I ask each of them to choose one of these cutouts. When each of them is holding his or her selection, I tell the class that I want them to imagine that they actually are the thing they have chosen, the sun, or the moon, or the clouds, and from that perspective to tell me about themselves. To give the exercise some structure, I ask them to describe themselves using their five senses (they've been studying them in school), and to use a simile in each line. Do they know what a simile is? There are several guesses, but no one really knows, so I talk a little about the root of the word, how it is like the word *similar* and ask if anyone knows what *similar* means. They do, and we go on to a discussion of what a simile is. I read them a number of examples from various books, all written by students about their age.

Then, to start, we do the exercise together once. I ask them how they would answer these questions about the sun:

- How does the sun feel?
- How does the sun taste?
- How does the sun smell?
- How does the sun look?
- How does the sun sound?

Once we have done this first example together, the students get to work. I have them write their answers directly onto the cutouts (which are large enough for this). When they are finished writing, they come to the blackboard, where I've put up a large blank piece of paper, and tape their cutouts to the "picture" wherever they want. As more students finish, our picture-poem gets more and more developed, and sometimes students change the position of their cutouts as they see where other things are being placed. I like how Lamont, who had written about a kiwi in the previous exercise, and who claimed that piece as his favorite, uses a comparison to a kiwi in this piece. It is also interesting that the main thing that comes to mind, when he thinks of how a tree might smell, is "poison spray." Another student wants to write "about that brown stuff—dirt!!" and is disappointed that I don't have a cutout of it.

When all the students have finished writing and have contributed their pieces to the picture, we stop to admire the scene we have put together. Then each student comes up to the front of the class and reads his or her piece. Later, the teachers offer to find a place for the picture-poem on a bulletin board where other students can see it as well. The kids really enjoy the exercise and like seeing the picture take shape. They also take pride in having something to call their own at the end of the class, a piece of the whole that they can point to and say, "That's mine!" Here are some of their writings from this day:

The Flower

I look like a girl and a beautiful flower.
I feel good.
I taste as sweet as a mango.
I smell like air.
Air smells like summer.
I am as quiet as the sun.

 —*Meagan Bermudez*

The Tree

I look like a giant sticking my hands up.
I'm as hard as a rock.
I taste like a kiwi.
I smell like poison spray.
I sound like a bear.

 —*Lamont Howington*

The Rain

I look as white as paper.
I feel as wet as water.
I taste as plain as soup.
I smell as stinky as glue.
I sound as drippy as a faucet.

—Jason Uddin

The Rain

I look like an umbrella.
I feel heavy.
I taste like macaroni.
I smell like rice cooking.
I sound like drums.

—Ahmed Aridimini

The Sun

I look like a yellow wheel.
I feel hot as a radiator.
I taste like hot cereal.

—Daquan Goodwin

The Moon

I am as big as the earth.
I am as hard as hard trucks.
I taste like a potato chip.
I am as white as a white flower.
I am as big as a gorilla and a big car.
I taste like a big apple.

—Jony Kamal

Creation Myths

After we had spent a number of weeks thinking, talking, and writing about the place of nature in the city, I wanted to provide a way for the students to bring together their ideas on the subject. To do this, I decided to have them work together to generate "creation myths" of New York City, using actual creation myths from around the world as models. I am drawn to creation myths for several reasons. Young children—like the people of the ancient cultures that gave birth to these myths—lack the scientific knowledge to explain the world around them, and so must use what they know and imagine to piece together an explanation. But while ancient cultures strove to explain the movement of the sun, the phases of the moon, the rhythm of the seas, and the peopling of the earth, these kids have the wonders of the modern metropolis to explain as well. I want to explore my students' understanding of how such a magnificently complex place as New York City arose from the primordial ooze, how the natural world begot skyscrapers and steel bridges and the world with which they are familiar. Such explanations allow kids to see nature not just in her component parts—plants and animals, the weather and the seasons—but offer a larger view of nature as generative force.

To introduce my students to creation myths, I use a children's book with myths culled from cultures around the world called *Marduk the Mighty and Other Stories of Creation*, by Andrew Matthews. The stories in it are strange and wonderful and fascinating, and the students are intrigued by them. I tell them that these stories were thought up long ago by people all over the world to explain how the world and everything in it came to be. Each story is an imaginative evocation of what was here "at the beginning of the beginning," and of how the trees, rocks, plants, animals, humans, mountains, and all the things of the world came to be. The students and I talk about how the stories are full of wild things: dreams, lies, made-up things. "From the boiling of her fury," a goddess makes "a great army of monsters—scorpion-men, lion-men, and flying dragons." The darkness at the beginning of the world "made God's fingers cold when he touched it." The world is held together by a "rainbow snake" who "keeps very still, but if he twitches the land trembles in an earthquake." We talk about some of these wild details for a little while, and the students are curious about who made up these stories and when and where in the world they come from.

When we finish our discussion, I tell my students that we are going to make up our own stories about how New York City came to be. "You can use anything you want in your story," I tell them, "and you can make it as strange or extraordinary as you wish." I reassure them that anything they don't know they can just make up, as did the tellers of the stories we just read. We talk briefly about all the sources they can draw from: stories they've heard, things they make up out of their own head, dreams, things they've studied in school, things we've talked and written about during my time with them. They are free to use anything at all to tell the story of what was here before New York City was here, and of how the city—all of it, the buildings, the people, the cars, the trees, the animals, and the parks—came to be.

Next I split the class up into four groups. Two groups work with the classroom teachers and two with me. I ask the kids to dictate the story to me, and let each student speak whenever he or she has something to add. My role is to write down what they say and help facilitate the taking of turns. The kids are a little shy at first, but once we have a beginning they are surprisingly forthcoming with the details, and the words pour out of them faster than I can write them down.

The things they say are as strange and wonderful as the stories I read to them and often very funny as well. From time to time I ask questions, but for the most part they just talk and I write. I think the strangeness of the tales in the book opens up possibilities for their own stories. They riff off each other, and what they have to say opens a window on their own world. The natural world means "messes all over the place." It means God and Mother Nature. There is religion, natural history, and fantasy. There are ideas on ethnicity, and bits and pieces of the many things they know all mixed together. The tales they tell weave together nature and the built world, just as these things are woven together to form the fabric of their life in the city. This is the world I inhabit, these pieces say to us, and this is how it all fits together.

Here are the stories:

In the Beginning

In the beginning of the beginning the dinosaurs were the first animals in New York City. The T. Rex ate meat. They ate other dinosaurs. The volcano blew up and all the dinosaurs died. People started coming from heaven to live in New York City. They wanted to go places like a restaurant, a supermarket, basketball games, a beach, and a park. They really wanted to go to the movies. The people from heaven were friendly. They didn't have guns. They were happy and they liked to work. This is how they stayed out of trouble. People lived in nice tents and brick houses. They ate a lot of rice and beans, macaroni and cheese, and crabs with lobsters. They liked to let their food digest and then they liked to play with each other. Everybody had a computer in New York City and they could talk to each other. The people from heaven learned how to make drums, flutes, pianos, and guitars and they played them. They loved to play together. They played games on the computer. When they went outside it was hot in the summer and cold in the winter. The trees had bikes and money on them. People had to try and catch leprechauns because they had the gold. The little kids liked to go fishing a lot. They loved to go on trips. Everybody in New York City lived happily ever after.

—*Rasean, Ahmed, Jonathan, and Joshua*

In the Beginning

In the beginning of the beginning of the world there were dinosaurs and T. Rexes taking over the world. After the dinosaurs died, Joseph and Mary were the first people to live in the world and they had to live in caves. It was just caves and swamps and birds and squirrels. There was just dirt and messes all over the place. There were rats. There were footprints of dinosaurs and skeletons of dinosaurs.

People used horses instead of cars. The people wanted houses because if they built their houses out of wheat and straw, when it rained and thundered their houses would fall down and they would be homeless. God built the first building. It was a skyscraper. It was made out of wood and bricks and metal. God just put bricks, bricks, bricks, bricks, bricks, and bricks. The first people on earth that God made, those were the people that made the jobs and the skyscrapers. Mother Nature made the plants. She had magic and she made the seeds out of her magic. The dirt came from the old times when God was living in the world. It took a long time for God to make trees because he had a lot of things to make so he took his little time to make trees. After that he asked Mother Nature for advice. She said, "You know how we make plants and wood? Maybe they should be made out of wood. Other things are made out of wood. . . ." And that's how God made the trees. First there were these little roots and then these little roots, they grew as the days passed until they were big. Then some squirrels came along and made a hole and ate nuts.

God made the water by dripping rain down. Drip, drip, drip, drip, drip. The rivers got made by ice falling down and then the sun came out and melted the ice, and that was the river.

This is how the people came: First God figured out the colors like light skin and brown skin and black skin. After that he made a round circle and after that he made the body and the shoulders.

The people built New York City with bricks and bricks and bricks. They built the roads with bricks and cement. The electricity came from a thunderstorm.

—*Monae, Daquan, Dionte, and Shanise*

In the Beginning

In the beginning there were caves and dinosaurs. The trees were not as they are today. There were trees with stars and trees with coconuts. There were people but they lived in tents instead of houses. The ground was covered with dirt and sand. The great waterfalls turned into the rivers that surround the city today. The tents were made out of sticks, grass, and leaves. Leaf-eaters died when they ate the poison plants. Travelers used their bones to make the Brooklyn Bridge.

God sent people down to build the first building. They used cement and bricks to build a skyscraper. This was the first twin tower. God said, "Hey, that building is cool. Let's make another one exactly the same!" God sent another group of people to build the second World Trade Center building. The Statue of Liberty did not exist until mine workers dug her out of the ground. A pedestal was built to stand her on. She now stands for freedom, as the miners let her free from the ground. Medusa used her eyes to create Central Park. She pointed her wand down at New York City and said, "Let there be a large park!" Central Park was spreading day by day until it was large enough. A very large beaver used trees from Central Park to make Macy's Department Store. Using wool, cotton, nylon, polyester, and linen, clothes were made. To buy the clothes the people had to dig for silver and gold stones.

This was the beginning and all we know about the city.

—*Erica, Tameeka, Rashida, Lamont, and Jason*

In the Beginning

In the beginning of the beginning there were dinosaurs. There was nothing but dirt and flattened-out leaves from the footprints of dinosaurs. It looked like a desert.

There was no Brooklyn Bridge or George Washington Bridge or Statue of Liberty. There were only coconut trees. There were no people. There were no houses. Sometimes it smelled fresh, and sometimes it smelled nasty.

The dinosaurs ate poison plants and then they all died. There was an earthquake. The world was flat and a baboon made the dinosaurs laugh and they laughed so hard that they fell on the floor and rolled over and rolled off the earth.

The first building was built by God, and then Mother Nature made the flowers with her magic seeds. The first skyscraper was made out of wood. The first building was made by slaves. They made the roads by making mud out of dirt. They also used melted steel. They made the mud really, really sticky, and then they put cement on it to make it hard. The electricity came from static electricity, TVs, lightning, radios, and from the man who flew his kite in a rainstorm. They made cars with metal and tires and motors and paint and a paintbrush.

The people came from God and Nature. They came from Adam and Eve.

—*Devonald, Rose, Jony, Megan, and Rayshana*

I had to search hard for children's literature on nature that spoke to my students about the particular world they inhabit, but I believe these books were important to the success of these writing exercises. They offered the students a way to look at and talk about the natural world they knew—or could know— and thus helped them to move from generalities about things with which they had limited experience, toward a wonderful specificity: the sprig of thyme that looks like "a skinny person with lots of arms," the bridge made of dinosaur bones, the rain that "smells like rice cooking," and the flower "as quiet as the sun."

Bibliography

Derby, Sally. *My Steps.* Illustrated by Adjoa J. Burrowes. New York: Lee & Low Books, 1996.

Koch, Kenneth. *Rose, Where Did You Get That Red?* New York: Vintage, 1990.

Martin, Jacqueline Briggs. *Snowflake Bentley.* Illustrated by Mary Azarian. Boston: Houghton Mifflin, 1998.

Matthews, Andrew. *Marduk the Mighty and Other Stories of Creation.* Illustrated by Sheila Moxley. Brookfield, Conn.: The Millbrook Press, 1997.

Shulevitz, Uri. *Snow.* New York: Farrar, Straus & Giroux, 1998.

Torres, Leyla. *Subway Sparrow.* New York: Farrar, Straus & Giroux, 1993.

Joseph Bruchac

The Land Keeps Talking to Us

I wonder if the ground
has anything to say?
I wonder if the ground
is listening to what is said?

Though I hear what the ground says.
The ground says it is the Great Spirit
who placed me here . . .
The same way the ground says
it was from me human beings were made.

—*From a speech given by Young Chief of the Cayuse in 1855*

I. Listen

"Listen," the old man said.

He had his ear close to the leaves of a maple tree that overhung the deck of the cabin. Beyond us, a lake that had been as starful and dark as the night sky began to reflect the first sunlight of a long Adirondack day.

I didn't say anything. In the many years I'd known Swift Eagle, a Pueblo Apache elder who had come to live in the northern New York town of Saranac Lake where he and his family worked in a tourist attraction called Frontier Town, I'd learned that silence is the only way to answer such a command. A breeze came walking across the wide lake, a pattern of ripples approaching. Then as that small wind touched that maple tree, the leaves fluttered against each other, making a sound that reminded me of a gourd rattle.

Swift Eagle smiled. "It all just keeps singing to us."

As long as we remember to listen, I thought.

The land is always talking to us. It is just that most people seem to have forgotten to listen. It is how I start each day, and each day never fails to bring me something new to hear. This morning I stood on the deck of another cabin, one just over the ridge from the homestead in the Kaydeross Range where my Abenaki grandfather was born. It was a hazy June dawn and the sun was wreathed in cloud and paler than the crescent moon had been last night. It's the time of day when I usually hear the sharp, repeated whistles of the pair of red-tail hawks who nest just across Bucket Pond in the tallest cottonwood. They ride the thermals of our ridge in higher and higher circles, wings spread wide. Today I heard what might have been a mourning dove. But this call was longer, more tremulous, and it was answered by another call a quarter-mile or so away. The two lovesick owls I'd listened to late last night were still chanting to each other.

As a teacher of writing, one of the biggest ironies I have always faced is that of living in a society that is both fixated on sound—the louder the better—and increasingly deaf. It's pretty much a certainty that the average student, no matter how young or old, has never been aware of the dawn cry of a circling red-tailed hawk or the late-night throaty calls of great horned owls. And as far as paying attention to the song of the wind in the leaves, forget about it! Contemporary world culture continues to lay down layer after layer of interlocking noise, a blanket of sounds that cancel out each other and stifle the old awareness that all our ancestors shared of a living, breathing, communicating world beyond ourselves. There is so much sound, so much coming at us from radios, televisions, surround-sound movies, CD players and boom-boxes and public-address systems—to say nothing of the less patterned cacophony of the internal combustion, electrical, and jet engines that are everywhere above, below, and around us in our cities—that *not* hearing, shutting the doors of auditory perception, has become necessary to preserve some semblance of sanity.

But we were meant to listen. As more than one Native elder taught me, we were given two ears and only one mouth. As long as we possess that ability to hear, it is one of our primary means to learn from the natural world. Thus, helping students open their ears again to what the land is saying has become one of my primary aims as a teacher of nature writing.

You can start in a classroom, even one in a city. N. Scott Momaday, one of America's finest writers and the author of the Pulitzer-prize-winning novel *A House Made of Dawn*, knows how to do that. He has sometimes begun the first day of classes at the University of Arizona by standing before his students and saying—in his wonderfully sonorous voice—"*Listen!*"

Then he says nothing further. He just stands there. Within a few moments, the students begin to get restless. They're not used to silence. They grow increasingly nervous, some of them start tapping their desks, clearing their throats, unconsciously doing things to reintroduce that familiar atmosphere of random noise. It's a great way to make it clear to people how hard it is for them to be comfortable with quiet. It is, by the way, one of the traditional ways used by the people of the Pueblos to introduce a story. Speaking the word that means "listen" or a phrase that might be translated to mean something like "daybreak" or "dawn," initiates the quiet start of the new day when all things begin to look and listen once again.

You'll find that word at the start of Laguna Pueblo novelist Leslie Marmon Silko's book *Ceremony*. And when that introductory word or phrase is spoken, those who hear it then have the responsibility of supplying the silence within which the story will come to fullness. But if there is no silence, no space for it to grow in, then the story cannot be born.

II. The First Drumbeat

You can start it that way in the classroom, offering silence as a metaphoric smoothing of the ground—just as you might take a hand and sweep clear a patch of soft earth before drawing shapes in it with a stick. Remind your class that the first step to getting in touch with nature is to remember how to listen. (They're not learning something new here, just recalling something very old. All of them started as listeners, long before they spoke or touched the earth or breathed in the air. Before their birth, they listened to their mother's heartbeat all around them.)

Have them close their eyes and listen deeply, hear everything that is around them—or even within them. When you sit long enough in silence you may begin to hear the sea roaring in your ears, the rhythm of your own beating heart. Students will certainly hear some of those human-generated noises, maybe the hum of the fluorescent lights, the creaking of someone's desk, sounds coming from the street outside or from another classroom. Then, after a few minutes, have them open their eyes and write about what they heard.

This can be done in two stages. The first, the literal, is to have the students simply write down what they hear. The second is to use similes to extend their descriptions: to write what those sounds were like, what those sounds made them think of. At this point, especially with writers of junior high age or older, I may quote for them the following poem adapted from an Anishinabe song:

> I thought it was a loon
> but it was my lover's
> canoe paddle

III. Going Out

The next step, whenever possible, is to go outside. Here, too, as with accepting the possibility of being quiet, you'll be walking on new ground with most students. Not just those who've lived all their lives in the cities—to whom the forest is that place where movie-style monsters are lurking to tear them apart. (Have you ever seen a 250-pound high school football player turn and run in terror from a frog? And not a really big frog at that!) I'm also talking about many of those who are environmentally conscious, but spend half their time in the forest talking to the others on their field trip as they whip through the woods at warp speed.

Get them to sit down. Alone. Without talking. Leave them there with their pens and their notebooks. Eyes closed or eyes open, their job is to listen and to absorb, to accept whatever is about it be given to them and to acknowledge it with the words they put down on paper. Such a quiet sit can last fifteen minutes. Or it can be much longer. My son Jim, a writer and outdoor educator himself, often uses this technique. He sometimes prepares special groups to do such quiet sits, not just for a few minutes, but through an entire night.

Alone. Quiet. Without talking. Without a campfire or a flashlight. During the experience itself, the natural darkness precludes writing. The writing can be done with the return of the light. This all-night exercise is easy to describe, but doing it is not that easy. When you succeed, though, you are left with something that will be with you for the rest of your life.

IV. The Names of Things

Talking about onomatopoeia can also lead into a writing exercise that comes from listening. I begin by pointing out to students that many words in English and in other languages come from sounds in the natural world. Take the word for *crow* in Abenaki (and also in Iroquoian languages). It is *gah-gah,* spoken in a nasal voice. In a sense, the crow speaks its own name. So, too, does the sea gull, whose Abenaki name is *kah-ahk.* After having your students identify words in English that come from natural sounds, they can then try making up new words from the sounds they hear. Have them write down the sound of a bird song, the sound of a pine tree's breath as the wind shushes through it on a high ridge. They can collect a whole new vocabulary of words given them by the wind. Then ask them to write a poem making use of one or more of those new words. They might also try to do a "translation" into English from the language of nature. Say in your poem what the wind is speaking, what the birds or animals are saying.

Using words from another language in our writing creates effects that can have powerful resonance. I tried this more than thirty years ago when I was teaching high-school-age students in Ghana. We first did this by incorporating words from their native Ewe into their poems written in English. It woke them up—in a post-colonial education system that gave little or no acknowledgement to their own African culture—to the value of their own traditions. We ended up creating a whole book of their brief, haiku-like poems that sprang from the world they lived in, not the distant realities of *Tom Brown's School Days* (a required text!). Here is one by a young man named Rejoice Nanevie, a poem about *harmattan,* the dry, dusty wind that sweeps down from the Sahara:

Harmattan.
The thirsty beggar
walks down my spinal cord.

I also discovered how many words in Ewe reflect their origin. (Of course, words in every language always do that. In a great many cases, the more you learn about a word's roots, the closer you come to the earth from which it sprang.) I still use some of those Ewe words—as in this stanza from a poem of mine called "Crossroads Song":

> Ko-ko-lio-kwayyy—
> that was the rooster's song,
> his claws rattling the rusted tin roof,
> wings clopping, the opening eyelids of dawn
> rising over red West African hills . . .

Having young writers create new poetry by taking a poem in a language they don't speak and then "translating" it word by word is a technique first introduced by Kenneth Koch and Ron Padgett many years ago. This, though, is a bit different insofar as it takes into consideration the context in which those natural "words" were given to the listener. Whichever approach is taken adds vocabulary. Adding vocabulary is an effective way to build strength for a writer, especially when it helps that writer better hear those messages always being spoken by the natural world.

Listen. That's how to begin and end it. Listen.

Bibliography

Silko, Leslie Marmon. *Ceremony.* New York: Viking, 1977.

Sam Swope

The Blackbird Is Flying, The Children Must Be Writing

I

Among twenty snowy mountains,
The only moving thing
Was the eye of the blackbird.

First we went over some hard words—*pantomime, indecipherable, Haddam, lucid, euphonies,* and *equipage.* Then, as I handed out copies of "Thirteen Ways of Looking at a Blackbird," I told my fifth graders, "This is a famous poem written by an American businessman named Wallace Stevens. I'm telling you that so you know you can be a writer and still have another career." I said, "Before we discuss it, I want you to read it silently."

Thirty-six children put their elbows on their desks and leaned over the poem. I had been this class' writer-in-residence for three years and knew them well. They were a smart group, immigrants to Queens, New York, from over twenty countries, speaking eleven languages. Many were poor, their sights set on doctoring as the clearest way up the American ladder, and although they enjoyed reading and writing, most had the idea that math and science were the only subjects that really mattered.

Their classroom was crowded, not much space for anything but students, tables, and chairs. But it was a bright, tall room, at the top of a fat old schoolhouse made of brick and limestone. The room's windows started eight feet up the wall, so that even when standing you had to look up to look out, and all you ever saw was sky. It was like being in a deep box with the lid ajar.

Twenty snowy mountains. It was late January, but seventy degrees and sunny. We were hot. "El Niño!" cried my students. "Global warming!" What could they know of mountains and of blackbirds? The school had no recess, and when the kids were not in class, most were stuck in tiny apartments, forbidden to play in the city streets. (A handful had visited their native countries, where they ran freely outdoors, but that was only for a few weeks every few years. Mostly, their childhoods were spent in man-made environments, and "nature" was something they knew from books and TV.)

The room was silent as the children read.

II

I was of three minds,
Like a tree
In which there are three blackbirds.

The moving "eye" of the blackbird becomes the "I" that is the poet, the black-birds an unsettling metaphor for the poet's thoughts. Throughout this poem, Stevens juxtaposes the actual blackbird with the blackbird of his mind. At least I think that's what he's doing, but it's hard to know for sure. It's a fair question: Is "Thirteen Ways of Looking at a Blackbird" too difficult for fifth graders?

Kenneth Koch, a poet whose useful, entertaining books on writing poetry with children have earned him my gratitude and trust, describes in his book *Rose, Where Did You Get That Red?* the way in which adult poems can inspire children to write their own poetry. Koch uses poems by Blake, Donne, Whit-man, Lorca, Ashbery, and others, each providing an example of what he calls a "poetry idea." He makes a special pitch for "Thirteen Ways of Looking at a Blackbird," finding in it both a "gamelike quality" that is appealing to children and an obvious poetry idea: Write about an ordinary object in as many different ways as you can. This assignment was well suited for my yearlong unit on The Tree, and I hoped it would help my students approach our subject from new and interesting directions.

I waited for the children to finish reading the poem. One by one they looked up, faces blank. "Uh-oh," I thought. The less confident cast sidelong glances round the room, checking to see if others were as lost as they. I told them, "This is a difficult poem. Don't worry if you didn't understand it. But before we discuss it, I'd like to hear your first reactions."

Not a hand went up. Everywhere I looked, eyes avoided mine.

I called on Simon, a bright-eyed kid with sticking-out ears. Simon was the baby of a Dominican family, so lovable and so well-loved he never was afraid to say he didn't know. "This is like a college poem, Mr. Swope," he said. "Why'd you give us a college poem for?"

"Yeah!" said Angelo. "I didn't understand a word of it!"

"Yeah!" said Alex. "I thought I was falling asleep!"

Smelling blood, everyone perked up, eager to join an uprising—yeah! yeah! yeah!

"It's not a poem!"

"It's like a set of instructions!"

"Directions to see a blackbird!"

"It's a how-to thing!"

"It's got numbers!"

"Yeah, it's like so weird!"

I was of three minds: I am a rotten teacher; this is a rotten class; Stevens is a rotten poet.

III

The blackbird whirled in the autumn winds.
It was a small part of the pantomime.

Stevens's economy of language is impressive. In just two lines he moves us from a single bird to the whole sky. If this were a scene in a movie, the soundtrack would be silent as the camera tracked the bird, then gradually pulled back to reveal an autumn panorama in which the ever-smaller blackbird soared.

"Now I'll read the poem out loud," I said. "Just make yourselves comfortable and listen." I turned out the lights; the room went gray and dusky. Several students put their heads down. It's a marvelous thing, reading to children. My voice, Stevens's poem, blackbirds in the room. No one fidgeted, no one whispered, and when I finished, the poem hung in the air.

"Reactions?"

Students lifted their heads, rubbed their eyes. I called on Miguel, a polite boy whose mother had been a schoolteacher back in Ecuador. He smiled apologetically, sorry to disappoint.

"Come on, Miguel," I said. "What did you think of the poem when you heard it read out loud?"

"When you read it, it made more sense."

"Yes," I said. "In what way did it make more sense?"

He smiled and squirmed, nothing to say.

Sageeta, a thoughtful Indian girl with beaded cornrows, put it this way: "When you read something, you can't explain the feeling—it's the feeling you have, whatever you do."

"What do you mean, 'whatever you do'?"

"When you read this, it's a feeling. It gives you a feeling."

"What feeling?"

"I can't explain it."

Is this enough? To read a poem out loud, cast the spell, give your students a feeling, and move on? Not talk about what can't be talked about? Perhaps, but even if we say that sometimes the reading of a poem is enough, is "Thirteen Ways of Looking at a Blackbird" that sort of poem? I doubt it. If I had let it go, Stevens's words would have whirled in the room and vanished.

It's a tough poem to hold on to. It has no characters, no plot, no humor, no rhyme, no clearcut beat, no uplifting sentiments, and its pleasures are subtle, quiet, abstract, intellectual. Koch is right. "Thirteen Ways of Looking at a Blackbird" is a puzzle, a Cubist collage—precisely the kind of poem you get to know better by talking about it. But how to do that with a room of ten-year-olds?

Following Koch's advice, I focused on the poem's more accessible sections, then asked the children to write about a tree in as many ways as they could. Most came up with four or five separate thoughts, of which these are typical:

It looks like eyes on the trunk.
A stick with a beehive on the end.
I wish it was Spring so my tree could grow leaves.
A tree is a place that keeps people trapped inside.
You are the wall I hate that covers the sun when I'm cold.

I was both heartened and disappointed. They had gotten the poetry idea, as Koch promised, yet they hadn't written poems. To help them do so, I decided we'd discuss the poem line by line, but in small groups, and then, using Stevens's poem as a model, write "Thirteen Ways of Looking at a Tree."

Later, after I explained this assignment, Sageeta looked at me and said, "Let me get this straight: You want us to use all thirteen techniques, but with different words, and about a tree?"

"Yes, that's the idea, but if a section seems too hard," I said, "skip it. Make up something all your own."

"No, no, it's not too hard," she said. "No problem."

The world around the tree
Was hectic and moving
Yet it stood still
With a brave heart.

—*Sageeta*

IV

A man and a woman
Are one,
A man and a woman and a blackbird
Are one.

Here the style of the poem changes. In plain, declarative sentences, Stevens announces a spiritual idea of unity. We are all one. There's nothing more to say.

I met with students in groups of five or six. What a difference intimacy makes! One group was all boys, and by the time we got to this part of the poem, each of them was fighting to be heard. Simon, the boy who scolded me for giving them a college poem, was so eager to talk he couldn't sit still.

"Simon, please don't stand on your chair."

"But I want to say what section IV means!"

"Okay, what's section IV mean?"

"It means a man and a woman get married and become one because they love each other so they're not two separate people."

Cesar disagreed. "No, it means like the man and woman do like a matrimony and then they look at blackbirds and see the blackbirds do the same."

"But a man and a woman and a blackbird are not going to get married!" said Lorenzo.

"No, not like get married exactly," explained Cesar, "but birds, people, they do basically the same—"

"No!" said Simon. "He said that a woman and a man and a blackbird are one. He's not comparing them."

"Then what is Stevens doing with the blackbird here?" I asked Simon.

He went quiet for a moment, then he said, "It might be that that bird's their pet."

Everyone liked this idea. "Maybe they are bird lovers," suggested Lorenzo. "The man and the woman, they get married, so then they treat the blackbird like a child."

Cesar smiled, happy at that thought. "Part of the family," he sighed.

> You are one.
> So am I.
> But trees are part of us
> Also.
>
> *—Noelia*

V

> I do not know which to prefer,
> The beauty of inflections
> Or the beauty of innuendoes.
> The blackbird whistling
> Or just after.

I begged him, "Salvador, write! Write something! Try!"

He hadn't written a thing for months, rarely had his homework, and in class he couldn't sit still. Salvador was immensely confident, capable of unusual, interesting thought, yet he was also lazy and disorganized, angry and socially awkward. He often drew while other children wrote, but he wasn't very good at it, and what he drew upset me.

"May I see?"

Salvador had scrunched his drawing in a corner of the page. It was typically sloppy and mostly indecipherable. There were scratchy men with limbs that didn't bend, and there were guns and bombs. At least he had a bird, an eagle decently drawn, but even it was bleeding from the heart. There were blotches of explosion and lots of smudgy death, not the joyful ruin happy children draw, no flashing zigzag lines and gaudy colors.

"Oh, Salvador," I said. "Why are your pictures always so violent?"

He smiled, happy to be noticed, and continued drawing. We had had this conversation many times before.

"It worries me, Salvador. It makes me feel like you're not happy."

"Oh, I'm happy, Mr. Swope. I just like drawing violence, that's all."

I knew him well enough to say, "This picture makes me think you're going to grow up and be a mass murderer, Salvador, and I think you can do a little better than that."

Salvador giggled as he kept on drawing.

"Do me a favor. Stop drawing and try to write. Write at least one way of looking at a tree, okay? You can do this."

"Okay," he said, and cheerfully pulled out his writing folder.

> It grows big
> but he
> is small
> although
> big things
> are happening inside.
>
> —*Salvador*

There are no euphonies here, and even though his poem isn't perfectly clear, it has some interesting innuendo going on, a lot of promise. I gave it a *Good!!!*

But it's hard to know what I responded to—the poem itself, or the boy behind it; my student as he was, or as I wanted him to be.

VI

> Icicles filled the long window
> With barbaric glass.
> The shadow of the blackbird
> Crossed it, to and fro.
> The mood
> Traced in the shadow
> An indecipherable cause.

This section was a class favorite, with its prison made of ice, its menacing shadow, and its goosebumps sort of evil. Yet when I asked Soo-jung how she'd do something similar, but with a tree, she shook her head and told me that was hard.

Her classmates disagreed.

"I know!"

"Through the icy window—"

"The tree—"

"Or its shadow—"

"It looks like a monster or something—"

"Suddenly the wind blows and you see this branch—"

"And it looks like a hand—"

"Yeah, and you get scared—"

"And you see a UFO!"

As other children huddled round and spun this silly horror, Soo-jung sat in silence. She was often quiet, not always by choice. Sometimes she'd join in a discussion, then startle us by going mute, eyes looking out at me as from a cell. She couldn't speak, not even when she wanted to. No one could explain these strange and sudden silences, least of all Soo-jung. It was as if she were under a curse, and in a way, she was.

Soo-jung had emigrated from Korea with her parents at age four. Three years later her mother up and left. Soo-jung's father didn't tell his daughter why or where her mother had gone, and Soo-jung never heard from her again. This is the stuff that fairy tales are made of: abandoned daughters locked in towers, wounded birds and goblins dancing in a circle, "No one loves you! No one loves you!"

When you suffer as a child and have the blackbird's shadow in your heart, do you lose the fun of fear, the happiness of horror? Throughout the years I had her as a student, Soo-jung never once wrote of a happy ever-after. No prince ever rode into her stories.

We want to know our students, and knowing, try to help. I searched her writing, certain that I understood, but is her life, as I have told it, her deciphered cause? Am I so wise? Can I say I know this child so well I see into the window of her soul? What arrogance is that?

Soo-jung's only comment on this section of the poem was, "I don't like looking out an icy window 'cause I feel like it's destroying my eyesight."

"Because you can't focus?"

"Exactly."

The tree is an angel
That god sent down
To watch over the earth.
But in the winter
The snow covers its eyes
So it can't see.

—*Soo-jung*

VII

O thin men of Haddam,
Why do you imagine golden birds?
Do you not see how the blackbird
Walks around the feet
Of the women about you?

It's hard to look at the world and really see it.

To get the kids outside and under, on, and around trees, we traveled to Central Park once a month and spent the day there, observing, writing, and playing. One day we were outside, and the kids were drawing trees. I was watching Angelo, a skinny Cuban kid with shiny blackbird hair.

"Angelo, why are you coloring the tree trunks brown?"

"'Cause that's what color they are."

"Take a look around you. What color is the bark?"

He squinted at some nearby trees and said, "It's brown."

"No, it's not. It's gray."

"No, it's not. It's brown."

"Look!" I told him. "Use your eyes!"

Angelo looked again, and when he saw that I was right, he said, "I don't care what color real trees are. In comics, trees are brown."

Angelo's parents were divorced. To support her son and daughters, his mother worked six days a week as a receptionist. She was a kind, decent woman with a sad smile, and she always looked tired. She came to school several times, worried about Angelo. He didn't read books, was bored by school, didn't do his homework, hadn't tested well. All he cared about was comics and cartoons. What should she do?

"Buy him paper and paints and markers," I said. "Send him to art class."

"I don't want to encourage him."

"His comics are really good. Maybe he'll be an artist."

"That's what I'm scared of," she said. "An artist's life is very hard."

"It's scary, yes. But if he is an artist, there's nothing you can do. You won't change that. It'll be better for Angelo, and better for you, if you encourage him."

This made her sad.

"Don't worry, he'll be fine. I think he's got a gift. Besides, there's money in cartoons."

It was easy to see him as an artist type. Angelo was a loner. He was quiet and sensitive, quick to cry, but he had a rattlesnake temper when roused. He loved to dance. Although happy if I let him make a comic and not write, if I didn't, Angelo would make a comic anyway, drawing one in words. It didn't matter what sort of writing I got him to do—essay or story or poem—it was always a comic strip struggling to get out.

When Angelo handed in his "Thirteen Ways of Looking at a Tree," I asked him, "While you were writing this, did you glance at a real tree even once?"

"No."

I threw up my hands and said, "Angelo!"

"Heh, heh, heh," he answered, mimicking Beavis.

But Angelo was right, just following the master. I don't imagine Wallace Stevens sat on some old rock while writing of the blackbirds at his feet.

O crazy mimes of Staten Island
Stop giving free performances

to the tree, can't you see the
Tree is one of you, you mimes,
The Tree is a very still mime!

—*Angelo*

VIII

I know noble accents
And lucid, inescapable rhythms;
But I know, too,
That the blackbird is involved
In what I know.

In the beginning was the thump, screech, and grunt. Then came words, or was the whistle first? Long before our noble accents, back when speech was being made, what models did our early wordsmiths use? Where did the sounds of language come from—the whoosh of wind, a gurgling stream, the songbird warble? Somewhere lost in time did Nature help to shape our tongue, and so inform our thought? Is that what Stevens meant: "the blackbird is involved in what I know"?

I asked Fatma, a gloomy Pakistani child and the school's top speller, what she had made of "Thirteen Ways." She hadn't liked it: "The thing is, it doesn't say very much, but then you don't understand it."

Good point. Even when his words are simple, reading Stevens is like trying to understand a language you don't know very well. You have to do a lot of guessing.

But Noelia, a carefree Caribbean child, showed her gap-toothed smile and said, "That's why I like this poem."

"Explain."

"Because I didn't understand it!"

"But why do you like that?"

"Because I learn new things," she said. "And it's kind of weird."

"Weird is good?"

"Oh, yeah! Weird is def-i-nite-ly good."

Noelia loved the funniness of words, their boing-a-doing and tickle: "In-you-EN-doe!" "YOU-fun-knees!" But with Stevens I suspect she loved the word *equipage* best of all, and when I said, "That word is kind of fun to say. Let's say it all together," Noelia pogoed up and down and shouted out of sync, "Equipage! Equipage! Equipage!"

Later, I told this story to a friend of mine, a fan of Wallace Stevens and a poet. When I was done, she asked, "That's how you pronounce it? Are you sure that it's eh-kip'-ij?"

"No, I'm not sure," I said. "How would you pronounce it?"

"It's French. I think it's eh'-kee-pahj."

"My God, how stupid, yes, of course you're right." Whatever was I thinking?

But then I looked *equipage* up, and found we both were wrong. A French word, yes, but come to us by way of England, its Gallic murmur filtered through a Henry Higgins nose. It's ek'-wuh-pij.

> The hands of
> the tree
> reach for the
> sunlight
>
> —*Lorenzo*

IX

> When the blackbird flew out of sight,
> It marked the edge
> Of one of many circles.

If Stevens were my student, I'd have written in the margin: "Interesting image, Wallace, but I'm not quite sure what you're referring to here. What circles do you mean exactly?"

I think about my students. I can see them in my mind—or sort of can—the whole class in a circle, holding hands.

> When the
> tree shakes
> its arms
> I still see the
> mark
> left behind.
>
> —*Polly*

X

> At the sight of blackbirds
> Flying in a green light,
> Even the bawds of euphony
> Would cry out sharply.

I told each group, "I have no idea what this section means. Don't bother imitating it. Just make up something of your own. Now, let's move on."

I didn't understand the section, true enough, but that's not why I hurried to get past it. I wanted to move on because of the word *bawd*. I had looked it up, expecting it to mean "a libertine," but *bawd* instead means "prostitute."

It wasn't that I didn't think the kids could handle that. They watched TV, they flipped the bird, they spat out words both coarse and sexual. Some of them knew a lot more than they should. My worry was their parents, who didn't know how much their children knew (or half-knew, even worse) about the whores who nightly worked the nearby strip with all the garish lights. My worry was the school board and the armies of the right.

> I looked out my window
> And there the tree stood,
> Gazing into my eyes
> Like it knew something.
>
> —*Sageeta*

XI

> He rode over Connecticut
> In a glass coach.
> Once, a fear pierced him,
> In that he mistook
> The shadow of his equipage
> For blackbirds.

This one's fun. The glass coach crossing Connecticut is a nice touch, almost surreal, with the rider—I see someone noble—vulnerable, exposed, as though inside a bubble. Then the sudden fear, a gasp!

"How would you do that, but with a tree?" I asked one of the groups, and had them write.

Whip-smart Polly needed time to think, but not too much. That girl could get her words down quick.

> As I ride the bus
> along the road
> I see the tree
> moving but not
> me, am I crazy?
>
> —*Polly*

Yes! She'd even got the startle right, the shock we feel when things aren't what we think.

Polly came from Hong Kong, skinny as a stick, and everything with her was fast, fast, fast. On Field Day when the whistle blew, off she'd fly and leave the rest behind. In class, no sooner did I give a task than snap! she had it done—and neatly, too. And when it came to math, her hand shot up, the numbers figured out inside her calculator head. There's more: eager to grow up, she was the first to place a hand upon her hip, to roll her eyes and say to me, "Oh, please!" And long before the other girls, Polly played the teen and wore short shorts, her shirt-tails knotted up above her little belly button.

On parent-teacher night, she brought her mom and dad to school. They knew only Chinese, so Polly told them what I said. We spoke, her parents smiled and nodded, looked confused, and left. A topsy-turvy world, the daughter telling grown-ups how things are. There were a lot of things that Polly didn't know, of course, but what's a ruthlessly efficient girl to do? To be not lost, she grabbed whatever models she could find, and they were all around her: Spice Girls! *Baywatch! Titanic!*

To counteract, I offer Art. Yet what can any poem do—a match's flicker in Times Square! And though the battle's always hard, it's harder still with poems as strange as Stevens's with its winter thoughts, all mind, no easy heart. But maybe that's why Polly worked with it so well. Clever thing, she tackled it like math.

> Two birds on a
> tree. Two minds
> in one. As two
> minds in one
> thought.
>
>   —*Polly*

Brava! Not only had she understood the birds as metaphors for thought, but she extended that and made them metaphors for love. I told her, "Polly, this is really good. Profound, in fact, and beautifully expressed."

She said, "I got this idea from a commercial."

"What idea?"

"The two always stick together," she said and slyly smiled.

I didn't understand, but Polly swatted at the air and gave a huff and told me, "Never mind!"

Noelia turned to me and said, "It's from a toothpaste commercial, and part of it is tartar control and part is whitening, and together they are one."

XII

> The river is moving.
> The blackbird must be flying.

Jessica always thought too much, which made her stories so complex and so confused that the only way she could think to end them was to write: "To Be Continued!" And when she made her first attempts to mimic Stevens, her words were typically perplexing:

> The land was
> of five minds
> like my tree.

I said to her, "Don't think. Just write whatever comes into your head!" When our work that day was done, among the other bits she handed in was this:

My tree is so big
that no one
really notices.

Some days later, I read this poem to the class and Jessica cried out, "But that's not mine!"

"It has your name. It's in your handwriting."

"I'd remember if I wrote it."

I handed her her paper, which she studied, disbelieving.

"You wrote it, that's for sure, and good for you," I said. "That is a good poem."

Jessica looked surprised. "It is?"

"Yes."

"Oh!" she said, and beamed with pride.

Then she got to thinking, and later said to me, as if confessing, "That poem I wrote that you liked? I don't know what it means."

XIII

It was evening all afternoon.
It was snowing
And it was going to snow.
The blackbird sat
In the cedar-limbs.

There's a lot of quiet in this poem.

Earlier, when Salvador discussed the blackbird whirling in the silent autumn winds, he said, "I think what Wallace was trying to say is like the blackbird would make no noise when he was going through the wind and so he was like part of the stillness of what was around him."

"But if he was part of the stillness," said Maya, "he shouldn't be moving, right?"

"Stillness can also mean quiet," I said. "It doesn't only mean motionless."

"Oh," said Maya, dreamy-eyed, her straight black hair so long that it was like a cape.

I asked Tomás, "What is Stevens doing in the last section?"

Speaking softly, Tomás said, "It's the end of his poem, so it's gonna be like it's gonna be darkness, and it's snowing a little, but it was gonna snow more, so he has to go home."

"Why does the poet end with this simple image?"

"Because he probably doesn't want to write no more and so he wants to end it in a way that people can understand."

"Mmm-hmmmm. How do we know that it's ending?"

"He's saying it's evening and he has to go to sleep or something."

Sleep, perhaps, or maybe there is here a deeper stillness, the blackbird on the snowy limb a metaphor for death. Many children heard the poem's darker echoes, but Maya, who loved horror, reveled in them. "Isn't thirteen a dreaded number?" she had asked me with a hopeful smile. "Isn't black an evil color?"

"Yes," I said. "That's in the poem, too."

Maya was a model student with a peaceful, pleasant manner. When we studied Stevens, I did not sense that anything was wrong, and did not know that her favorite uncle had just died, or that her best friend in the class had recently betrayed her. It wasn't until sometime later that her mother called to tell me Maya was often overwhelmed with tears and cried out to her parents, "I want to die! I want to die!"

> As still as night
> as night is
> still
> The wind blows
> the bird chirps
> the dog barks
> but still
> the tree is still.
> The bark falls off
> but there is no sign
> of pain, or suffering.
> How can this be?
> No pain,
> no nothing that a
> human has.
> So giving
> and strong,
> nothing really
> in its way.
>
> —Maya

We worked with Stevens for two weeks. And then, at the end of a February day, several children read their poems to the class, and we said goodbye to blackbirds. Everyone was tired, yet everyone seemed happy. It was time to go home.

"All right," I said. "That was good. Thank you. That was very interesting."

When I asked Simon if he liked the poem now, his face lit up. "Oh, yeah, a lot!" he said, and others quickly cried out they did, too—oh, yeah! yeah! yeah!

Bibliography

Stevens, Wallace. *Collected Poems.* New York: Vintage, 1990.

Eleanor J. Bader

Thinking Green

Writing the Advocacy Essay

SCENARIO: For months you've been thinking about your upcoming trip to the seashore, a favorite site since childhood. You've been dreaming of the long walks you'll take and the sunbathing you'll do. Indeed, you can almost smell the salty mist as you let your mind wander.

The day of your vacation finally arrives, your car is packed, and you set off for your destination. Six hours later you emerge, inhale, and . . . a vile, sulfurous smell hits you in the gut. Shocked, you recoil in horror.

You now face several choices. You can get back in your car and return home; scream and yell at your nearest and dearest; organize a political response to right the situation; or take hold of a legacy popularized by such people as Allen Ginsberg, Audre Lorde, Henry David Thoreau, and Adrienne Rich, and write something to rile the masses.

Let's say that, after some hooting, stomping, and hollering, you ultimately decide to go with the last option. Where to begin? What to do? Before putting pen to paper or finger to keyboard, you should contact local, state, and national environmental groups and see if they are aware of the problem. You should also file a complaint with those agencies responsible for overseeing natural resources. That done, it is time to begin writing your agitational message.

Your first task is to choose a genre. While poems, fiction, and news articles can stimulate social change, an equally effective tool is the advocacy essay. Short, punchy, and direct, the advocacy essay or editorial can shift public opinion, sway lawmakers, and compel Joe, Jane, and the community to take action. In fact, a sustained editorial campaign can inspire the resigned and apathetic to act in their own collective interest—and win.

But how to do this? While there is no formula for successful advocacy writing, a few rules of thumb exist to guide your efforts:

• Keep your writing simple. Assume that your reader knows nothing about the situation. Explain, but do not condescend. Start with a statement of fact: What is the problem? Why are you concerned? Why should others share your worry?

• Your lead paragraph is the most important part of the essay. If it seems overwritten, muddled, or boring, you'll lose the reader and turn off the audience you are aiming to activate. Keep your opening statement free of hyperbole and rhetoric. The situation you uncovered at the beach is horrifying enough; you do not need purple prose to embellish its impact.

Staying with the beach example, you might begin with a description of the coast as you remember it from childhood. What did this particular locale mean to you when you were coming of age? What did you feel upon arriving a decade or two later to discover once-pristine sands overtaken by industrial fumes?

A word of caution: Most folks *will* be able to identify with your desire for a vacation, and your disappointment at finding the beach ruined will resonate. But be careful not to go on too long: there is a fine line between the personally compelling and the self-indulgent.

• A paragraph about your experience should be followed by a paragraph outlining how the situation affects the entire community. This section should be grounded in fact. Do the research needed to identify the chemicals that are fouling the air. Call the Environmental Protection Agency or other environmental regulators, speak to community activists, and dig for the history of the company or companies that are responsible for the pollution. Once you can prove the source of the problem, name names, but be certain that you can prove your accusations.

• Use concrete examples. Of course your personal experience is useful, but so are statements about the environmental impact of the sulfurous fumes on tourism, sea life, plants, and animals.

• Use statistics sparingly. A few numbers can go a long way in conveying urgency; too many, however, will put off even interested readers. In addition, when using statistical references, be sure to let the reader know the origin of your data. Most people trust authority and want to know that your numbers have been derived from a reputable, knowledgeable source.

• Use the words of experts to buttress your observations and claims. Before you start to write, you should interview environmental scientists, activists, community residents, and politicians—not to mention representatives of the corporation that is spewing the noxious chemicals into the air. Particularly with the latter, your goal should be to get a representative to say something about the company's environmental safety policies. If you can get a corporate spokesperson to admit something damaging about company practices, you will not need to indict the company; the spokesperson will have done the job for you. On the other hand, a well-placed "the XYZ Corporation had no comment" can also be damning.

Those of you who have never done journalistic interviews before should keep the following advice in mind:

• When scheduling and conducting your interviews, be as direct as possible. Tell the potential interviewee who you are and what you are doing (unless you are attempting to go undercover, a risky if gratifying prospect, but not one for the novice or faint of heart). Indicate approximately how long you expect the interview to last so that you can arrange a mutually convenient time for it. Anticipate a longer rather than shorter interview, since there is nothing worse than a rushed conversation that leaves both parties feeling hassled or misunderstood.

• Before you begin the interview, know the general areas you wish to discuss. Do not use the meeting to fish for information that is already available. If your source has been interviewed by the *New York Times,* for example, refer to the article. This lets him or her know that you are prepared, and affords you an opportunity to rectify anything that was previously unclear.

• Be flexible. Even though you have determined what you wish to ask, if your source says something unexpected, be sure to stay with the comment and ask appropriate follow-up questions.

• Don't be embarrassed to ask for clarification or elucidation and do not be afraid to ask the person to repeat an answer if you are unclear about it. People, especially those trying to hide something, sometimes speak in riddles to confuse you and get you off their backs. Don't fall for it. Stay focused and polite, but make it clear that you expect a forthright response. If necessary, rephrase the question and ask it again.

• Capture direct quotations when possible. It is a lot safer to use the person's actual words than it is to use a paraphrased summary. Although it is up to you to take notes or use a tape recorder, always call your source if you later discover that your jottings are unclear or if his or her comments seem to make little sense. Checking quotations is especially important when citing someone you are likely to want to contact again. People remember being misquoted and often hold grudges that are hard to undo.

• End all interviews by asking your interviewee if he or she has anything else to add. Be open-ended. Let your source ramble. Sometimes the best material comes out of unstructured time in which people are encouraged to tell their stories, to share their ideas, or to wax philosophical.

• As a finale, check the spelling of all names. As with misquoting, getting a name wrong is likely to ruffle feathers and tarnish an otherwise congenial relationship.

Once the fact-finding and interviews are completed, it is time to write your essay. Remember your goal—ending corporate pollution of the beach so that it can be restored as a vacation spot—and do not let yourself go off on tangents. Tell your story, then use statistics and quotations to flesh out the structure you have assembled. Someone from an environmental or public health group can delineate the long- and short-term health risks posed by the fumes; a corporate lackey can hem and haw, or offer a justification for the emissions; and Rick and Rosie Resident can provide a close, personal look at what it is like to live in a community riddled with toxic fallout.

Your essay should be short: 750–1000 words. If you find, however, that there is an abundance of material relevant to the issue, you might divide the data into several subject groups and write a series of editorials. This is also a way to keep the issue in the public eye and build support for a movement.

Lastly, if you opt to write an advocacy essay, be prepared to stay in the limelight once the editorial is published. Comments from the corporation you have criticized are likely, and you may need to engage in ongoing public debate until other people become actively involved. Use this time as an opportunity to hammer your objections home.

Endnote: Six months have passed. You return to the shore for a long weekend of rest and relaxation. You breathe deeply, letting the salt air into your lungs and throat. The sun smiles down on you and you search for the perfect rock on which to sit. A novel in hand, you begin to unwind. The beach is just as you remember it: beautiful, clean, and refreshing.

Kim Stafford

Wild Child Words

"DO LADYBUGS LIVE ALONE?" The stub of a boy looked up at his father, just as the ladybug in question, at the tip of his tiny finger, snapped open its wings and flew away.

Does this child think ladybugs are really little ladies, and prey to loneliness? Shall we explain that "lady" bugs may be male or female, and that they have been observed to mass together to survive the winter? Yes, let's explain all that, but first—*first*, let's write down the question that came from the child, to honor the child's curiosity, and to record the poetry of the error.

I know the importance of writing down exactly what the pre-literate child may say about the natural world because I was that child. That question was mine, and my father wrote it down: "Do ladybugs live alone?" The child observer and the adult scribe (or maybe a sixth grader and a younger sibling) can team up for one of the purest exercises of nature writing for both parties. The wee ones see things, and see things in such wonderfully oblique ways that anyone "skilled" enough to read this essay may find it hard, if not impossible, to remember what happens there, at the beginning. This is what the act of writing is for.

A Nez Perce friend once explained to me that she grew up learning native words for particular trees—not identified by species, but by that tree's particular situation. Of course, she said, there are Nez Perce words for cedar, ponderosa and lodgepole pine, alder, willow, and spruce. But there is also a vocabulary to describe an individual, regardless of the species: a word for the tree that lives by itself in open country—whether a pine, a cottonwood, or douglas fir; for the tree old enough to wear lichen on its bark; for the cedar old enough to give generously of its roots; for the tree "twins" that grow side by side. Such naming demonstrates the sophistication of the intuitive, which my own culture tends to diminish by more exacting ways of knowing. My body—crossing open ground—knows the particular beauty and importance and kindred feel of a tree alone there. Why doesn't my language have a name for that? I think an observer too young to know how to write might have such a name. Principles of the wild yet reside in the child, and part of fieldwork might well include attention to that font.

Do ladybugs live alone? What happens if an ant gets lost from the colony? What about a widowed goose? I still want to know. I brought that ladybug on my finger to my father, and asked about her sometime in the early 1950s. And today I have a record that I asked that question, because my parents had the habit of keeping a journal of what their children said, long before we could write on our own. By the time we were little writers, in fact, there was already a family book of what we had observed, thought, wondered, and said.

My parents called their book *Lost Words*, and it is one of the most precious volumes in the family library. Often we mangled the language, but our parents, both of them teachers and good observers of the learning process, simply honored our eager trials. They were scientists of the exact process of our learning, in nature and at home. They noticed that our utterance had the compact potential of a seed, but what amazing things might grow from that beginning? They saw us learning how to help our spirits survive—the spirit of enabling curiosity—as we played with words in the presence of tree, stream, and sky.

They say that if you observe young raccoons at the edge of a pool or stream, you may be tempted to identify their "instinct" for catching bugs and frogs and crayfish—anything that moves. But a more observant witness has suggested that the young raccoons may have an "instinct" simply to play: with a pebble, with a stick, with mud. And in the process of that play, if a polliwog, minnow, or grasshopper blunders into range, the young raccoons find that lively toy more interesting than the pebble, or stick, or mud. Polliwog, minnow, grasshopper. And so, in play, the little ones learn how to survive.

So it must be with our kind. Words in the mouth taste good. My father's first word was "Moon," a delicious one that began his career as a poet. His mother wrote it down. And so my own father and my mother kept track of what we said when we were small. They kept the journal that folded in the dreams, ideas, quick poems, and sayings of the little tribe, a notebook at the kitchen table to recall the catch of the day.

Like all children, we tried to puzzle out the way the world worked. My brother asked, "Does something ever look so pretty, robbers won't tear it down?" I asked one day, out of nowhere, "What do you do when your teeth catch on fire?" And my sister, "Daddy, why is God such a good boy?" And my brother again, explaining history to me: "First there was the cavemen, then Jesus, then Davy Crockett." These experiments with words are bracing explorations when you are very small.

When it came to the natural world, we tried to explain what we saw—both in terms of fact and of metaphysics:

The sky felled on the school ground.

—*my sister, age 2 (describing fog)*

You don't stand in the dark wind.

—*my brother, age 3*

We wanted nature to live in the house, and we wanted wild creatures to do what people do, so we could know what they know:

Let's make a hole in our house so a rat can come in and live.

—*my brother, age 3*

Why do birds always blow their whistles?

—*my sister, age 3*

Reading our tattered book, *Lost Words,* I am struck by the parallel between how I see the world through the eyes of these little ones, and what I now consider the playful sophistication of Native American story. In a Nez Perce creation myth, the trickster character Coyote can be childlike in his nonchalant exchanges between the human and natural worlds. Similarly, a sense of belonging in the natural world may be native to the very young. What happens to that common wisdom as we "grow up"?

I'll go outdoors and just keep on walking.

—*me, age 3 (when angry)*

I'm going to go jump in the daylight.

—*me, age 3 (when happy)*

Daddy, the birds could stay up all the time, couldn't they,
after everyone was dead?

—*my sister, age 4*

The child wants to understand the world, and its relation to family life. The parent or other listening adult wants to understand the child, and to regain some of what the child sees, to sense a kinship the child feels with the world outside.

Lakes are made out of water, but the ocean is made out of waves.

How old is a cow?

How much cloth would it take for a coat for a germ?

The rabbit is happy because he likes to see things happen.

I'd like to be a squirrel, and just live in this happy tree.

My culture often diverts such essential awareness in two directions. One is into the formality of science ("knowledge"). The other diversion is into the cartoon animal or the (sentimental) greeting card. But the child may see the whole living being. The child may wed the observational power of science to the intuitive kinship of what we used to call "primitive" people, but whom we now recognize as our elders, our teachers.

We're made of animals. We're made of monkey hands. We're made of dogs'
feet. No—we're made of cooney hands.

—*me, age 4*

Does our sky hook onto Donna's sky?

—*my brother, age 5 (when we moved away from his best friend)*

It is not simply that my brother died at forty that makes his utterances precious,
but also the sense that in childhood he was most purely himself. That time was
not a preparation for another time—for maturity, adulthood, profession, inde-
pendence—it was when he was who he was beyond anything we knew. And all
of us then expressed the core of our being in small ways:

The moon is melting . . . the moon is dying.
(Seeing the moon through mist)

Is God still working on the world? The worms help him, I believe.

See that family of trees going up the hill?

I'm going outside to get the nice feel of the night.

Daddy, you know what I like best? The world to be in. It's the best place.

When my own daughter first began to speak, I found myself alert to the
early babble of her words, and began compiling a book for her. Long before she
could manage every sentence correctly, she was delving into deep issues:

Papa, why the music is over?

I don't like bad times, I like our times.

I saw the bash men. They push you down, and don't give a hug.

Can we just go fishing this time all our life now?

Papa, we have a cuckoo clock instead of a television, right?

I really love the way you can impossible make things up on the piano.

Some people use their heads just to look, not to think.

Some people hit to say words.

She exhibited an early and sustained interest in exactly what happened before
her in the natural world:

I heard two robins in the night. They wake me oftenly.

Do ducks wobble along?

All of the birds crept out of their eggs and said, "Yay!"

A kiss lasts a long time on your face, but finally it's worn out and drops on the ground where worms clean it and take it to their children—then you need more kisses.

Dad, you're lucky—if you had no flowers, your house would only be searched by green.

The bumblebee is having a drink of water in the blue flower.
(Crouching to look into a chicory blossom)

We will see cows, and pigs, and the bee-light will blow the corn away!
(Preparing for a drive in the country)

What can that mean? Is she seeing pollen on the wings of bees, and remembering the wind? And once she announced, "Skunks blow their horns, and make suddenly smoke!" What helped her know so much in so concise a form?

One evening, as I worked in the garden at dusk, she came charging around the corner of the house, and made a long announcement to me:

Dad! I came to the Earth on a rocket, and you walked. Look! there are blueberries on this Earth. And look, a house! Let's go in it and see if there's a bed for me.

We went together, exploring our way into the house, back to the alcove with her bed.

There is! And a blanket!

Back to the yard she led me.

Look, raspberries! I love this Earth. It's the only one with magic. I sprinkled magic on the air and it made this Earth magic! All this stuff is new! The other Earth by Japan and Disneyland doesn't have magic. Would you like some magic? Here, put it in your pocket so it won't fly away. I love this one Earth. Can we live here forever?

This became what she called "The Earth Game," and for many nights after, we would go out into the yard after dark, shining a flashlight on one thing after another, exclaiming, "Look! a rose bush . . . a fence . . . dirt!"

I will never forget the day in my college biology class when my teacher, a distinguished research geneticist, made a confession. "The one thing I lack as a scientist," he said, "is the intuition of an eight-year-old. If I had that, along with my scientific training, the breakthroughs of our time would be mine."

How can we preserve that treasure—the inkling of a child, the insight, the integrating genius—as school buries our curiosity under a mountain of knowledge? It may be that the simple tool of the notebook, held by an alert parent or teacher while the young are babbling in the presence of the natural world, will be our salvation. My parents read us poems and stories, and they recalled in detail the magic of their own childhood rambles into the fields. And then they wrote down what we said.

CLOSE LOOKING

We are Nature, long have we been absent, but now we return,
We become plants, trunks, foliage, roots, bark,
We are bedded in the ground, we are rocks,
We are oaks, we grow in the openings side by side
. . .

We are what the atmosphere is, transparent, receptive, pervious,
   impervious,
We are snow, rain, cold, darkness, we are each product and
   influence of the globe,
We have circled and circled till we have arrived home again, we
   two,
We have voided all but freedom and all but our own joy.

—*Walt Whitman, from "We Two"*

John Tallmadge

A Matter of Scale

Searching for Wildness in the City

IT WAS NOT A HAPPY DAY when I learned that my family and I would be moving to Cincinnati, Ohio. A job is a job, and a good job even better. But Cincinnati? What wilderness lover would ever dream of living deep in the Rust Belt, downstream from places with names like Nitro, West Virginia? It was a long drive from Minnesota, every mile falling farther and farther away from the Boundary Waters where big pines still towered over virgin forests and lakes. At the time, it felt like hurtling into exile. But now, after ten years spent in the heart of it, I find the city a startlingly rich environment, a scene of instruction as fruitful as any storied landscape out of the classic nature writers. Reaching this point has been a long, fantastic voyage that has revealed, among other things, how much the sense of wildness depends on the scale of our perceptions.

Imagine a late winter walk—after a thaw, let's say, with ice still lingering in the gutters and the trees beginning to bud. The sweet air carries a scent of liquid water; the trees are full of sky, the lawns moist and earthy, smelling of damp straw. Overhead, cumulus clouds ride east on a buoyant wind that must have started out high in the Rockies and then swept onto the plains to rush unimpeded clear across Kansas, Missouri, and Indiana. My outspread fingers tingle at its touch, as if they could almost feel bare granite and sublimating snow. That's all it takes. For the next block I move as mechanically as a sleepwalker. My body may be in Cincinnati, but my mind has fled to high peaks and wide open spaces.

Later, brooding at the desk, it becomes clear that while we encounter wilderness "out there," we normally *think* about it "right here," that is, in the cities and suburbs where most of us actually live. The very idea of wilderness presumes the viewpoint of one immersed in civilization, gazing into the distance. Wilderness is a landscape of desire predicated upon a sense of loss, degradation, nostalgia, or incompleteness, all of which stem from daily life and work. The Wilderness Act of 1964 defines wilderness as a landscape where "the earth and its community of life are untrammeled by man [*sic*], where man is a visitor who does not remain." Such an area is required to contain at least five thousand acres, so that a person crossing it must have the experience of sleeping out. These ideas, contributed by pioneer wilderness advocates Aldo Leopold and Robert Marshall, reflect the belief that primitive travel in remote places can help us get back to our origins as precultural animal beings. Wilderness enables us to "evade for a while the clamor and filth and confusion of the cultural apparatus," as Edward Abbey says, in order to clarify our vision and ground ourselves on the bedrock of reality, "the bare bones of existence."

Like Thoreau, who challenged his readers to wedge their feet down through the slush and muck of opinion until they reached "a hard bottom and rocks in place, to say 'this is, and no mistake,'" wilderness writers have celebrated an ascetic process of stripping off the habits of civilized living. The landscape becomes a strict discipline conducive to mental health, and wilderness becomes not just a scene of recreation, but a "necessity of the human spirit," as Abbey says. No wonder, then, that we think of wilderness as something big, with big trees, big animals, and big scenery, a place of "mountains and rivers without end." It's a place largely free of people and their works. And it's far from where we actually live. Vastness, purity, and remoteness—such are the field marks of wilderness in our time.

Leaving aside the obvious objections—for instance, that Native Americans practiced land management for thousands of years, or that there's no place on earth untouched by human activity, as ozone depletion and alien species attest— this strict view of wilderness invites only momentary and romantic relations such as observation, travel, research, or vision quests. It is not conducive to dwelling, husbandry, or any sort of ethic grounded in participation, community, interdependency, or intimacy. That's because it encourages us to reject nature "right here," where we live, in favor of nature "out there," where we dream of adventures and visions. We face, it seems, an impossible choice between culture and nature, home and adventure, wildness and civilization. Small comfort to those who reverence both and aspire to what Gary Snyder prophetically terms a "practice of the wild."

But what happens when we adjust the scale of our perceptions in space and time? This is the sort of thing that writers can do, not just because of "poetic license" (which covers a multitude of sins) but because imagination is also a form of perception. Writing, like mathematics and quantum physics, can take us beyond the range of our senses, not just to create and explore imaginary worlds, but to expose the invisible dimensions of our own. To illustrate, let's step out my back door in search of wildness. It takes only three steps to cross the concrete patio; a half dozen more and we reach the edge of the lawn, pleasantly lumpy underfoot and blessed with flowering plants like indian strawberry, purple wood violet, and blue-eyed grass. Beyond the lawn are woods as lovely, dark, and deep as any jungle, especially at the height of summer, though in truth it's only forty feet south to the neighbor's yard or two hundred east to the city park with its soccer field. The woods offer an abundance of distractions, even in winter when the sky pours in and the light gets tangled in a chaos of wiry, expressive limbs. At such times it can certainly feel wild and strange, even remote. But can it compare to "real" wilderness?

Consider, first of all, the trees: at fifty years, they have not attained full growth though they tower above us—black tupelo, northern pin oak, shagbark hickory. In the old days, big animals like wood buffalo, black bear, elk, and wolves roamed here. Now, amazingly, we still have deer and coyotes coming through, plus raccoons and possums. Smaller mammals such as rabbits and squirrels thrive here, along with mice, moles, and chipmunks. As for birds, more than two dozen species have passed within a block of my house, from great blue herons and pileated woodpeckers to juncos, warblers, and house sparrows. Move down the scale and you find still more diversity and abundance. Hundreds of fireflies ascend to the treetops on hot June nights; crickets rasp and locusts whine all through July. Every seventeen years, millions of cicadas emerge from the ground to swarm, mate, lay their eggs in slits of tree bark, and die; the neighbors, grumbling, sweep up their husks like chaff. Turn over any rotting log or clump of decaying leaves, and you'll expose a host of wriggling invertebrates, some barely visible without a lens: thrips, centipedes, grubs, springtails, roundworms, annelid worms, and nematodes. A microscope would reveal even more, tiny crustaceans, mites and spiders, transparent rotifers bulging frantically into view, plus all kinds of protozoans, ciliates bumping along like barrels, flagellates whipping around, clots of blue-green algae, delicate meshworks of mycelia destined to fruit eventually as yellow honey mushrooms or red-capped boletes, perhaps even the gloppy plasmodium of a slime mold programmed—who knows how?— to gather one day into a bright, chrome-yellow dollop, soft as mayonnaise, on the surface of some damp, unassuming log. Not to mention, of course, the myriads of bacteria, many unknown to science, whose job it is to perforate, ferment, digest, and otherwise transform all the vast residuum and waste of "higher" life into the nutrients those very forms can use. Without them, the planet would be no more than a gigantic landfill, clogged with junk.

Interestingly, as we go down the scale, the living world becomes more prolific and diverse and thus less easily distinguished from what we would find in a wilderness. On a larger-than-human scale, the woods behind my house do not seem very wild, but at subhuman scales the sense of wildness increases until, when we reach the teeming metropolis of the soil, there's little difference. Perhaps that's why the great naturalist E. O. Wilson once declared that if he were to be reincarnated, he would like it to be as a microbial ecologist so that he could, among other things, take "Magellanic voyages" around the trunks of backyard trees.

Time offers the writer a similar venue for thought experiments with the sense of scale. Our Cincinnati landscape bears dramatic testimony to the Ice Age: moraines, changed drainages, canyons cut by meltwater, even the present course of the Ohio River itself. The ice stopped here on several occasions before retreating north as the climate warmed. A glance at the weather map shows that Cincinnati still rests on the isotherm between two climate zones; our winters seesaw between ice and thaw, wreaking havoc on city streets and concrete bridge abutments. Walk out the front door in January a few days after a snow and you'll find water running in the gutters, cutting small canyons in gray slabs of remnant ice. Up close, the ice resembles that found at the snouts of glaciers, congealed to a waxen uniformity by repeated cycles of freezing and thawing, studded with all kinds of sharp debris pried from the circumambient landscape—in this case, particles of sand and concrete lifted from the pavement itself as well as chips of wood and bark, seed husks, bits of broken glass, perhaps a bottle cap or twist tie (not to neglect the human world), or even a feather dropped by some passing bird. All these are first embedded, frozen in, and then released by scouring water, washed downstream, and eventually deposited in the elbow of a curve against the ice or else in a small delta fanned out on the lip of a storm sewer grate. Thus one can see, in the brief compass of a winter day, the same processes at work that created the vaster landscape over a span of tens of thousands of years. The seeds of future glaciations seem to present themselves at one's feet. All at once, time begins to lengthen out. It becomes harder to distinguish the present and future from the past. The landscape begins to shimmer, seems less permanent; its present "damaged" and domesticated state appears as little more than an eddy in the larger flow of climate, ecosystems, and advancing or declining species.

One need not imagine geologic epochs to appreciate how apparent wildness depends on the sense of time. Imagine a smooth granite surface in Yosemite's High Sierra—specifically, the top of Sentinel Dome. A crack has formed, and, over the years, it begins to fill with sand weathered out of the bedrock. Soil forms, and one day a blown seed catches in the crack and sprouts. A tree begins to grow—specifically, a Jeffrey pine. It hangs on for a hundred years, buffeted by prevailing winds, until its trunk extends like a twisted arm far out above the bare rock surface, while its twigs and needles bristle upward, stiff as a comb. One day a photographer—Ansel Adams—frames it at high noon against a dark horizon. In the remorseless light the tree looks totally exposed, no cover anywhere between it and the churning clouds. The awed viewer sees it as an icon of rugged individualism and endurance, like a climber achieving some first ascent by "fair means" alone. Its splendid isolation and tortured form seem an expression of character, as if its entire history were bodied forth. We think: This is what it means to be wild, to be in the wilderness and survive.

Now imagine another smooth rock surface—specifically, a concrete sidewalk in downtown Cincinnati. Soil has accumulated along a joint, and one day a ragweed seed lodges and sprouts. It grows for a hundred days, buffeted by wind and sun, gnawed by insects, beaten and bruised by passers-by. It is small, dusty-looking, of no more account to the casual eye than any of hundreds of other vigorous, opportunistic, and street-tough weeds that flourish like some green stain at the edge of the human world. By summer's end it too has attained an eloquence of form that testifies to a lifelong spirit of survival. Both plants are dead now, yet who can say that one was more wild than the other? Both lived out their allotted time, accumulating a history expressed in their very shape and so achieving character. The only difference is that the pine lived longer than a human life and grew in a place removed from human work. It therefore acquired an air of sublimity that Adams, with his art, converted into the radiance of an icon.

It is easier, I admit, to dream of remote and glorious places than to exercise the imagination upon the humble and near-at-hand. An icy gutter or a spoonful of garden soil cannot match the glamor of an Alaskan fjord or a tropical rain forest—unless you are willing to shift your perspective dramatically. Yet that is precisely what nature writers are called to do. By discerning the wildness in familiar things, they help the rest of us learn how to see the unseen. And that is the first step on the path to the world's healing.

Exercises for Writing about Time and Scale Using Urban Nature

1. Treasure Walk

Give each student a small pocket notebook, then proceed to the school entrance. Have them cross the threshold one by one and walk slowly around outside, taking note of everything new or surprising they see in the natural world. Ask them to wander as they like within a hundred feet from the building. Back in class, have them write from their notes. They can write descriptions of things they experienced, or tell the story of their walk. What did they notice growing, blooming, creeping, flying, scurrying—and how? What surprised them most? What did they feel? What was the high point? What would they tell someone else? What did they learn?

2. Power Spot

Take students outdoors—to a park, to a vacant lot, to the schoolyard—and ask them to wander around until they find a spot to which they feel attracted. Ask them to spend five or ten minutes each day at that spot, writing down what happens. At week's end, have them look for a story in their observations and thoughts. (This can be done alone, but is also fun to do in groups.) If it's not practical to visit the power spot during school hours, students can do this exercise as homework.

3. Giving Voice to the Voiceless (Gestalt Exercise)

Take the students outside. Ask them to wander about and find some object or creature that attracts them. Reconvene in a circle and have each student speak to the group as if he or she were that object or creature witnessing to its life, experience, reality. Example: "I am moss growing in a cushion at the base of an oak in the schoolyard. I am green and springy, soft to touch yet firm. I carry dewdrops each morning without breaking them. The sunlight makes me glow. Ants tickle me. Twigs fall without breaking me. Even in winter I never turn brown. I keep low to the ground but still reach for the sun."

This exercise has many variations. For example, try having each student choose a local plant or animal and write or tell its autobiography as if it were speaking, then respond to questions from the audience. Or, ask the students to describe the neighborhood (home or school) as that organism would experience it. I like to encourage students to choose creatures more distant from the human scale, such as insects, protozoa, lichens, fungi, herbaceous plants, or migrating birds. For inspiration, see Sally Carrighar's *One Day at Teton Marsh* (Lincoln: University of Nebraska, 1979).

4. Stories in the Land
Have each student research the history of the land on which they live (e.g., their home or their neighborhood), going back at least 10,000 years. Then write its story. Share in groups. For inspiration, see John Hanson Mitchell's *Ceremonial Time* (New York: Houghton Mifflin, 1984).

5. Ecological Powers of Ten
Have students pick spots; these could be their local power spots (see exercise 2) or any places they know well. Ask students to imagine how these places will be in five days, five months, five years, fifty years, five hundred years. Have students write these future histories and then share them in groups, discussing what lessons may be drawn.

Suggestions for Further Reading

Lueders, Edward, editor. *Writing Natural History: Dialogues with Authors.* Salt Lake City: University of Utah Press, 1989. An excellent collection of conversations with contemporary nature writers describing their practice and concerns.

Murray, John. *The Sierra Club Nature Writing Handbook.* San Francisco: Sierra Club Books, 1995. An instructive primer for aspiring nature writers.

Tallmadge, John. "Writing as a Window into Nature." In *Into the Field: A Guide to Locally Focused Teaching.* Great Barrington, Mass.: Orion Society, 1999 (Nature Literacy Series # 3). Techniques and exercises for using writing in place-based environmental education.

Trimble, Stephen. *Words from the Land: Encounters with Natural History Writing.* Salt Lake City, Utah: Gibbs Smith, 1988. A fine anthology of contemporary nature writing with a long introduction based on interviews with the writers in which they discuss their art and techniques.

Mary Oliver

Pen and Paper and a Breath of Air

FOR AT LEAST THIRTY YEARS, and at almost all times, I have carried a notebook with me, in my back pocket. It has always been the same kind of notebook—small, three inches by five inches, and hand-sewn. By no means do I write poems in these notebooks. And yet over the years the notebooks have been laced with phrases that eventually appear in poems. So, they are the pages upon which I begin. Also I record various facts which are permanently or temporarily important to me—when I first see certain birds in the spring, addresses, quotes from books I'm reading, things people say, shopping lists, recipes, thoughts.

Some of the phrases and ideas written down in the notebooks never make the leap into finished prose or poems. They do not elaborate themselves in my unconscious thoughts, apparently, nor does my conscious mind pluck at them. This does not necessarily mean that they are of a casual or fleeting order of things; it could be that they are seeds broadcast on a chilly day—their time has not yet come. Often I find the same idea will emerge through several phrases before it gets worked on.

I don't use the pages front to back, but randomly, in a disorderly way. I write wherever I happen to open the notebook. I don't know why this is. When the notebook is fairly full, I start another. In the spring and fall notebooks especially, there are pages where the writing is blurred and hard to read. Spring and fall are the rainy seasons, and almost all of the entries are made somewhere out-of-doors.

What I write down is extremely exact in terms of phrasing and of cadence. In an old notebook I can find, "look the trees / are turning / their own bodies / into pillars of light." In a more recent notebook, "the refined anguish of language / passed over him." Sometimes what is written down is not generally understandable at all, but is a kind of private shorthand. The entry "6/8/92 woof!" records for me that on this day, and with this very doggy sound, I first came upon coyotes in the Provincelands. Both the shorthand and the written phrase are intended to return me to the moment and place of the entry. I mean this very exactly. The words do not take me to the reason I made the entry, but back to the felt experience, whatever it was. This is important. I can, then, think forward again to the idea—that is, the significance of the event—rather than back upon it. It is the instant I try to catch in the notebooks, not the comment, not the thought. And, of course, this is so often what I am aiming to do in the finished poems themselves.

Who would tell the mockingbird his song is frivolous, since it lacks words?

❧

Do you think the wren ever dreams of a better house?

❧

Though you have not seen them, there are swans, even
      now
tapping from the egg and emerging
      into the sunlight.
They know who they are.

❧

When will you have a little pity for
every soft thing
that walks through the world,
yourself included?

❧

When the main characters of one's life die, is there any replacement? Or, is there anything *but* replacement?

❧

I hope I don't live to be a hundred
in the arms of my family.

❧

When you first saw her—beauty, the dream—the human vortex of your life—or him—did you stop, and stand in the crisp air, breathing like a tree? Did you change your life?

❧

The small deadly voice
of vanity.

❧

It's better for the heart to break
than not to break.

❧

Elly Ameling during a masterclass at Tanglewood, talking to a young singer: "No! No! No! Make it like peaches in your mouth!"

❧

All my life, and it has not come to any more than this: beauty and terror.

※

Something totally unexpected,
like a barking cat.

※

Sharpsburg: "One well-read member of the 9th New York wrote long afterward: The mental strain was so great that I saw at that moment the singular effect mentioned, I think, in the life of Goethe on a similar occasion—the whole landscape for an instant turned slightly red."
    —B. Catton, Mr. Lincoln's Army

※

The sword, after all, is not built just to glitter like a ribbon in the air.

※

But I want to say something more uncomfortable even than that.

※

"And then, who knows? Perhaps we will be taken in hand by certain memories, as if by angels."
    —M. Yourcenar

※

Molasses, an orange, fennel seed, anise seed, rye flour, two cakes of yeast.

※

Culture: power, money, and security (therefore).
Art: hope, vision, the soul's need to speak.

※

All culture developed as some wild, raw creature strived to live better and longer.

※

Dreams don't have time/space constriction. Of course, in a way Adam naming the things of this world was narrowing his horizons.
Perhaps dreaming is meditating, before language existed. Animals certainly dream.

※

Language, the tool of consciousness.

※

The line is the device upon which the poem spins itself into being. Verse, versus, *vers*, turn the plough, turn the line. It is impossible to measure the frustration I feel when, after making careful decisions about where the lines should turn, an editor snaps off the long limbs to fit some magazine's column-girth or print-line.

❧

Who are you? They called out, at the edge of the village.
I am one of you, the poet called back.
Though he was dressed like the wind, though he looked like
a waterfall.

❧

F. has been to visit us, and now he is gone. The power of last resort, is the power to disrupt.

❧

M. arranging the curtains in the next room. "Hello there, darling moon," I hear her say.

❧

If you kill for knowledge, what is the name of what you have lost?

❧

The danger of people becoming infatuated with knowledge. Thoreau gassing the moth to get a perfect specimen. Audubon pushing the needle into the bittern's heart.

❧

I took the fox bones back into the dunes and buried them. I don't want to hold on to such things anymore. I mean, I'm certainly full of admiration, and curiosity. But I think something else—a reverence that disavows keeping things—must come to us all, sooner or later. Like a gift, an understanding, a more happy excitement than possession. Or, of a sudden—too late!—like a stone between the eyes.

❧

Everybody has to have their little tooth of power.
Everybody wants to be able to bite.

❧

About poems that don't work—who wants to see a bird almost fly?

❧

With what sugar in your voice would you persuade
the beach plum
to hurry?

❧

After a cruel childhood, one must reinvent oneself.
Then reimagine the world.

❧

van Gogh—he considered everything, and still went crazy with rapture.

❧

A snapping turtle was floating today on Little Sister Pond.
Goldeneyes still on Great Pond.

❧

Laughing gulls fly by the house laughing.
Maybe a hundred pilot whales off the point.

❧

All July and into August, Luke and I see foxes. An adult fox with a young pup.
The adult serious and nervous and quick. The young one trailing behind, not
serious. It reached up, swatted the pine boughs with a black paw before it vanished under the trees.

❧

To Unity College, in Maine, and back. We stayed in Waterville, saw two bald
eagles flying over open rivers, though there was still much ice, and snow. A good
trip, friendly people, an interested audience. Luke and Bear were quiet throughout, except that Bear threw up on me just as we arrived in the parking lot. I hope
he learns to ride better than that.

❧

Hundreds of gannets feeding just offshore, plunging, tufts of water rising with
a white up-kick. Scary birds, long wings, very white, fearful-looking beaks. We
opened the car windows and there was no sound but the sound of their wings
rustling. They fed at three or four places, then were gone much farther out. We
were at the right place at the right time.

❧

"I am doing pretty well, gathering energy, working . . . and every now and then
timor mortis descends over me like midnight."
    —Letter from D. H.

❧

Just at the lacy edge of the sea, a dolphin's skull. Recent, but perfectly clean.
And entirely beautiful. I held it in my hands, I was so excited I was breathless.
What will I do?

❧

Three deer near the path to Oak Head—of course now they always make me think of Luke. Happiness by association.

❧

Who knows, maybe the root is the flower
of that other life.

❧

Money, in our culture, is equal to power. And money, finally, means very little because power, in the end, means nothing.

❧

Lee, as he was dying, called out, "Strike the tent!" Stonewall Jackson said at the end, softly as I imagine it, "Let us cross over the river and rest under the shade of the trees."

❧

Today I am altogether without ambition. Where did I get such wisdom?

❧

You there, like a red fist under my ribs— be reasonable.

❧

Little myrtle warblers
kissing the air

❧

Let's not pretend we know how the mule feels.

❧

Hearing a crow, the first one in a long time. I listened to it, deeply and with pleasure. And I thought: what if I were dead, lying there dead, and *I heard that!*

❧

Which would you rather be, intellectually deft, or spiritually graceful?

❧

The sugar of vanity, the honey of truth.

❧

When I was young, I was attracted to sorrow. It seemed interesting. It seemed an energy that would take me somewhere. Now I am older, if not old, and I hate sorrow. I see that it has no energy of its own, but uses mine, furtively. I see that it is leaden, without breath, and repetitious and unsolvable.

❧

And now I see that I am sorrowful about only a few things, but over and over.

❧

Fairy tales—the great difference is between doing something, and doing nothing. Always, in such tales, the hero or heroine does *something*.

❧

The new baby is all awash with glory.
She has a cry that says *I'm here! I'm here!*

❧

Give me that dark moment I will carry it everywhere
like a mouthful of rain.

❧

There is a place
in the woods
where my swift
and stout-hearted dog
turns and wants to climb

into my arms.

❧

Don't engage in too much fancy footwork before you strike a blow.

❧

So much of what Woolf wrote she wrote not because she was a woman, but because she was Woolf.

❧

I would like to do whatever it is that presses the essence from the hour.

❧

A fact: one picks it up and reads it, and puts it down, and there is an end to it. But an idea! That one may pick up, and reflect upon, and oppose, and expand, and so pass a delightful afternoon altogether.

❧

From my way of thinking, Thoreau frequently seems an overly social person.

❧

The cry of the killdeer / like a tiny sickle.

❧

The translation of experience into contemplation, and the placement of this contemplation within the formality of a certain kind of language, with no intent to make contact—be it across whatever thin or wild a thread—with the spiritual condition of the reader, is not poetry. Archibald MacLeish: Here is the writer, and over there—there is "the mystery of the universe." The poem exists—indeed, gets itself written—in the relation *between* the man and the world. The three ingredients of poetry: the mystery of the universe, spiritual curiosity, the energy of language.

❧

And what is the universe, as far as we are concerned?

❧

Leo Frobenius: "It was first the animal world, in its various species, that impressed mankind as a mystery, and that, in its character of admired immediate neighbor, evoked the impulse to imitative identification. Next, it was the vegetable world and the miracle of the fruitful earth, wherein death is changed into life. And finally . . . the focus of attention lifted to the mathematics" of the heavens.

❧

Art cannot separate from these first examples which willed it into existence. Say such forces belong now only to dream or nightmare or to Jung's (our) collective unconscious—or to the ecologically sensitive—I say it's entirely more primal than that. Poetry was born in the relationship between men of earth and the earth itself. Without perceptual experience of life on this earth, how could the following lines be meaningful?

> *It is the east, and Juliet is the sun.* Or,

> *And what rough beast, its hour come round at last,*
> *Slouches toward Bethlehem to be born?*

❧

I think as an ecologist. But I feel as a member of a great family—one that includes the elephant and the wheat stalk as well as the schoolteacher and the industrialist. This is not a mental condition, but a spiritual condition. Poetry is a product of our history, and our history is inseparable from the natural world. Now, of course, in the hives and dungeons of the cities, poetry cannot console, it carries no weight, for the pact between the natural world and the individual has been broken. There is no more working for harvest—only hunting, for profit. Lives are no longer exercises in pleasure and valor, but only the means to the amassment of worldly goods. If poetry is ever to become meaningful to such persons, *they* must take the first step—away from their materially bound and self-interested lives, toward the trees, and the waterfall. It is not poetry's fault that it has so small an audience, so little effect upon the frightened, money-loving world. Poetry, after all, is not a miracle. It is an effort to formalize (ritualize) individual moments and the transcending effects of these moments into a music that all can use. It is the song of our species.

❧

Hasn't the end of the world been coming absolutely forever?

❧

It takes about
seventy hours to drag
a poem into
the light.

❧

delirious with certainty

❧

It's almost six A.M. The mockingbird is still singing. I'm on my way to the ocean, with the sun, just rising, on my left shoulder, and the moon, like a circle of pale snow, lingering on my right.

Birds in the City
A FIELD SKETCHBOOK

by Barbara Bash

Walking down the street I look up - pigeons are easy to spot. They used to be known as ROCK DOVES when they nested along the cliffs of Dover.

Now they like to roost in the nooks & crannies of old buildings and railway overpasses.

A big storefront letter becomes a nesting spot

BABY PIGEONS- sketched through a bathroom window

What amazing features!

AT A BUSY INTERSECTION

NEST

SMALL OPENING TO ENTER

Everyone is racing
along all around me.
I stand still and
watch a house finch
slip quietly inside
a street lamp to tend
its eggs - laid in the
bowl of the lamp -
kept warm by the
heat of the lamp.

hen I notice a pair of sparrows
ringing grasses to the pipe
at the top of
the traffic
light pole.

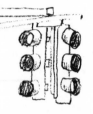

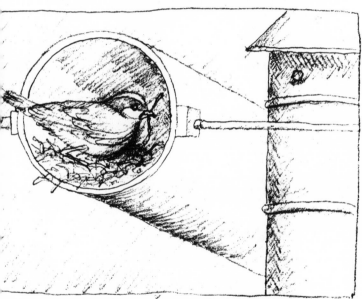

the bird pauses, looks
around to make sure no one
is watching – it doesn't notice
me! – then disappears into
the pipe with its twig.

I see sparrows
nesting in the
hollows around
building ornaments.

One spring a mourning
dove laid her eggs in a
potted geranium on my
back steps.

And last spring
a friend noticed a
pair of wrens trying to nest
in his trousers hanging on the
line. He tied up the pant legs —
so the twigs would stop falling
through — & donated his pants
to the wren family for the season!

At twilight I listen to large crow gatherings in the winter trees of the park. Their wings rustle as they land. Then the calling out begins – rattling, squeaking, gurgling – even cat-like cries – it all mixes together in a cacophony of sound until the light fades and quiet descends.

Looking up under some eaves —
a family of swallows held in
their mud-lined nest...
Looking down on the edge of
a gravel parking lot — a camouflaged clutch of killdeer eggs.

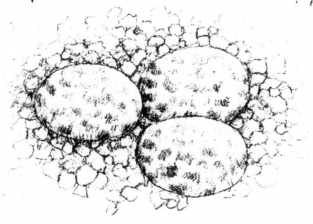

On the 24th floor of New York
Hospital overlooking
the East River
I sit by a
window
& quietly
watch...

a mother peregrine
falcon perched on a
long stick attached to
a sand filled nesting
box. She keeps a
close eye on her chicks

FALCONS IN NEW YORK

Brought back from the edge of extinction, peregrine falcons now thrive in the cities - a world of high stone cliffs & deep canyons... and plenty of food to hunt in the form of PIGEONS...

It's a good home.

the babies call out to their mother - continually staying in touch.

Birds and
their urban
roosts.

Sarah Juniper Rabkin

A Great Excuse to Stare

Seeing through the Eyes of a Gifted Drawing Teacher

> Student: "How do you draw grass?"
> Jenny Keller: "You need to ask the grass.
> Otherwise you miss out on all the things grass is."

I TEACH WRITING at the University of California, Santa Cruz. Recently, I overheard a conversation through the half-open door of my office. A student out in the hallway was exclaiming in a tone both admiring and wistful: "Wow! That's beautiful. Look at those feathers! That one's *AMAZING*. You're so *GOOD!*" Then, with a defeated sigh: "I wish I could do what you do. I can't even draw a stick figure."

Eavesdropping, I realized that this young woman was paging through a friend's sketchbook. Then came a second voice, confident and reassuring: "Oh, anybody can learn to draw. I really believe that now." I knew what she would say next: "You just have to have the right teacher. Like Jenny."

Jenny Keller helped establish UC Santa Cruz's Science Illustration Program in 1986, and has been teaching field sketching and natural science illustration courses there ever since. As a writing instructor who loves to sketch, I have learned a great deal from her—not only about drawing, but also about teaching my own craft. When Jenny and I work together, the parallels between our respective disciplines pop up so frequently that we have begun to think of writing and visual art as mutual metaphors. I believe the reason Jenny can mentor me from across the disciplinary divide is that, while she teaches field sketching and I teach nature writing, we share essentially the same set of attitudes. It is a spiritual stance: a deep admiration for the threatened integrity of land, air, water, and living things, and a desire to help our students cultivate their own passionate relationships with this world.

Colleagues for more than ten years, Jenny and I have sat in on each other's classes; we have also co-taught summer journal-keeping courses in the rust-and-jade canyon country of southern Utah. We have spent countless hours out in the field in different states of the Union, bent side-by-side over our notebooks. Once, Jenny grinned over at me mid-sketch and declared, "That's the main reason I love to draw: It's a great excuse to stare at things!"

On a June morning on the banks of the San Juan River, at the foot of a copper-colored wall filigreed with Anasazi rock art, Jenny was giving a first lesson in staring. Gathered were the seventeen students in our week-long floating workshop "Reflections on the San Juan," organized by the Four Corners School of Outdoor Education.

"That's what artists do," Jenny was saying. "It's nothing tricky. They force themselves to *look*."

"But there's so much to see," said a student. "How do you know what to draw?"

"The world is gigantic," Jenny replied. "You have to narrow it down to what matters at the moment. Choose a subject that *beckons* to you: a shell, a person, a landscape, whatever. You don't have to think you can draw it. If it interests you, it's important. That interest will take you through the tough spots."

In writing as in drawing, it's the heart's resonance with a subject that leads to satisfaction and a sense of vitality in the act of creation. Both disciplines can help us turn our gaze on some bit of the natural world that calls to us to enter into an ongoing conversation with it. "What makes me want to finish a drawing is intensely *wanting* the thing I'm going to end up with," said Jenny. "Artists see the world and snag it and make it their own." Like most good teachers, Jenny balances her exhortations with explicit instruction. "First of all, let me just say that drawing is a learnable skill," she assured us. "You all have the manual dexterity it takes to draw; the trick is training your hand and eye to work together." She told a story about having learned, in just a few days after breaking her right arm, to draw with her left. "Coordination is a little part of it, but seeing is everything."

As I listened, I mulled over my own experiences with drawing—an activity at which I usually feel humbled. But I have had some successes: going into the backyard with a sketchbook and pen, sitting down in front of a clematis blossom, and letting the flower teach me. On a good day, I can keep my attention on the plant itself, ignoring concerns about making a "good" picture. At those times, the process of looking and drawing loosens my cramped spirit, opens my pores, and wakes me up. I come away tingling, as after a run. Achieving this open, attentive state is what imbues drawing with meaning and delight.

The same is my goal as a writer. Fundamentally, I write in order to awaken to a bit of the world as it comes alive to me, and when I teach writing I try to help students to do this. Of course, I do teach nuts-and-bolts of writing—just as Jenny does with drawing, offering countless tips for sharpening "coordination." But these lessons are siding, roof, and trim. *Seeing*, in the broadest sense, is the framework and foundation of what we both do and what we both teach.

On the trip down the San Juan, Jenny's first exercise was blind contour drawing. This involved looking closely at an object, focusing on the boundary between the thing and its surroundings. Once we'd each chosen something to sketch—a plant, a petroglyph, the hand we weren't drawing with—Jenny had us picture a bug slowly crawling along the object's edge. "Imagine that your eyes are faithfully following the bug's progress," she suggested. "Think of your drawing hand as somehow mechanically coupled to your eyes, moving at exactly the same speed as the bug. Try not to let your eyes or your hand jump ahead. Without looking at your paper, trace the bug's path onto your sketchbook page."

We weren't allowed to peek at our drawings until, after several minutes of trance-like concentration later, Jenny called time. She wandered around, peering appreciatively at everyone's sketchbooks, assuaging nervous giggles over the wild, squiggly strokes that strayed off the page's edge. "There are actually little pearls of truth among these crazy lines," she said.

"Usually what stalls us in drawing is getting critical," she continued. "In blind contour drawing, you *can't* decide what looks good or bad. In fact, the finished drawing doesn't really matter. Properly done contour drawings end up looking wild, anyway, kind of like possessed steel-wool. What *does* matter is the process: learning to move your eyes and hand at the same slow pace. The drawing you are left with is just a by-product, but you will see in it parts of the personality of your subject.

"Another thing that can cause problems in drawing is unconsciously relying on memory. What we've memorized before can actually get in the way of what we see now. But when you do a contour drawing and have to focus so intently on your subject, preconceived ideas of what something should look like just can't get in the way. You draw what you see, not what you think you know. Even though the proportions or placement may be distorted, the personality will be there."

Looking at the datura blossom I'd outlined roughly on my page, I thought about the similarities between doing contour drawings and writing field notes. With field notes, you try to collect information as thoroughly and accurately as possible. As in drawing, you try not to impose any preconceptions on the subject, and you wrench yourself away from concern with the finished product. The writing usually comes out more authentic and alive if you focus at first on your initial sensory impressions themselves rather than the way they land on the page.

The next exercise Jenny had us try was gesture sketching—which is fast and loose, whereas contour drawing is meditative and slow. In gesture sketching, you study the subject attentively, holding your notebook up so that you can see the paper and the subject at the same time, and work in quick, expansive motions with your whole arm.

"Making a hasty gesture sketch without really looking first is like writing a summary of an article you haven't read," Jenny said. "So before you begin drawing, hold your pen in the air and swirl it around your view of the subject to get a feel for what you'll be drawing. Once you begin, let your pen explore on the page. Use flowing, continuous lines, and don't stop to erase 'stray' marks. Think big to small; look at the whole form at once. Start out as if you only have a moment to capture the object, and in the first five seconds, have something down about every important feature."

Jenny stopped us when her watch beeped thirty seconds. "This is an excellent way to begin any drawing—loose and gestural, to get to know your subject," she said. "When you see what you can do in thirty seconds, you realize, 'Hey, I have time to draw!' And speed allows you to cut through to the essential—to evoke the essence of the subject."

Later that morning, Jenny passed the teaching baton to me, and we heard echoes of her last lesson in my instructions for the next exercise, in freewriting. In freewriting, a common technique for getting ideas onto paper, you also work quickly and continuously, moving too fast to let critical second thoughts stall the pen. As in gesture sketching, the point is not the finished product—though that may have power and personality—but the process of contacting the mind at its most energetic.

Over the next seven days, as our group of students, instructors, and boat guides wound its way down the sluggish San Juan, we continued alternating between drawing and writing, and Jenny and I kept seeing parallels. When Jenny gave a lesson on drawing "negative space"—the gaps within and between objects rather than the objects themselves—she said, "If you draw the negative spaces, the positive shapes will take care of themselves. Ditto if you draw the shapes of the shadows: the cliff face will still look like a cliff face." Quoting art historian Roger Hinks, Jenny offered a literary metaphor for visual negative space: "Words are like the threads in a piece of lace. Who can say whether it is the threads themselves or the voids between them that make the pattern?"

The comparison prompted me to devise a complementary writing exercise. I had the students freewrite for five minutes, then I told them to look for the negative spaces—what's not said, but limned, by what they had put down on the paper. "Now," I said, "spend three minutes drawing out those negative spaces in words."

I also learned about teaching from watching Jenny work. One day she brought up the subject of composition in sketching. "Talking about composition is a bit like talking about how to drive a car," she said. "Learning about all those controls can make you lose your natural grace for a while. But eventually it all becomes like second nature. The same applies to drawing. You already have a natural sense of composition. Don't let what I tell you freeze you up. Take it in, then forget about it." As teachers, we don't always have to offer something new. Often our most important function—as when writing instructors encourage writers to invent their own forms or write about their unique experiences—is to draw out what students already know.

This led me to recall an experience a few years before, when I was auditing Jenny's field-sketching class. On a warm, breezy October morning, we took a trip to local Lighthouse Field. We could hear sea lions barking, prop planes buzzing overhead, surf washing against the cliff a block away. In spite of the lovely day, I found myself becoming more and more miserable as I struggled to draw a Monterey cypress. It came out stiff, mute, graceless. When Jenny walked over to see how I was doing, my frustration poured out.

"You are in a class, after all," Jenny reminded me. "This is your place to make mistakes and do experiments. Allow your curiosity, rather than a feeling of obligation, to rise and hold you focused. If you're stuck, you need to keep trying." She showed me how to build up wedge-shaped strokes with my pencil to suggest clumps of foliage. "Sometimes when you're having the most trouble," Jenny said, "it's because you're standing at the border of your safe territory and you're trying to expand it. Don't think there's something wrong just because it's a struggle. That's how it ought to be when you're learning at the edge."

In writing instruction, experimentation with forms and with points of view can minimize students' frustrations, by redirecting their focus toward playfulness. When teaching I now make a point of inviting students to try approaches that are new to them: to write a poem in which each line contains the name of a color, or to write descriptive prose in which the speaker is the river running past our campsite. Students get so taken with the novelty of the exercise that they forget about executing it "well." It's easier to let go when an assignment feels more like play than work. There's time later to practice and polish.

I saw this principle at work in Jenny's sketching class, and experienced it firsthand: the more I could "play" at an assignment, the more I enjoyed it and learned from it—and, often as not, the more I liked the finished product. Nevertheless, I continued to notice in myself a tendency to look for the "good" and the "bad" performances in the class—to judge, on the basis of some quality of line, stroke, or composition, which of my fellow student-artists "had it" and which didn't. I evaluated my own work with equal harshness.

Jenny anticipated the potential of competition, envy, and self-criticism to poison the class atmosphere. Before the first "critique," when all of the students were to post our finished drawings on the wall for commentary, she headed us off at the pass. "Whether you feel intimidated or inspired by someone else's good work is your choice," she said. "You can ask the creator of something you admire how he or she did it. Learn from them." I felt enormously relieved by this simple, seemingly obvious observation, and have repeated it ever since in almost every class I have taught.

For me as a teacher, it was useful to return to studenthood for a while, and to be tutored by a teacher gifted in the art of group dynamics. Like Jenny, I strive to encourage in my classes a sense of common endeavor and individual self-respect. When I form peer response groups and guide students through the process of giving and receiving constructive editorial criticism, I aim to model a way of treating each other with mutual curiosity and respect. Because it necessarily involves such lessons, teaching writing—like teaching art—*is* teaching philosophy, citizenship, and ethics. They really aren't separable—especially when we are trying to teach a sustainable way of relating, not only to other people, but also to the planet that nourishes us all.

Clare Walker Leslie and Charles E. Roth

Nature Journaling with School Groups

NATURE JOURNALING is a powerful tool for breaking the bonds of viewing our world through isolated and separate disciplines. It incorporates sciences, local social and natural history, math, language, art, and physical education into one, integrated practice. The developmental sequence in journaling usually begins with recording simple objects and events; in time it progresses to putting these objects and events into contexts that stress the connections between them. The accomplished journalist comes to focus on whole systems and their meaning to his or her life. Journaling can become a personal journey to a real sense of place and a holistic vision of life.

We have observed hundreds of students exploring the outdoors, paper and pencil in hand, carrying abundant energy and varying degrees of curiosity, then finding a squirrel or leaf or spider to attach their attention to. The connection is made and the students are amazed at how good their drawings can be. There is no such thing as a child who does not love nature; all kids simply need to be taught ways to connect.

At this change of millennia, schools are in another cycle of reform, of trying to be sure that they teach young people what they really need to know to lead worthwhile lives. The longtime industrialized approach, the so-called factory model of schooling, has failed many; some of the new reforms still focus primarily on developing more efficient, productive workers. The better reforms focus on developing healthy, holistic learners who can meet the challenges of creating truly sustainable societies and economies on what has become a somewhat diminished planet. Nature journaling, by helping students become observant or immersed in—and reflective on—the world around them, sets the stage for lifelong self-learning from primary sources.

This "curriculum web" (see next page) shows one way of understanding the interconnected topics, skills, and traditionally defined disciplines that nature journaling links together. This reflects Susan Stranz's (a teacher from Barnstable, Massachusetts) understanding of the process; you may want to develop your own web.

EARTH SCIENCE

- Plants
- Insects
- Birds
- Other animals
- Trees and shrubs
- Habitats and seasons

- Weather
- Observing
- Identifying
- Measuring
- Comparing
- Listing

SOCIAL STUDIES

- Local History
- Natural and human communities
- Environmental health in history
- Mapmaking

PHYSICAL EDUCATION

- Walking and exploring
- Outdoor activity
- Hiking

Nature Journaling

MATH

- Measurements
- Charts
- Graphs
- Mapmaking
- Computation

LANGUAGE ARTS

- Written: poetry, prose, fiction, nonfiction
- Oral: description, problem-solving, communication
- Listening: group communication, sharing, and oral learning

ART

- Hand-eye skills
- Self-confidence and social skills
- Learning to compose work supportively

- Observational drawing versus imaginative drawing
- Different forms of art expression
- Mapmaking

The Teacher Leader Role

As a teacher or leader, you need to create learning situations that stimulate learners to begin writing or drawing in a journal. As time passes, start asking students what connections they see between recorded objects and the rest of the world around them. Stimulate them to record the broader context for each object and event they're attending to. Finally, urge them to record how they feel about what they are observing, and what meaning the observations have in *their* lives.

It is important for you to journal along with your students. This demonstrates to them that journaling is an important activity, not just another directed student task. It also helps them see that learning is an ongoing, lifelong activity—particularly if you share some of the things you learned during the journaling session.

A teacher with students

If you are using nature journaling in a classroom and wish to assess the individual journalist's progress, it is wise not to try and assess all aspects of his or her development at once. Choose only one or two aspects at a time. There are also benefits for the journal keeper who engages in assessing his or her own journaling skills. There is the satisfaction in seeing tangible evidence that one is truly learning something. This recognition motivates the journal keeper to continue the effort.

Creating Windows Into Perception

Looking at the journals of other people can give you insight into how they see their world, interact with it, respond to it, challenge it, and accept it. The best way to encourage your students to see and observe is through careful questioning, rather than critical commentary. The developing journalists need to develop the confidence and trust to honestly record their own observations, thoughts, questions, and insights. Journals are not the copying of the observations and thoughts of others; they are an individual's direct responses to physical, social, and internal environments. In essence, a journal should a personal, hands-on personal activity for the journal keeper—so try to limit your input.

Journaling as a Part of an Interdisciplinary, Hands-on Curriculum

Education today is moving toward interdisciplinary study, hands-on learning, critical and creative reasoning, and a mix of group and individual activities. Nature journaling meets all of these reform goals. Journaling activity can take place both in class and out, thus providing both in-class work and homework. The journal becomes a database from which the learners can mine material for creative writing, art, and science projects. Keeping the journal fosters a variety of skills, including observational skills, critical and creative reasoning, communication skills, and drawing skills.

Moreover, the journal provides an ongoing record of students' progress in developing these skills. Comparison of journal pages over time helps track the progress of each student. It also helps students to perceive changes that are going on about them all the time—they can see for themselves just what they are learning.

Prompting the Process

Particularly with beginning young journalists, offering prompts may help them focus their observations. These suggestions can help guide the journaling activity, leading to growth in all areas—awareness, understanding, concern, and action. The prompts should be open-ended questions—specific enough to help learners focus observations and ideas, but not so specific that they restrict students in any way.

You can provide prompts on a separate sheet of directions for each day's activities, or you may want to create small looseleaf journal booklets, with prompts for each small project written at the top of each journal page.

A page from a young student's nature journal

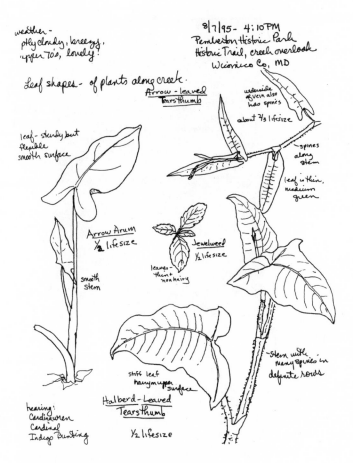

weather -
ptly cloudy, breezy,
upper 70's, lovely!

8/7/95 - 4:10PM
Pemberton Historic Park
Historic Trail, creek overlook
Wicomico Co, MD

Leaf shapes - of plants along creek.

Arrow - leaved
Tears thumb

underside
of vein also
has spines
about 2/3 lifesize

leaf - sturdy but
flexible
smooth surface

spines
along
stem

leaf is thin,
medium
green

Arrow Arum
1/2 lifesize

Jewelweed
1/2 lifesize

smooth
stem

leaves -
thin,
non hairy

stiff leaf
hairy m upper surface

stem with
many spines in
definite rows

Halberd - Leaved
Tears thumb

1/2 lifesize

hearing:
Cardinal wren
Cardinal
Indigo Bunting

A page from a college biology teacher's nature journal

Projects to Encourage Learning and Reflection

Make sure your students read over their journal entries regularly, so that they reflect on what they have observed as well as what they may have missed. Encourage them to return to a particular journaling site again and again, on different days of the week and at different times of the day, to see what has changed or what they may have missed before.

Students shouldn't see journaling as merely another form of busy work. With your guidance, students may find that journaling can be a joy, a rewarding exercise in self-expression, creativity, and discovery. Here are some journal projects and activities you can try with your students:

Give an Open Journal Pop Quiz. Based on questions you create while observing your students journaling at a site, give a pop quiz later in the week or mark-

A pair of college students and their nature journal

ing period. Let enough time pass that their short-term memories of the session have faded. Tell students they can use their journals to research answers to the quiz. This will help them see how journaling supports and builds memory.

A Writing Project. Challenge students to write about something that relates to their journaling activities in an essay, short story, haiku, or other type of poem. Encourage them to use material directly from their journals, and have them include notes at the end of their pieces indicating what they used. Ask them also to note what they *couldn't* find in their journals.

You can also challenge the students to create a place in their journals for their own poetry, personal responses to things observed, or quotations they like from writers on nature.

Teenagers and adults enjoy reading the writing of poets and nature writers such as Rainer Maria Rilke, Henry David Thoreau, Rachel Carson, Robert Frost, and Matsuo Bashō. *Earth Prayers from around the World,* edited by Elizabeth Roberts and Elias Amidon, contains works of many good writers to expose students to.

You can also ask students to try one or more of the following:

• Write a poem about fall: colors, smells, sounds, feelings.

• Write about a little experience you just had while being outdoors—playing soccer, bicycling, noticing the moon, or sitting by water that is reflecting the fall colors, for example.

• Describe in poetry or prose a flower still blooming near you.

• Choose favorite poems or prose passages and copy them into your journal.

An Art Project. Ask students to create a detailed drawing or painting based on sketches and notes they created in their journals. Ask them to indicate what they couldn't find, but wished they had noted when journaling.

A Science Project. Have students create a science research project based on observations and questions from their journals. They should detail the question they want to explore, the observation strategy or research activities they plan to follow, and the kinds of data they expect to record as they proceed.

A History Project. Have students select a particular area—a school site, vacant lot, farm, housing development, or industrial park—and then find out what the area was like before its present use. What (and who) was there before? Are there stone walls, glacial boulders, or giant trees on the site? Are any of these mentioned in property deeds? How did the walls and boulders get there? Can you find foundations of old buildings on the site? Are there plants—such as lilac, apple trees, or lily-of-the-valley—that are clues to former occupants of the site? If students perceive problems in the current land use, have them determine how these problems came about. Who is responsible, and what social forces led to the problems?

A Math Project. Have your students choose a local area, and then locate old maps of that spot. What system of measurements was used? Investigate such terms as rod, chain, acre, mile. What are the relationships among such measures? How do the measurements on the map translate into metric system? How can you measure objects you find without a standard ruler? Develop a measuring system using your own body parts. Figure out your own pace and stride. Translate these field measurements into standard units.

A Music Project. Record all the sounds you can hear from a particular observation point. Do the same from several other places. Can you develop a picture of a place based solely on the soundscape? Make landscape drawings based on the soundscape. Then create a song based on a particular soundscape, adding musical sounds that evoke that soundscape.

Bibliography

Roberts, Elizabeth and Elias Amidon, editors. *Earth Prayers from around the World.* San Francisco: Harper San Francisco, 1991.

Christian McEwen

O Taste and See!
Using the Five Senses to Write about Nature

language, tangerine, weather, to breathe them,
bite, savor, chew, swallow, transform

—Denise Levertov

FOR THREE YEARS NOW, I've been teaching poetry in a town called Central Valley, about an hour and a half drive from New York City. The school is small and beautifully appointed, its parking lot edged with trees and flowering shrubs. Most of the students are of Irish, Polish, or Italian heritage, with a scattering of African American and Vietnamese. Sometimes I work with the third grade classes, more often with the fourth and fifth. After years of teaching junior high and high school, I'm struck by the ardor and inventiveness of these younger children, their coltish grace, their giddy sense of humor. They have a buoyancy that frees me to take risks.

In the exercises that follow, I asked the children to slow down and pay attention, focusing in turn on each of the five senses. Such "isolations" felt strange to them at first. They didn't see the point. Writing for them was about facts: listening closely to what the teacher said, and then repeating it. They weren't used to writing from the body, finding words for what they knew as living, breathing human beings. But as they moved from sight to sound to touch, and on to memories of taste and smell, they surprised themselves with their own expertise. Their work became richer, dreamier and noticeably more personal. Both the world and their part in it were remarkably enhanced.

Being Blind: Acrostics

Again and again, teachers of nature writing emphasize the value of "close-looking." They urge their students to attend to what they see, from the sudden blaze of dandelions beside the road to the chickadees squabbling on the backyard feeder. But for many children, reared on the exotic close-ups of the TV nature documentary, such local moments can seem thoroughly humdrum. They simply are not interested, either in the natural world, or in their own ability to describe it. One of the best exercises I know for counteracting such an attitude is, quite simply, pretending to be blind.

At Central Valley, everyone brought scarves or bandannas from home, and we trooped outside to an open grassy area, framed on one side by the town library and parking lot, and on the other by the swings and slides of the school playground. The teacher and I pointed out these boundaries to the children. Then we asked everyone to choose a partner. One was to cover his or her eyes with the bandanna, while the other was to act as guide. For precisely six minutes (and I made it clear that I'd be timing this) the guides were to lead their partners around "blind." It was their responsibility to make sure that no one tripped over rocks or roots or bumped into trees. They also had to find things for the "blind" students to investigate: a feather, a leaf, a piece of bark, the crumpled petals of a flower.

As for the "blind" students, their primary instruction was to pay attention, feeling their way down through the soles of their feet and out through the palms of their hands, noticing what they noticed, with fingers, ears, and interested noses. I emphasized how important it was to stay close to their guides. "But don't be too obedient! If your guide abandons you or hurries you along too fast, you should feel free to stop. Tell your buddy to wait, to slow down a little. And if he or she doesn't listen to you, pull off the blindfold."

The children nodded, shuffling their feet. Some already had their blindfolds on. They wanted to get started. Others stood back from the crowd, bashful and uneasy.

"Remember you are going to trade places," I told them. "After six minutes, everyone will switch."

I rang the bell, and the teacher and I stood back under the trees, watching the blindfolded children blunder about. The girls held hands and led each other carefully around roots and tussocks. "I heard Sherelle whispering to me that everything will be all right," one told me later on. Another wrote of "letting my friend Anna be my eyes to the world." The boys were far more casual. One led his partner to the top of the library steps and watched with interest as he fell and scraped his knee. Someone else stumbled into a pine tree and got sap on both his hands.

Not surprisingly, these different experiences showed up later on the page. Priya, a fifth grader, wrote a grateful acrostic for her friend Laura, using Laura's name as the spine-word:

Likes to take me to weird places
Actually gave me something cool to see
Understands when I'm going to get hurt
Reassures me when I'm scared
A really great guide.

C.J.'s six minutes with his buddy Paul (also told in the form of an acrostic) were clearly much more volatile:

Paul led me
All around like a rag-doll. I
Underestimated what it is
Like being blind

My leader Paul made me laugh. 6th graders looked at me like I was a ballet-
    dancing
Yak. Paul

Led me up hills and I
Erupted from a volcano. He led me down hills and I fell from an
Avalanche.
Don't
Ever let me
Re-hire Paul as a leader!

Brad too was less than delighted with his experience. He wrote an acrostic
with the spine-word BLINDFOLDED, which he somehow coerced into rhyme.
There was a grouchy, middle-aged tone to this that made me laugh:

Being blindfolded isn't all that fun.
Little things can make you run.
. . .

Everyone was bumping into trees
Don't try this, just take it from me.

But for the most part, the children seemed to value their blind walk, which
(as I'd hoped) served to heighten their appreciation for the remaining senses.
David, for example, wrote that being blindfolded made him think a lot harder
"about what I was hearing, touching, smelling, and what kind of land I was
walking on. Whether it was bumpy, hill-like, or if it had twigs for me to hurt
myself." Brett wrote of this in acrostic form, using the spine-word BLIND:

Brings extra feeling to your other senses
Like being
In the middle of a dream.
Nothing you can see or
Do but trust.

Elytie and Meagan also wrote lucid, thoughtful pieces:

I heard children laughing. I started to be led up to something. I held my breath.
This was scary. I felt something rough. "Trees?" I said. I felt something silky and
soft. "Moss?" She laughed. I didn't understand. Why was she laughing? "Spider-
web," she said. I jerked my hand away. (*Elytie*)

I felt a feather. It was soft and felt silky. I touched tall grass, short grass and small plants. I felt large trees with rough bark. I felt the warm air from the back of a fan. . . . As I was walking I felt twigs, sticks, and rocks underneath me. (*Meagan*)

This was the kind of accurate observation I'd been hoping for, the crucial foundation to all good nature writing. Given the long association of nature and spirituality, it came as no surprise that it should sometimes flower into a moment of private revelation, as in this last contribution by Corey:

The smooth rock glides through my hands and flower petals flutter to the ground. My mind is blank except for thoughts of heaven. Angels dancing around singing the songs of a bird. The roughness of a tree trunk protects its content from exposure to a human world, keeping its spirit within. A mist comes and the world disappears.

Silence: "The White Horse" by D. H. Lawrence

Because teachers spend so much time asking their students to please keep quiet, children have a bad reputation when it comes to noise. It's as if they themselves would prefer to live in a perpetual racket. But the fact is that most children have a deep appreciation for silence and the kind of spacious attention it makes possible. Since this too is one of the essential skills for the beginning naturalist, I like to take the time to elicit it in school. Ideally one would do such work outside, in smallish groups. But even in a classroom setting, one can make a good start, working partly from memory, partly from immediate experience.

At Central Valley, I introduced sound and silence to a fourth grade class by asking everyone to shut their eyes and put their fingers in their ears. We all did this for maybe as much as a minute.

"What did you hear?" I asked the kids.

Of course, in a class of twenty or twenty-five, very little had escaped them. They'd heard the blood beating in their veins, the tiny movements of their fingers squinching against the inside of their ears. They'd heard a pencil falling, papers shifting, someone scraping the metallic legs of their desk against the floor. And there were more distant noises: the teacher bellowing instructions down the hall, the lawn-mower in the field outside, a far-off plane.

Silence is rarely absolute. Almost always it is shaped (enlivened, accentuated) by tiny outbursts of sound. This is true in the country and in the city too. I told the kids about my old apartment in Manhattan, how even in the middle of the night I could hear the hum of the refrigerator, the television talking to itself from the floor below.

And then I read them this little poem by D. H. Lawrence:

The White Horse

The youth goes up to the white horse to put its halter on
And the horse looks at him in silence.
They are so silent they are in another world.

After making sure everyone knew the meaning of "youth" and "halter," I read the poem again, explaining that in real life we would probably be able to hear the horse munching grass or the boy breathing. But something else was going on here, some particular harmony between the two of them. It was a special kind of silence, not what people call a "dead" silence, but something more interesting and engaged, a "live" silence, if you will.

"Where have you experienced that?" I asked. "Where have you yourself felt especially calm and tranquil?" And then I stood ready at the chalk-board, and the children called out their responses.

"In church—"

"In the library—"

"In the basement at home—"

"In the middle of the woods."

When we had a good list of especially silent places, I shifted the question to silent times. "Is winter quieter than summer? Or night quieter than day?" The children had plenty to say about this too. In their opinion dawn and sunset were especially quiet, and of course the middle of the night. Winter was quieter than spring. Being alone was almost always quieter than being with someone else.

"What about silent creatures?" I asked. "Birds and fish and all the different mammals?"

Again we came up with a list. Cats were quiet, most of the time, the children told me. And so were deer and snakes, and rabbits and ants and spiders.

One by one, I wrote these up on the board, sometimes asking an extra question. "A deer isn't so quiet when it's racing away through the underbrush. When is a deer most silent?"

Finally, I paused, and explained that I was going to ask a different kind of question altogether. "If silence were a color, what color would it be?" There was no right answer, I emphasized. But what did they think?

The children were happy to tell me. The question didn't faze them in the least. Silence was white, silence was black, silence was silver, silence was goldish-blue. Silence was transparent, it was pink and peach and lemon, the softest, palest color of the sky.

I asked about noise too. "What color might noise be?" By then the arms were flailing. Noise was tie-dye, noise was purplish-red. It was white if silence had been black, and black if silence had been white. Noise was all the colors of the rainbow.

I didn't bother to make a list of colors on the board. But I did write up the words *silent* and *silence*—hard words for fourth graders to spell; also *quiet* and *quietness.* And then I asked the children to write a poem about what silence meant to them: an image or two in each line, if possible.

Silence is goldish-blue.
It is like seeing the moon in the rain.
Silence is like standing by the window
when all you can hear is the sound of the wind blowing past you.
It's like standing in front of a gate in heaven.

—*Joseph*

Silence is a walk in the park at midnight
Or a hard decision you have to make, Now or Never.
The dead of winter, the spring rain, they are all
silent. Driving on a backroad at dawn.
A restless night. This is silence.

—*Brian*

These two poems were my favorites, both written by nine-year-old boys without a moment's hesitation. But many of the other poems had terrific lines as well:

Silence is black as charcoal and its sound is transparent as a piece of glass
Silence is a worm digging into the black cold earth

—*Alex*

Silence is the wind rolling over the tall grass of the plains
Silence is a pair of scissors sliding through a piece of paper like it was air

—*Justin*

Some children preferred to use the word *quiet:*

Quiet is midnight when an owl looks down on me.
Quiet is a spider making a web to sleep.

—*Brett*

It is very quiet when I am in the car driving some place far away.
It is quiet when butterflies are flying around in the afternoon. It can be quiet
     when I am drawing on my porch.
It is quiet when two girls paint their nails.

—*Kathryn*

Then, of course, for the speedy writers, there had to be some poems about noise. Julie Ann described it with a cool exactitude, as if she were a journalist filing a report on NBC:

Loud noise of thunder hit the ground with a horrifying roar. People huddled in their basements with fear. A twister round the land as far as you can see. When the torching night was over people thanked god they were alive.

Other children held to more familiar, domestic images. For Jessica, whose silence was "a gray cat sleeping, a long book, a walk in a park, a deep sleep, the dew just falling on the grass," noise, by contrast, was:

big bright colors
screaming in excitement
chatting to a friend

while for Cynthia,

Sound is a warm bath and a towel to put around you . . .
Sound is a laugh when you can't stop.
Sound is the end of this poem.

"My Busy Hand": Rilke and Concrete Poems

In the same way that nature writing depends on close looking and attentive listening, so too it benefits from a considered sense of touch. Like so many of us, children tend to take this sense for granted. They don't realize what touch has already taught them, or how that expertise translates into their connection with the larger world. Helping them to focus on the story of their hands (their history, appearance, interests, loves and hates) can be a powerful experience, even within the constraints of a forty-five-minute session.

At Central Valley, I began my class with a tiny anecdote borrowed from Diane Ackerman. A musician went over to her friend's house and sat down at the piano. "At the moment," she said, "I have a lovely piece of Schubert in my hands."

"What do you have in your hands right now?" I asked my fifth graders. "The grainy feel of the orange you ate for breakfast? The memory of a bike accident last weekend? Your newfound skill at a particular video game?"

The children called out answers, and I told them about Rilke, making sure to write his name up on the board. "Hands have a history of their own," he wrote. "They have indeed their own civilization, their special beauty, their own wishes, feelings, moods, and favorite occupations."

"What do your hands love to do?" I asked the kids. And the answers came tumbling out. They loved to climb trees. They loved to stroke dogs, cats, gerbils, guinea-pigs. They loved to write things down.

And what did they hate? Later Brad wrote his entire poem on that subject:

My hand hates burns, bites, frostbite, hot bulbs, elevator doors, car tires, Chinese finger traps, arm wrestling, writing, drawing, scrapes, blisters, blowing my nose, fractures, broken blood vessels, bugs, papercuts, rug burn, puppets and shock.

Meanwhile the rest of the class was busy pondering the next two questions. "If your hands could wish or dream, what would they wish? What would they dream?" Some answers were unabashedly ferocious. "My hand dreams of punching my brother in the face," wrote Brandon later. But most of the children were more playful and imaginative:

"My hand wishes it could have a name," wrote Rebecca. "It dreams about wearing a sweater or pants and a shirt."

"My hand dreams of sticking itself in a sack of money," wrote John.

As for Lynsey, her hand liked doing her hair and painting her nails. "It dreams of one day holding a microphone while I sing in front of millions of people."

When all the children had told their hand stories, I asked them to calm down a little, and settle themselves in their seats. Then I led them in a very short guided meditation.

I asked everybody to choose one of their hands and look at it as if it were completely unfamiliar, following the veins in their forearm, staring at the network of lines in their palm. I explained that it could have been different. They might have ended up with claws or spines or feathers or scales. Instead they had this naked human hand, with its opposable thumb. Long ago, before their oldest ancestors were born, that hand was a fin in some ancient sea. And in fact it was a fin again, before they themselves were born, when they were moving about inside their mother. But now they had this special thumb and those good fingers. I asked them to wriggle their fingers, and to look at each one very carefully. "What do they look like? What have they had to learn?" I reminded them of the way each of us grows and changes, from a tiny infant to a baby and a toddler, and then to an older child who can tie shoe-laces, write his or her name, use a computer, catch a ball.

When the time came to write, some children focused on the leads I put up on the board:

My hands love . . .
My hands hate . . .
My hands wish . . .
My hands dream . . .
My hands remember . . .

Here are some examples of what they wrote:

My hand dreams of holding an ice cream cone and touching the cold drizzle
   that slides down.
My hand loves to feel the softness of a velvet cloth.
My hand wishes it could be a bird and fly above trees all over the world
My hand grips around an umbrella through dark rain. . . .

   —*Jackie*

My hand loves to feel the leather of Northeastern steerhide on my baseball glove.
My hand hates the freezing ice cubes I grab out of the refrigerator ice maker.
My hand is sad when there is nothing left to do, or when I go to sleep.

   —*Matt*

Others preferred to concentrate on what their hands looked like, while yet
others were intrigued by the notion that each hand had its own particular history. Here are some of my favorites, drawn from both categories:

Fragile little
Inches of skin and bone
Nothing to protect them from
Getting broken or scratched
Elegantly picking up objects,
Rolling
      Sliding.

   —*Lauren*

My hand is almost like a person, different personalities from one another.
My thumb is like the Commander of the Army, strong, thick, and short, but
   size doesn't matter.
My pointer is like a tattle-taler telling where things and people are.
My middle finger is like a super-model, taller than the rest and more elegant.
My ring finger is like a regular person with hopes and fears, but special in its
   own way.
My pinky is like a little girl sweet and quiet. Though weak, she is bendable.
Together they make my hand which tells so many stories I can't say now.

   —*Janelle*

My hand is a door hinge, swinging whenever moved.

   —*Daniel*

My hand looks like four rivers flowing in opposite directions.

   —*Kevin*

My hand is a shovel building a sand castle by the beach in the sun.

—*Ben*

My hand remembers the feel of the air going through my fingers as I ran through the alleys back in the Bronx.

—*Steven*

There were some surprising responses too, among them, the letter one girl wrote to her left hand from her right:

My Busy Hand

Dear Lefty,
You are so lucky. Since I am the righty hand, I have to do all the chores. I do the dishes, practice piano, snap, write, type, color, scrub, pick up heavy things, and raise myself while you just sit there doing nothing.

—*Kim*

One student took the time to consider what life would be like without hands:

Without your hands you couldn't feel the leaves on the tree.
Without your hands you couldn't glide through the water.
Without your hand you couldn't touch your mother's or father's soft gentle hand.

—*Stephen*

In the course of writing about their hands, children often reached for scrap paper and began to trace around them. This led naturally to concrete poems. I gave out copies of Reinhard Döhl's "Pattern of Poem with an Elusive Intruder," which is arranged in the shape of an apple. Its entire text consists of the word *apfel* repeated over and over, except for the one intruding *würm*.

The kids loved the idea of making a poem in the shape of the thing it described, and searching for the worm was always a success. I also showed them Emmett Williams's "Like Attracts Like" (in which two *Like*s merge together) Eugen Gomringer's "Silencio" (a box made of repetitions of the word *silencio*, with an empty space in the middle), and Robert Froman's "Skyscratcher" (in which the words reach up and around the shape of the building).*

---

* You can find the Williams and Gomringer poems in *The Teachers & Writers Handbook of Poetic Forms*, under "Concrete Poem"; see the Bibliography at the end of this essay.

With this range of models, it was easy to provide some options for the children's own concrete poems. They could decide on a shape and fill it with text, either new or recycled. They could write their poem around its edges. They could stretch or shrink words and letters as they pleased. When they traced their hands, children often filled each separate finger with the words that described it:

> My hand is fat. Like a sumo wrestler about to jump. My middle finger is like
> an overweight man eating a donut.
>
> —*Matt*

Later they could make a fair copy on plain white drawing paper, cut out the shape, and glue it to a poster-sized sheet of colored construction paper, signing their names with a flourish at the end.

Taste and Smell: Pablo Neruda's "Ode to the Watermelon"

The last of the five senses are taste and smell. These are almost entirely neglected in most schools, despite the enormous amount of energy they generate among the children, and the value of such a focus for the future nature writer. In Central Valley, I tended to teach the two of them together. But first I introduced the form of an ode.

I began by teaching everyone the basic facts: that the ode is a song or lyric poem that celebrates a person or thing; that its name comes from the ancient Greek word, *acidein*, to sing; that people have been writing odes for about 2,500 years; and that the first we have were written by the Greek poet Pindar, to be sung and danced by a chorus. For many centuries, odes were addressed to important people or to abstractions: emperors, generals; freedom, joy. But since the 1950s, when Pablo Neruda published his *Odes to Simple Things* (which included an ode to his socks, an ode to an artichoke, etc.), the subject matter has broadened enormously, and contemporary poets write odes to whomever or whatever they wish.

At this point I handed out copies of Neruda's "Ode to the Watermelon."

Ode to the Watermelon

The tree of intense
summer,
hard,
is all blue sky,
yellow sun,
fatigue in drops,
a sword
above the highways,
a scorched shoe
in the cities:

the brightness and the world
weigh us down,
hit us
in the eyes
with clouds of dust,
with sudden golden blows,
they torture
our feet
with tiny thorns,
with hot stones,
and the mouth
suffers
more than all the toes:
the throat
becomes thirsty,
the teeth,
the lips, the tongue:
we want to drink
waterfalls,
the dark blue night,
the South Pole,
and then
the coolest of all
the planets crosses
the sky,
the round, magnificent,
star-filled watermelon.

It's a fruit from the thirst-tree.
It's the green whale of the summer.

The dry universe
all at once
given dark stars
by this firmament of coolness
lets the swelling
fruit
come down:
its hemispheres open
showing a flag
green, white, red,
that dissolves into
wild rivers, sugar,
delight!

Jewel box of water, phlegmatic
queen

of the fruitshops,
warehouse
of profundity, moon
on earth!
You are pure,
rubies fall apart
in your abundance,
and we
want
to bite into you,
to bury our
face
in you, and
the soul!
When we're thirsty
we glimpse you
like
a mine or a mountain
of fantastic food,
but
among our longings and our teeth
you change
simply
into cool light
that slips in turn into
spring water
that touched us once
singing.
And that is why
you don't weigh us down
in the siesta hour
that's like an oven,
you don't weigh us down,
you just
go by
and your heart, some cold ember,
turned itself into a single
drop of water.

—*Translated by Robert Bly*

The kids glanced at the poem doubtfully: it looked long and daunting. Before I read it aloud, I talked it through, as if I were telling a story. I spoke about hot summer days when the sun seems to beat at us with "sudden golden blows," when our shoes feel scorched from the city sidewalk. I reminded them how our feet hurt, as we've had to walk on tiny thorns. And worst of all, we are so thirsty! We feel as if we could drink waterfalls. I threw my head back, as if I were standing under a rushing torrent. ("Glug! Glug! Glug!") Neruda is exaggerating, of course, I told the kids. He knows you can't really drink a waterfall, or the dark blue night, or the North Pole. But he imagines you could because (in the context of the summer heat) they all sound so wonderfully refreshing. Then, as he's writing about his thirst, it's as if an image pops into his mind, like a thought-bubble in a comic strip: "the coolest of all / the planets crosses / the sky, / the round, magnificent, / star-filled watermelon."

You can't really have a watermelon planet. But a watermelon is big and impressive the way a planet is. And it does have things inside that look a little bit like stars. "Seeds!" chorused the kids.

So there we have it, the "fruit from the thirst tree." Neruda compares it to a green whale, calling it "the green whale of summer" because a whale is a large roundish creature with a rough gray skin, and a watermelon is a large roundish fruit with a tough green skin. And if you split it down the middle (changing the metaphor), you get two halves that look like a sort of flag: green and white and red, the green of the rind and the white under it, and the juicy red of the fruit itself.

Neruda praises the watermelon in extravagant terms. He calls it a 'jewel box of water," the "phlegmatic queen" of the fruit-shops. That's because it's so much bigger than the other fruit. I asked the kids to think for a minute of a grocery store, with boxes of oranges and apples and bananas and kiwi fruit, maybe an occasional pineapple or melon. The watermelon is bigger than all of these. It's like the empress. It can seem a little cold and reserved, not easily excited. That's what "phlegmatic" means. But if you break open that watermelon, it's so luscious and delicious, it's as if it's full of rubies. And we're so thirsty (Neruda has involved us now, he's written us into the poem), that we want to bury our faces in it—even our souls. It's as if that watermelon is a mirage shimmering on our horizon, "a mine or mountain of fantastic food." It looks huge. But when we finally get to meet it head on, when we actually eat it, then it changes into cool light inside us, into spring water. And that's why it doesn't weigh us down in the siesta hour. (Here I paused to find out if anyone knew what "siesta" meant, and to explain it if they didn't.) It's not like eating potato pancakes or a big plate of hamburger and French fries. The watermelon just dissolves in us, it's like a "cold ember," the glow of coals that the fire leaves behind. It turns into a single drop of water.

At this point, having expended maximum energy and enthusiasm in my exposition, I read the poem itself, as plainly and simply as I could. I made time for vocabulary questions (the kids needed help with "fatigue," with "firmament," occasionally with "profundity" and "abundance." The rest they got easily enough from the context).

By now we were about a third of the way into the lesson, and the children were eager to get started on their own poems. If I'd had more time, I might have taken them out into the field behind the school, or handed out little vials of coffee and cinnamon and lavender to elicit memories of smells. But usually this is not an option. The next piece of preparation has to be done imaginatively.

I asked the children to shut their eyes and allow their sensual memories to roam. "What tastes do you remember that truly delight you? What special smells?" Once again, I began to accumulate a gargantuan list up on the board. Taste-treats ranged from mangos to mashed potatoes, from pizza to fresh-baked chocolate chip rainbow-sprinkled peanut butter cookies. And the smells were even more various. The scent of lilacs or the salty breeze commingled with third and fourth grade favorites like blue pen ink, gasoline, and scented body glitter.

When the board was crowded with beloved tastes and smells, I asked the kids to look at Neruda's ode again. There are innumerable ways of structuring an ode, but this one is set up fairly simply. There are three different sections, starting with the one that introduces the idea of heat, exhaustion, and summer thirst, and culminates in the magical appearance of the "planet watermelon." The second section praises the watermelon with all sorts of elaborate metaphors, and the third section describes what it is actually like to eat the fruit.

Some kids preferred to work with a simple form like a list poem, picking their own favorite items from the board. But others decided they'd like to try an ode. I talked them through the various sections: the longing, the encounter, and then the final engulfment. "How does it feel to want an ice cream?" I asked. "And then to feel that first sweet trickle on your tongue? And what is it like afterwards when you've eaten it all up?"

The kids were eager to answer. They wrote odes to mashed potatoes, odes to pizza and spaghetti, odes to milk and lemons and watermelons, odes to chocolate-covered strawberries. Here are a couple of complete poems by fourth graders:

Ode to Mashed Potato

Oh the smell!
Oh the taste!
When it goes down my throat I feel like I'm in heaven.
I savor every moment.
It slides down my tongue to my tummy. Delicious.
It's like a quilt over a baby in the winter.

—*Kristen*

Ode to Bread

I like the taste of bread
All different kinds

The bread tastes good to me.
Bread to me is like chocolate melting in my mouth.
It tastes so good, too good to be true
When I come home from school
I gobble my bread into crumbs
and no bread for you.

    —Chris

Here is a selection of some of my favorite lines:

Strawberries covered in chocolate on a summer night.
Strawberries covered in whipped cream on a hot day.
Strawberries cut in half in a silver bowl.
Strawberries bitter and sweet a great treat.

    —Natalie

When you drink milk it is like sailing through a cloud of sweetness. It is like diving in a pool of delicious taste of desire.

    —Joseph

A watermelon is like a raging river flowing into my mouth. It's a monument
    in my refrigerator.
When you spit out the seeds it makes a whole new generation of planets.

    —Justin

There were terrific list poems too, some praising taste, some praising smell, all of them tinglingly specific. Here, for example, is Nicole on tastes:

chocolate chip cinnamon bread
fresh and juicy watermelons
creamy white chocolate
ice cold lemonade.
cotton candy the first bite

and Jen on smells, both delicious and disgusting:

The smell of mashed potatoes my mom makes.
Picking raspberries in the woods . . .
The smell of cotton candy from a circus.
The chewy of gum
The smell of popcorn from a movie . . .
The smell of car exhaust. YUK!
Smell gasoline from a car. YUK!
The smell of gunpowder. YUK!
Smell the cigars that men are smoking. YUK! YUK! YUK! YUK!

As with the hand exercise, or indeed with either of the other lessons, poems to taste and smell can easily find a new identity as concrete poems. Students have shown me poems in the shape of an ice cream cone or a carton of French fries, poems in the shape of mangos and raspberries, poems written around the outline of a rose.

Another alternative is to make an entire book to honor one particular poem. One African American girl wrote a poem about her hands. She liked to wear green nail polish, and for her book she created a brown construction-paper cover in the shape of a hand, each finger with a carefully shaped green nail. A "blind" enthusiast made his book in the shape of a carefully twisted bandanna. Someone else cut out two enormous, staring eyes.

The fact is that children love to make such things. Ending a residency or semester with a day of colored paper, gold paper-fasteners, scissors, and glue is a real delight, whether the ultimate product is a small book or a concrete poem. Computer images are perfect, yes, but they are also boring. Children know this, and much prefer to make their own, celebrating their work in all its clumsiness and accuracy, its sheer exultant humanness, the delicious specificity they've been writing about all along.

Bibliography

Ackerman, Diane. *A Natural History of the Senses.* New York: Vintage Books, 1990.

Bly, Robert, translator. *Neruda and Vallejo: Selected Poems.* Boston, Mass.: Beacon, 1971.

Lawrence, D. H. *The Complete Poems of D. H. Lawrence.* Collected and edited by Vivian de Sola Pinto and F. Warren Roberts. New York: Viking Compass, 1971.

Levertov, Denise. *O Taste and See!* New York: New Directions, 1962.

Macy, Joanna. *Despair and Personal Power in the Nuclear Age.* Philadelphia: New Society Publishers, 1983. (See p. 102 for the meditation on the hand.)

Padgett, Ron, editor. *The Teachers & Writers Handbook of Poetic Forms.* New York: Teachers & Writers Collaborative, 2000.

Suzanne Rogier Marshall

A Walk through the Woods

From Looking to Writing

As a child I remember looking long at the Minnesota woods, curling back purple-veined leaves in search of a "jack-in-the-pulpit," watching the finches weave pine needles and lacy leaf-skeletons into a nest. Later, I brought my journal along and sketched the tangle of bittersweet, captured the quick flight of a cardinal with a blur of red watercolor. I first used brush strokes and then later words to record these images, and I found, in doing so, that I began to feel a part of the natural world.

Most children now spend little time close to the earth. Their lives are scheduled and fast paced, dominated by technology. There is little time to be still and to reflect. So I have tried to reconnect my upper elementary students at Potomac, a private school in suburban Washington, D.C., with the acres of forests, wetlands, and meadows surrounding it. To lead my students on the journey back to nature, I have found that I must first teach them to look. By going from looking to writing, they begin to develop a greater understanding of and appreciation for the natural world.

I begin with something still: a single plant, a wildflower, a tree. If I ask in the classroom, "What is a tree?", the students respond from their symbolic memories: "Brown trunk, green leaves." When I lead them outside to a specific tree, such as a mulberry, they see that the bark is not brown, but instead a series of gray, flat ridges, tinged by orange, and that the leaves are not merely green, but silvered underneath, lime where the sun shines through. Observation makes the tree real, and so this serves as our beginning point. The students each choose a tree, or wildflower, or bush, and they sit alone, silently observing. They notice the colors, shapes, movements, small details, the patterns of light, the surroundings. They feel the bark, the leaves, the contrasts. They smell their plant. They listen to it.

This beginning stage is quiet and meditative. The quiet has a way of connecting the observer to the object observed. After a few minutes, I ask them to write notes about their observations. I encourage them to use specific words. What is the shade of brown in the bark? What is the sound of wind moving through leaves? After intense scribbling, we share images. I encourage them to connect verbs with their images and to select just the right word to convey that sense of action. Leaves no longer "move," they "shudder" or "shiver." These sharpened word choices lead to new thoughts and more notes.

We return to the classroom to draft our poems. This stage is sometimes difficult for students. How do you move from a page of scribbled notes to a poem? It helps to look at the work of other poets. I often choose models with different styles, for example, William Carlos Williams's poem "Young Sycamore" and Denise Levertov's poem "The Willows of Massachusetts":

Young Sycamore

I must tell you
this young tree
whose round and firm trunk
between the wet

pavement and the gutter
(where water
is trickling) rises
bodily

into the air with
one undulant
thrust half its height—
and then

dividing and waning
sending out
young branches on
all sides—

hung with cocoons—
it thins
till nothing is left of it
but two

eccentric knotted
twigs
bending forward
hornlike at the top

—*William Carlos Williams*

The Willows of Massachusetts

Animal willows of November
in pelt of gold enduring when all else
has let go all ornament
and stands naked in the cold.

Cold shine of sun on swampy water,
cold caress of slant beam on bough,
gray light on brown bark.
Willows—last to relinquish a leaf,
curious, patient, lion-headed, tense
with energy, watching
the serene cold through a curtain
of tarnished strands.

    —Denise Levertov

Williams's poem rises, like the young sycamore, image by image from "firm trunk between the wet pavement and the gutter" to the top. In her picture of the willows, Levertov instead selects images of color and light to emphasize a theme of enduring strength.

After reading the examples aloud, I bring up the idea of selection. The painter Georgia O'Keeffe wrote, "It is only by selection, by elimination, by emphasis that we get at the real meaning of things." A poet, like a painter, selects details to show the object as he perceives it or to express a feeling or thought arising from the object. On their notepads the students then highlight ideas that they want to use, decide on a logical order, and begin to draft, placing words in meaningful "chunks" on a line.

When they finish drafting, I encourage them to read their poems aloud. How does it sound? They change words, repeat words or sounds, add words, and omit words, until they are pleased. Then I have them look at the shape of the poem. How does it look? Do they like the shape the words make on the page, the shape of the white spaces? They make more changes.

Several students compose poems that are Georgia O'Keeffe-like, enlarged images of a single flower or vine.

Pansy

Fragile like glass,
trying to sway but caught by the stem,
petals of yellow and purple,
moist like the air on a humid day,
the designs of butterfly wings
in the summer.

    —Alex Emsellem, fifth grade

Bittersweet

Bittersweet,
Dying wrinkled berries,
A deep, endless red,
Intersecting branches

Bending and twisting,
A deadly brown,
Faded,
Tiny twigs still clinging to it,
Little bumps sticking out
Like a herd of antlers
Without its deer,
Alone, breaking, dying,
Gentle, but cut off from the world,
Sighing,
Spiky, yet soothing,
Bitter, yet sweet,
Dying in its own grave,
Bittersweet.

 —Amanda Gutierrez, sixth grade

Others stand back and observe trees. It is interesting to watch the same tree change character from the autumn to the spring. It is also interesting to watch the same tree convey different feelings to different observers. The children's poems become self-portraits, reflecting the way they look at the world:

Red Maple

A dark chocolate brown trunk,
rough and coarse,
lit up with sunlight,

long, thin branches spreading far,
casting shadows against
the grass and rooftops,

light green seed pods
edged with red,

leaves enveloped with sunlight,
turning almost gold,

and ending
with the hushing of branches,
whispering out.

 —Claudia Vasquez, sixth grade

Maple

Images of dancing spider webs
on the ground,
patches of grass
in between the intertwining roots,

a gray bark of tiger fur twisting
in a forever imaginary pattern,
slender branches
boasting,
with only a few crusty splotches
along its smooth bark.

—Andrew Meriwether, sixth grade

Japanese Red Maple

Winding, curving like a peacock
in an empty meadow,
beige green with glints of sparkling lights
in tufts of beautiful, elegant leaves,
leaves like a flaming, flickering fire
rustling in the wind,
smooth, tender branches with grooves
leading the way,
a pungent red
bristling in an afternoon breeze.

—Ajay Premkumar, fifth grade

Mulberry

The thrusting branches
push against the sky,
one,
then three,
then seven branches I see,
branches are light
while the trunk lurks
in darkness,
limbs lean from
side to side
as if trying to hide.

—Ben Weisgall, fifth grade

Seventh grader Drew Durbin adopted a tulip poplar tree as an earth science project. He visited and revisited the tree many times during the year, recording notes in his field journal. His notes eventually turned into a poem.

My Tulip Sapling

Ascending vulnerably,
enduring
incessant scarring.
Moist,

protruding,
dark brown grooves
swirl in tapering figure eight patterns.
The fraying edges of
harshly inflicted wounds
glimmer in the first light of dawn.
Soaked indents teem with
clusters of speckled, pale green lichen.
The trunk, dividing and separating,
creates an ebbing tide of branches
laden with lush green leaves.
Their smooth texture is broken only by the
slight veins
receding to a mere meandering maze
of dimensionless curves.
Their deep green trim is lobed
to a shape identical
to the wings of a vivid butterfly.
My tree stands out
like an artist's pallet
filled with vibrant natural colors

Like an artist's still life, a flower or a tree is a good subject for beginning poets because it stands still; it is patient with the observer. As the students gain experience in looking, they are able to look more quickly. They are ready to note energy and movement. In nature, a cardinal may appear as only a flash of red against the green. Animals are often merely glimpsed, so the poet must become a quick-sketch artist. I often find it useful to start with animals that have been brought in from the wild, captured for a moment so students can observe them. Later, as students gain fluency in observation, they can take their journals to the woods and record the unexpected: a fox blinking at us through a tangle of wild roses, or a red-winged blackbird clattering overhead.

I bring different animals into my classroom: minnows and tadpoles in an aquarium, crayfish in a white enamel pan, a snake in a terrarium. The children cluster around the animals for many minutes, watching the silver flickers of darting minnows, tentatively touching the crusty backs of crayfish. They scribble notes, sharing ideas as they write. I push them to find new words. They move from "silver" to "moon-lightning-flashes," from "brown" to "tawny bay color," from "swim" to "zig zag," "back pedal," or "shiver."

After notetaking, we read three model poems: "The Dragonfly" by Robert S. Oliver, "The Salamander" by Muriel Rukeyser, and "Bee Song" by Carl Sandburg. The children point out descriptive phrases they particularly like, such as "a cage of legs" or "yellow moons trimming black velvet." I encourage them to find interesting verbs, look for comparisons, and notice the use of repetition. Then, selecting details from their own notepads, they sketch quick, small poems. They use short lines, repetition, and rhythm to reflect the movement of these animals.

Bullfrog Tadpoles

Two beady eyes,
    watching,
        watching.
One obese head,
    moving,
        moving.
One slender tail,
    swishing,
        swishing.
Whole body,
    growing,
        growing
into a bullfrog.

    —Aja Ewing, fourth grade

Crayfish

Round, black beady eyes,
mermaid tail
in the back,

Tiny lobster
with small,
sandy brown
pinchers,

Hopping
backwards,
sliding,
slipping

Scraping,
darting,
making path with his tail,
hides.

Plop,
plop,
plop,
it goes.

    —Briana Evans, fourth grade

Crayfish

Black, spherical eyes
sprouting stiffly
from short stalks
on a brownish yellow shell.

—*Wesley Fleuchaus, fourth grade*

Minnow

silvery eyes
see-through body
skeleton inside
tickling the water
smelly water
looping—

looping—

sprints in the water

—*Tribbie Nassikas, fourth grade*

Minnow

Transparent sparkles,
glimmering, shimmering,
glow in the dark.
Flitting, dancing,
flying through water.
Moon-lightning-
flashes
of bright glowing
light.

—*Kate Jones, fifth grade*

Corn Snake

A flash of sunburn red
Jets across the hot sand.
Slowly ducking,
Black eyes gleam in the burning sun.
He lounges on a piece of jagged wood,
His tongue entering and re-entering gracefully.
A pretzel,
Tired,
Tanning
Snake.

—*Phinney McIntire, fifth grade*

Later, they are able to use their sharpened eyes to record notes in the field. They are able to describe the flight of a blackbird.

Red-winged Blackbird

A shrill from a red-winged blackbird
Fills my ears.
Then I see him.
He sits on a decrepit log
High above the lake,
His black velvet belly protruding
As he makes his call to the world.
Then he moves.
Two red spots hang onto his wings
As he flies to another perch
To make his call again.

—Lauren Shuler, sixth grade

As their artistic vision sharpens, they become ready for more complex subjects, for entire scenes. We hike to the woods or pond or meadow. At the edge I give directions to enter quietly, to find a place alone, and then to sit and observe. When they find their places, I tell them the names of some of the trees and birds around us. As we stop talking, they begin to hear the far-off cry of a mourning dove, the "gawk" of a crow. Then they write notes about what they see, what they hear, what they smell, and what they feel. I encourage them to connect action words with their images. They notice maple seeds whirling above them, and a wren, bobbing in the thicket of green with his tail tilting up and down. The world becomes rich with detail.

When we finish notetaking, there is a glut of images recorded on their notepads. How do we choose? The artist frames his vision by selecting details; so does the poet. We look at different ways of framing a landscape. In his poem "10/22," William Carlos Williams presents a composite of visual images, a collage of individual snapshots presented in separate stanzas. He writes what he sees and then what he sees next and then what he sees next. Color and contrast play important roles:

10/22

that brilliant field
of rainwet orange
blanketed

by the red grass
and oilgreen bayberry

the last yarrow

on the gutter
white by the sandy
rainwater

and a white birch
with yellow leaves
and few
and loosely hung

and a young dog
jumped out
of the old barrel

   —*William Carlos Williams*

In her poem "Vermont Spring," Letha Elliot strings her images together in
a more narrative form. She takes us on a walk through the woods, focusing on
a final image that she carries back to her life in the city:

Vermont Spring

Walking in spring
never far from the sound
of rushing water,
I came to a clearing
in the woods.
A silver birch stood
with me, silent.

A woodpecker beat time,
momentarily,
with my pounding heart,
and, in a marshy pond,
swollen with liquid snows,
something small, unseen,
broke the surface
to breathe the air.

Back in the brittle city,
where voices and corners
are sharp,
the surfaces concrete-hard—
important—
and silence is a memory,
something small, unseen
within me
breaks the surface
to breathe the wooded air.

   —*Letha Elliot*

The styles of these two poems are different, and the children are usually drawn to one or the other. I ask them to highlight the images on their notepads that combine to create a mood or feeling; some choose spooky images, others beautiful ones. In assembling the landscape poem, the tendency is to include too much. It becomes important to pare down, or the picture becomes cluttered. I encourage them to look for the unusual, something unseen by others, a surprise for their reader. Then they consider order. What did they notice first? What did it lead to? Were there contrasts? Finally, I have them reflect on the entire landscape. Did they leave with any thoughts or feelings? Can they come to a conclusion?

After an October walk, students selected images of autumn:

October

October has gone far away,
where no one knows.
Yellow leaves, like a yellow fire,
wave in the breeze.
A dim trail of a satellite zooms
into the distance
while the cool breeze runs
through my fingers.

    —Jimmy Miller, fifth grade

Autumn

Dripping orange leaves
swirling and whirling,
coating the ground with color.

Crackling brown bark
with ragged branches
against a blurry white-gray sky.

Rakes scraping
against scattered leaves
to be pitched into dead black bags.

The smell of freshly laid mulch,
that hot tea smell
mixed with the bitter wind.

    —Sammy Rocks, fourth grade

In April, they collected images of spring:

Swinging

The grass grows long and wild,
a little diamond drop of dew
crowning each blade.
Tall tulip poplars
support sweet-smelling,
heart-shaped buds.
Daffodils,
a glowing yellow,
rest on silver-green stalks.
The trees are blanketed
in purple-tinted moss.

Up and down it all goes
as I see it from my swing.
The sun on my arms,
the old, strong wood carrying me,
my hands gripping the fraying rope.
Butterflies flit in my stomach
as the wind races past my ears.
I smell fresh water,
a perfume of lilacs,
and a sweetness
like apples still on a tree,
a sweetness I can taste
on the tip of my tongue.

    —Katie Jerman, fifth grade

One class sat in the tall grasses by the pond to write these poems:

Poem of the Woods

Chilling on a bamboo stick
protruding from the water,
the turtle wastes time
while having a silent conversation
with the bugs.

Gliding along the pond edge,
the camouflaged bark-color snake
creeps to its hole,
not wanting to be seen.

A puff of summer snow skips by,
frightened.
Wait . . .
shy little rabbit hops out from curiosity,

a staring-eye contest,
one on one,
then disappears into darkness,
and the gloom of the poison ivy.

The crow's laughter,
the red-winged blackbird's screaming,
the cardinal's continuous siren
warn all the wood creatures of the human's approach.

   —*Ashleigh Carson, sixth grade*

Pond Poem

The rattling creak
Of a red-winged blackbird
Shatters the stillness.
Suddenly, everything is alive.
The minuscule mousy-colored bricks
Of a snake's coils bend the lush, green grass.
A gold-eyed jewel-frog hovers,
An emerald on the silver
Surface of the pond.
The iridescent blue sliver
Of a dragonfly
Hovers just above
A tiny blue star-flower.
A small, slick, night-black creation
Surfaces quickly, then vanishes.
Ripples bend the silver of the surface,
Spreading, spreading,
Until they break the
Bittersweet at the edge,
And a black streak
Touches the grass at my feet.
Then, the blackbird rattles
Once again,
And everything is gone.

   —*Maud Taber-Thomas, sixth grade*

Other classes took a walk through the woods, stopping on a bridge or beneath a tree to write poems:

The Forest

River whispers
by the sleeping moss-covered rocks
while the ants
march on the ferns.

Crows laugh,
sparrows bounce from branch to branch
while the woodpecker hammers
on the old oak tree.

The gnats crawl
on thorny leaves,
mosquitoes buzz by
into the mist.

A walk through the woods—
it feels like a walk
in a prehistoric jungle.

—*Andrew Johnson, fourth grade*

11/4

Trees and rich leaves
blazing and bending,
twisting sideways.

Leaves
shimmering and shaking
off wet soggy bark
with birds chirping
in the background.

Dead branches with
a rich maple smell
that is cold and gives you the chills.

Watching the
blazing red, dashing yellow,
wild orange,
with a dove in the tree.

When you stand
and watch the trees,
look,
you see life and death.

—*Jeffrey Diamond, fourth grade*

In learning to look, the children begin to see the natural world, perhaps for the first time. They see the crayfish's "black, spherical eyes sprouting stiffly from short stalks," they hear the "rattling creak of a red-winged blackbird," they smell the "hot tea smell" of freshly laid mulch, they feel the grooves of a tulip sapling "swirl in tapering figure eight patterns." As they begin to look at the earth and begin to record what they see in words, they discover, as Jeffrey discovered in his poem, "When you stand/ and watch the trees,/ look,/ you see life and death."

Bibliography

Dunning, S., E. Lueders, and H. Smith, editors. *Reflections on a Gift of Watermelon Pickle and Other Modern Verse.* New York: Lothrop, Lee, and Shepard, 1966.

Elliot, Letha. "Vermont Spring." From *Wild Song: Poems of the Natural World.* Edited by John Daniel. Athens: University of Georgia Press, 1998.

Hannum, Sara and John Chase, editors. *The Wind Is Round.* New York: Atheneum, 1970.

Levertov, Denise. *The Sorrow Dance.* New York: New Directions, 1965.

Lynes, Barbara Buhler. *O'Keeffe, Stieglitz, and the Critics.* Ann Arbor: U.M.I. Research Press, 1989.

Prelutsky, Jack, editor. *The Beauty of the Beast: Poems from the Animal Kingdom.* New York: Knopf, 1997. (Contains the Robert Oliver and Carl Sandburg poems mentioned in the text.)

Rukeyser, Muriel. *Waterlily Fire.* London: Macmillan, 1948.

Williams, William Carlos. *The Collected Poems of William Carlos Williams, Vol. 1: 1909–1939.* Edited by A. Walton Litz and Christopher MacGowen. New York: New Directions, 1986.

Holly Masturzo

With My Artist's Eyes I See...

Encounters of Estrangement with Natural Forms

> He had caught a far other butterfly
> —*Nathaniel Hawthorne, "The Artist of the Beautiful"*

IN ONE WAY OR ANOTHER, many of us have played the game of looking at something in the natural world and trying to see in it something else: spotting animal shapes in clouds, discovering fallen sticks in the shapes of letters of the alphabet, or seeing shadowy faces in rock formations. Observing the natural world can be a wondrous experience, one of discovery and identification. Ideas are stirred to the surface by observing how a bird's movement through grass raises insects. Imagination drives through series after series of associations.

I often begin my writing residencies with activities that involve encounters with the natural world. Many of my students, however, slip these initial encounters into known plots that reflect their recent studies and newly acquired facts. They seem anxious to show off their knowledge, to assimilate a new encounter with nature into a conventional framework. Their initial written responses often are demonstrations of what they have learned to identify, details of food chains, habitat, "natural law," etc.—observations that are more "recognition" than discovery. Observation via recognition is a useful and necessary skill, but it does not often meet the challenge of imaginative writing.

The Russian critic Viktor Shklovsky wrote: "After being perceived several times, objects acquire the status of 'recognition.' An object appears before us. We know it's there but we do not see it, and, for that reason, we can say nothing about it. . . . The achievement of art is the transformation of the object, describing it as though for the first time, communicating its particularities. . . . The purpose of the image is not to draw our understanding closer to that which the image stands for, but rather to allow us to perceive the object in a special way, in short, to lead us to a 'vision' of this object rather than mere 'recognition.'" Here Shklovsky is praising Tolstoy's ability to present images, to describe objects and acts with which we are familiar, yet in a manner that seems surprising and new.

While I did not expect all my young students to become Tolstoys, I did want to introduce to them the thinking processes that generate fresh and complicated images, to create encounters for them that would go beyond mere recognition. I hoped to avoid our knee-jerk reliance on common phrases and tracks of thought, what Nietzsche calls "worn-out metaphors which have become powerless to affect the senses." In the past, I had been somewhat frustrated in my efforts to communicate this to students; whatever natural forms I brought in to the classroom seemed to lose their specificity, and on outdoor excursions, even sightings of squirrels, birds, and trees seemed too easily explained or understood. My students appeared to be dealing with types rather than actual particulars. "As certainly as no one leaf is exactly similar to any other," Nietzsche wrote, "so certain is it that the idea 'leaf' has been formed through an arbitrary omission of these individual differences, through a forgetting of the differentiating qualities, and this idea now awakens the notion that in nature there is, besides the leaves, a something called the 'leaf,' perhaps a primal form according to which all leaves were woven, drawn, accurately measured, colored, crinkled, painted, but by unskilled hands, so that no copy turned out correct and trustworthy as a true copy of the primal form. . . . The disregarding of the individual and real furnishes us with the idea, as it likewise also gives us the form; whereas nature knows of no forms and ideas, and therefore, knows no species but only an *x*, to us inaccessible and indefinable." I realized that what Nietzsche terms "individual" and "real" were the kind of details I looked for in my students' writing.

The challenge for me as a writing teacher, then, was to find ways for students to write with a newness of experience approaching Emerson's "original relation." Looking at a leaf or shell or wing and seeing its "differentiating qualities" would also, I hoped, make my students aware of their own abilities to see uniquely. In order to "return sensation to our limbs, in order to make us feel objects, to make a stone feel stony," Shklovsky writes, "man has been given the tool of art." The process of such discovery operates through a device that Shklovsky terms "estrangement," *ostranyenie* in Russian, a neologism often translated as "defamiliarization."

One of the turning points in my teaching—I work as a writer-in-residence in Houston-area elementary schools—was my discovery of Kjell B. Sandved's book *The Butterfly Alphabet.* This book presents close-up photographs of butterflies' wings. Taken using special microscopic lenses and strobe lights, Sandved's photographs reveal in the patterns and coloration on butterfly wings letters of the alphabet and the numerals zero through nine. On facing pages two photographs of the same butterfly appear: one at normal range, the other in extreme close-up, showing the sector of wing where the letter or numeral was discovered. My students had seen countless butterflies, yet never as media for letters and numbers. That we can recognize our alphabet in patterns on butterflies wings would startle them, I thought. Here was the "defamiliarization" I was looking for: Sandved's book opens a door to an imaginative way of observing nature, ironically by showing something of our own, something human, in a natural context—one that was both familiar and unfamiliar. So I decided to develop an assignment that used *The Butterfly Alphabet* as a springboard for writing.

Prior to introducing the Sandved book, I spent four to six class sessions fore-grounding the importance of detail, image, and description in creative writing. My exercises emphasized "real-world" objects and called for original, yet pre-cise, observation and description. With Sandved's photographs, we moved from seeing "scientifically" to seeing "artistically" (a false dichotomy here, but initially useful).

I read out loud Sandved's introduction, a one-page letter to the reader that conveys his passion for his project and provides compelling details of its exten-siveness (decades of rough travel to over thirty countries in extreme locations). Several of the alphabetical letters are difficult to see in the "normal-range" pho-tographs, but Sandved encourages the reader by noting that "if you use your imagination, I am sure you will find other fascinating images in the patterns of the wing." This became our jumping-off point.

In the first photograph, the two brown lower wings of a birdwing butterfly both have four orange As along the curve of the wings, a clear marking dis-cernible to the naked eye. While students recognize the A, seeing it in a vibrant orange in the feathering of a butterfly's wings transformed their expectations not only of butterflies, but of letters and words. As we proceeded into the book, the students took pleasure in looking through the photographs, confirming with their own eyes what Sandved's special lenses were able to capture. They wanted to see where the small yellow Bs make a chain-link border on the brown-and-white wings of the African Atlas moth. The close-up photograph of the B is so tight that the location of the letter on the butterfly is difficult to determine. I waited until all of the students had been able to find the small Bs trimming the wings. As Sandved warns, some of the letters are more difficult to discern than others. We had a hard time finding the K, until one girl saw a pattern that looked like a river with its tributaries stretching off in several directions.

We discussed the kind of vision Sandved had, what was involved in his stud-ies and travels. The students talked about patience and hard work, many throw-ing in words from our writing vocabulary, such as *observation* and *imagination*. We talked about what it means to possess artistic vision, a type of vision, I assured the students, that they were all capable of. "How many of you have ever seen something in the shadows on the moon? Or shapes in the clouds?" I asked them. I told them how as a child I looked for sticks in the shapes of letters. "Have any of you done something like that?"

You can also do this exercise without the Sandved book. If you have a pre-served butterfly at hand, let the students pass it around, looking for letters and other significant or unusual markings. Most butterfly wings have some kind of Y or an elongated E in the veining on the wing that can be seen by the naked eye.

To push the defamiliarizing experince even further, the next phase of the assignment involves creating butterfly images using colored inkblots. Depend-ing on class size and time, we either make one as a class or each student makes his or her own, following a method I demonstrate. Using craft or tempera paints in four or five different colors, I have the class tell me which colors to use and how many "blobs" of paint to drop onto the white paper (8½" x 11" is fine, but larger sheets make a more impressive display on a classroom wall). Once at least one-half to two-thirds of the paper is covered randomly with blobs of paint (enough to smear but not enough to run), I fold the paper in half and rub it lightly in circles with my fingers to spread the paint. While making the blots, I reveal nothing about the result. The magic is in the moment of revelation.

The unfolding of the paper is like the slow opening of a butterfly's wings, but this is an unusual butterfly, simultaneously recognizable and foreign. The unveiling is met with outbursts of sightings: "I see an *o, a, q,* an *e!*" students cry out. If the paint blobs don't readily form letters, I encourage students to say if they see other things. Some describe animals, trees, or cars. When one student sees something that others do not, I remind everyone about the importance of vivid imagery and specific details. The students then work on honing their descriptions. In the process, they discover that concrete description and details, like those in more "scientific" observations, are what help to communicate our associative visions to others.

For some students, seeing in this way is difficult. Some worry that they are fibbing or stretching the truth if they say what they think they see. These students need permission to take this leap, to feel it's OK to see something that is not clearly there. Others, however, shouting in delight, may need no such reassurance.

Rarely do I tell my students what I see, for this immediately colors their perceptions. Once the others begin writing, I might share what I see with a student who's having difficulty. I'll point out a busy part of the inkblot, where shapes touch and colors mix, and say, "A lot seems to be happening here. Does it remind you of anything? What do the colors make you think of?" I stress that we each see differently, that I am interested in what he or she sees, not in a particular vision or "right answer."

When the discussion comes to a boil, I ask the students to freewrite from the inkblot we have made (or from their own), using the prompt "With my artist's eyes I see. . . ." I write this phrase on the board and ask them to see what they can discover. For some students the writing is fast and furious. Others may need help grasping that what they see does not have to correspond directly to reality, that shapes and colors in the painting can resemble other objects, people, animals, or scenes. So as they freewrite, I ask questions designed to focus their thoughts and to yield fuller and more specific responses: "Is there a specific place all the items you see are from? Where? In this country? On this earth? If you see people, what are they saying? What other sounds might you hear? What might you smell? Are things sitting still? If they're moving, how are they moving?"

Because the focus is on a new way of seeing, the writing process itself should not be a new or unfamiliar experience. Therefore I leave the writing open-ended; students write in poetry or in prose—whichever they are most comfortable with.

Many, their energies fully engaged, simply write descriptive paragraphs or lists. Some perceptions are described more fully than others. As I read the lists, I look for items that might be "activated"—that is, expanded upon in a new piece of writing. Often, the students' lists are compelling pieces in their own right:

In a Butterfly

With my artist's eyes I see . . .
a fish with no tail,
a lollipop with no stick,
the sun about to set,
blue moon over the fish,
a sunflower seed,
emeralds shining brightly,
a smiling circle with lines all over,
an apostrophe,
an amethyst,
a green lion frowning,
a heart floating by the sun and
an eclipse.

—*Kailey Caplan, third grade*

Satisfied with her list and her experience of discovery, Kailey was not interested in revising her piece. I asked her to reconsider the sequencing of her images, and the possibility of cutting a few. She did remove similar images (she had listed several varieties of gem stones) and added a few modifiers.

Other students focus more directly on the butterfly image:

Colors

A butterfly with white, red, blue,
green and yellow blobs on its wings.
Because it has a tangy twist.

—*Chelsey Cartwright, third grade*

Chelsey's poem does not use the prompt. Like Kailey, she did not want to revise her work, but was excited by her creation. In her class, each student made an inkblot. For Chelsey, looking at her inkblot in parts was perplexing, for she saw her butterfly only as a whole. She frequently wrote about colors, and began this poem like many others she had written. The addition of "tangy twist" is her registration of the newness of this butterfly.

I wanted the girls to continue writing, but was not sure how to encourage them to expand what they had written. Chelsey's tablemate, Reed, had missed the early parts of our discussion. After quickly making an inkblot, she began to compare hers with Chelsey's. They asked if they could work together to make a book, having decided on names for each butterfly. Every free moment for the rest of the week they crawled under a table to create another page of their book together. Each page, a different color of paper, bore a crayon-and-marker drawing of their butterfly-characters hovering above a stanza of a poem. Their writing reminded me of the mobile imagism of H. D., particularly of her poem "The Dancer," with lines and rhythms that roll out of each other and circulate in the poem.

The Blue Butterfly and the Rainbow Butterfly

Blue butterfly
fly up high
to the sky
oh beautiful butterfly.

Go eat pollen
and flutter into the garden
sit on a flower.

Go play
with rainbow butterfly.

Go flutter
in the garden
with your friends
make your wings
flow in the air.

Sing a song of joy
to all the butterflies.

Smell the fresh air
go high in the sky
to touch the sky.

Flow in the air
like the clouds
and remember your friends
the blue butterfly
and the rainbow butterfly.

—*Chelsey and Reed*

While the experience of estrangement did not produce fantastical visions, it did enliven the writing of these two girls—and began a new friendship.

Frequently, when certain threads in students' early drafts suggest narratives with setting, actions, and characters, I point out one or two and ask the student to consider elaborating on these threads. Katie's first draft was a short list: a king and two boys, a colored ball. "What's happening between them?" I asked. "Do they know each other? What are they doing?" She responded to my questions with a complicated oral narrative that I urged her to write down:

The Baker King

With my artist's eyes I see . . .

A king who is a baker, with a green hat as a crown.

Two boys sitting on the ground, their noses are so long, they have no friends. They are the king's sons.

There are lights on a ceiling that are blue, yellow, and purple.

The king has his hands in his lap and he is sitting in his royal throne asking his cooks for their finest recipes.

There is a ball that comes to the boys. They are happy because they think they will make friends, and they do.

One friend is a boy and one is a girl. The kids have lots of fun, and so does the king, for he gets married to a queen.

—*Katie Sayre, third grade*

The butterfly wings have become virtually untraceable. I suggested to Katie that she might drop the first line (the prompt), but she was attached to it.

Jordan's first response was also a poem:

The Rainbow People

The rainbow people have lots of colors
Not like all the others
They have blue, green, white, and red
But they don't have any other colors, quite a dread
They say they're big and rough
But they really just bluff
In rainbow land a Dalmatian
has lots of animation

—*Jordan Astrich, third grade*

The estranged moment, the discovery of the rainbow people, remained undeveloped. In our conversation, Jordan revealed that there was a planet where these rainbow people lived. I asked him to tell me about this world, and he began a new piece of writing:

The Rainbow People

There once was an enchanted planet called Rainbow Mania. Everything was going fine until one day a rainbow person complained her baby was normal; it wasn't rainbow. And on Earth, a lady complained her baby was rainbow. On Rainbow Mania, in Rainbow Land, the baby didn't do what all the rainbow people did. The place was so colorful it scared the baby. On Earth, the rainbow baby grew up very fast. He was already five years old and in school. As for the baby, he was not lucky, for the rainbow people got so sick of him they put him in a rocket and sent him to Venus. Nobody knew what happened to him after that, however, aliens from Venus took care of the baby and named him Pinky.

The next day, most students were ready to move on to something new, but Jordan was excited about continuing his story. While the class began a new activity, Jordan kept going:

After five days had passed on Earth, the rainbow baby wasn't a baby anymore because he was now thirty years old. He wanted to find out where he came from so he started walking down the side of the road. After he had walked for a few miles he found a man in rags. The man told him that "if you walked for another mile or so" he would find two passages. One would be filled with many lovely colors and the other would be black and white. "Take the black and white one to get to Rainbow Land. But whatever you do don't take the other one or you will get stuck on Venus!" So the rainbow person did what he was told, and when he got to the passages he stared at the one filled with colors for a moment. Then he thought that man probably didn't know anything and so he took the rainbow passage. The man was right and the rainbow guy was on Venus and when he looked back the passage was gone. So he started walking on that strange green planet until he found a rocket that was rainbow. He thought there must be a rainbow person somewhere on this planet and started looking. And before he found anybody he thought again if I fix this rocket I can go to Rainbow Land. But the rainbow people saw that he came in the rocket that the baby got sent to Venus in, so they never believed that he was a rainbow person or took good care of him. He did not live a good life. The End.

When our writing sessions together came to a close, Jordan told me he planned to continue his story yet further. Chelsey and Reed had moved on, but were still riding the wave of their enthusiasm. For many students, the Butterfly Alphabet assignment had been a breakthrough, a turning point in their writing.

Because the Butterfly Alphabet assignment shows students that writing—and, by extension, art—is a process of discovery, it is excellent preparation for a field trip to see modern art. It is also a good way to introduce the concept of image, and could be followed with literary examples that foreground image, metaphor, and moments of estrangement, such as Wallace Stevens's "Thirteen Ways of Looking at a Blackbird" or A. R. Ammons's short poems "Mirrorment," "Late November," "Night Post," and "Poem (In a high wind the)." The experience of a whole class seeing a variety of images highlights the existence of multiple perspectives, and thus serves to introduce a discussion of point of view.

"Art is a means of experiencing the process of creativity. The artifact itself is quite unimportant," Shklovsky wrote. "In my opinion, estrangement can be found almost anywhere (i.e., wherever there is an image)." The success of this lesson is not really dependent upon Sandved's photographs—though they are inspiring. One might use the veins of leaves, the splotches and graining on bark, or even the lines on the palm of the hand as catalysts for writing. A teacher could also take her class outside and have the students lie down and observe clouds before writing.

After my first Butterfly Alphabet session, I walked around for the rest of the day looking keenly at the world around me, surprised and emboldened by the connections firing in my mind. In the break room, the classroom teachers I had worked with slid over to peer into my satchel for a glimpse of Sandved's "butterfly book." We looked for the letters we did not get to discover in class.

"Can I see N ?" asked one teacher with a name that starts with N.

"We're like the children," another said, and we giggled.

Bibliography

Ammons, A. R. *The Really Short Poems of A. R. Ammons.* New York: Norton, 1990.

H. D. (Hilda Doolittle). *Collected Poems 1912–1944.* Edited by Louis L. Martz. New York: New Directions, 1983.

Emerson, Ralph Waldo. "Nature." *The Collected Works of Ralph Waldo Emerson. Vol. 1.* Cambridge, Mass.: Belknap Press, 1971.

Hawthorne, Nathaniel. "The Artist of the Beautiful." *The Centenary Edition of the Works of Nathaniel Hawthorne. Vol. 10.* Edited by William Charval et al. Columbus: Ohio State University Press, 1974.

Nietzsche, Friederich. "Truth and Falsity in an Ultra-moral Sense." *Early Greek Philosophy and Other Essays. Vol. 2. Collected Works of Friederich Nietzsche.* Edited by Oscar Levy. Translated by Mazemilian A. Mügge. New York: Gordon Press, 1974.

Sandved, Kjell B. *The Butterfly Alphabet.* New York: Scholastic, 1996.

Shklovsky, Viktor. "Art as Device." *Theory of Prose.* Translated by Benjamin Sher. Elmwood Park, Ill.: Dalkey Archive Press, 1990.

Stevens, Wallace. *The Palm at the End of the Mind.* Edited by Holly Stevens. New York: Vintage Books, 1971.

Ann H. Zwinger

The Nature of Nature Writing

> In the end, we will conserve only what we love,
> We will love only what we understand,
> And we will understand only what we are taught.
>
> —*Baba Dioum, Senegalese conservationist*

TEACHING NATURE WRITING involves teaching the discipline of firsthand field work and research as well as the craft of nonfiction writing. In my classes, I try to convey that nature writing is more than just sighing over how exquisitely dewdrops bespangle a spider web at dawn. I try to give students a firm idea of the requirements of nature writing as a base from which to develop their own styles. The range of nature writing spreads wide, from the personal to the scientific, from the philosophical to the practical and political. "Classic" nature writing begins with firsthand field experience, the "been there, seen that, done it" factor. This is what is involved in identifying the resident plants, animals from big vertebrates to microscopic invertebrates, fungi—that whole range of creatures that inhabit the surrounding world. Upon the quality of those observations is based good, solid research in many fields—geology, botany, archaeology, astronomy, history, to name only a few. Then those discoveries must be organized and presented in a graceful and enticing fashion, so that readers can absorb fairly complex concepts in a pleasant way, will learn fairly difficult information without being aware of it, and will be encouraged to delve further and to make their own discoveries. I base the course on these three skills.

Even if my students don't become professional nature writers, they will become, by default, "amateur naturalists." They will have gained a greater understanding and appreciation of, in the widest sense, their one-and-only home. Above all, they will never be bored, for there is always something of matter going on "out there": a cricket doing Michael Jordan jumps, an evening-primrose opening at dusk in the cupped warmth of your hands.

*   *   *

I've been teaching ever since I graduated from college with a degree in art history. After time out to be an at-home wife and mother, I taught studio art to high school students as well as nature writing/outdoor workshops for adults. For me, art history proved a superb background training for a naturalist, since it is based upon perceptive and precise observation. (My lack of scientific training makes me more aware of the challenges facing non-scientific majors!)

As an adjunct professor at The Colorado College, I teach a course called "Writing the Natural History Essay." Because Colorado College is on the block system, students take only one course at a time for three-and-a-half weeks. This, of course, influences how I teach, for I can take students out in the field for extended periods of time, an absolute necessity for nature writing. The flip side is a formidable challenge: time is so compacted that students can't leave their essays to ferment for a week, coming back to them with the necessary objectivity to edit them effectively.

Although I shall describe a course structure here in linear fashion, most assignments run concurrently. I lecture only on the first morning, presenting my definition of nature writing and identifying the two major assignments of the course: that students become acquainted with the body of natural history literature, and that they write their own essays. The writing—producing an essay of around twenty pages—is of primary importance.

I also expect them to read other natural history writers throughout the three-and-a-half weeks. I commonly use John Elder and Robert Finch's *The Norton Book of Nature Writing* and Stephen Trimble's *Words from the Land*. Both books contain an exhilarating variety of authors and styles. Each student chooses an author he or she particularly likes, reads other essays or a book by the same author, and leads a class discussion after reading favorite passages from the chosen author.

In the first class, I pass around a sheet for each student to write down why he or she is taking this class, what his or her aims are for the course, and his or her hopes and dreams. I collate these and hand back a list of goals for all of us, including myself, to keep in mind. Then we go outside and poke around campus, get acquainted with the immediate natural world, identify some plants, talk about the land forms (which include Pikes Peak) we can see from campus, watch a bee going about its business, and chat about how what we're seeing could translate into an essay. This is a "what-if" time of easy-flowing discussion, of noticing little things like a grasshopper with a gimpy leg, what leaf miners have done to one tree's leaves, or the interesting gall at the end of a willow branch. We end up in the library, where one of the reference librarians shows the students how to find natural history sources and makes sure that they are proficient in using the library.

At the end of the first day, I give students two assignments: to write a one-page essay using all the clichés they can think of, and to write a one- to two-page description of where they live, being as accurate as they can. (This gives me a good look at their descriptive abilities and their skill levels in writing and organizing.)

The second morning I have a few willing students read their cliché assignments to the moans and groans of their listeners. I then can acknowledge their superior use of cliché, adding that since they have used up and/or heard every cliché available, there is no need to use them again in this class. At the same time I remind them that clichés *do* have their place because of the cultural baggage they carry, and a good writer knows when or when not to use one. I reassure them that no one writes perfect prose every day, and that sometimes you just write garbage to get something out of the way, and that's excusable as long as it's not the end product. An awareness of banalities is an awareness every writer needs. Sometimes we have to write poorly before we can write well, and occasionally we find in the dross some nuggets that we can use later. We raise our right hands and solemnly give ourselves permission to write garbage when necessary, and the wit to know it.

Throughout the course, I use writing games and exercises that I've picked up from other teachers, such as the cliché assignment I describe above. For another, I divide the class into groups, one to list nouns, one to list verbs, one to list adjectives on long strips of paper. Then we combine and read them. Often among the untenable combinations there are surprising and totally unexpected juxtapositions that can give a writer fresh, unexpected, and often usable material.

A third exercise involves practicing simple editing skills, also something essential to good writing. I ask each student to assume he or she is an editor of a natural history magazine who has just had a very hackneyed short essay, in desperate need of editing, dropped on his or her desk. The next issue is due to go to press within the hour. I cram the ersatz essay with passive and mundane verbs, dull vocabulary, and egregious grammatical and spelling errors. As editors, they need to correct the piece, to enliven the writing with active verbs and more pungent nouns and spicy adjectives—in other words, to make the paragraphs fresh and readable. Despite their general lack of familiarity with editing, they quickly pick up on the techniques involved, techniques that will help them in editing their own work. Being cognizant of bad art—or bad writing—is extremely useful in helping to define what good art and good writing are.

Ideally, I like to have three or four class days on campus before taking students into the field. Because of the freedom of the block system, I've taken students for a week at a time to the American Museum of Natural History Research Station at Portal, Arizona, in the Chiricahua Mountains close to the Mexican border, or to the Colorado College adjunct campus near Crestone, Colorado—places set amidst stunning mountain ranges. I believe that even the scabbiest piece of land, if you're out there and curious about the environs, offers challenges for study and perhaps even more potential for writers. But I also understand that a good tablespoon of gorgeous scenery with your morning coffee can do a lot for a beginning writer's psyche.

Nascent nature writers need "a place of their own to write about." I begin field work classes by taking a long walkabout the first day, to all the different habitats a given venue has to offer: high, dry meadows; north-facing shaded slopes; south-facing sunny slopes; ponderosa pine woods; trickling streams;

aspen groves; damp meadows. I suggest, contrary to youthful cynicism, that a habitat *will* speak to them, and that that space is where they should settle in to write about. Only one caveat: they *must* be well out of sight of each other.

And students do find places they like, tucked away here and there, that over the week provide them with some unexpected delights. After they've picked their places and I've checked them out, I expect all of them to spend at least half if not more of their working day in their chosen haunts, including a dawn or sunset, and/or a night spent in a sleeping bag.

Generally we all meet first thing in the morning and spend some time talking about the selected sites, how they see them, how one spot is different from someone else's, and the challenges each site presents every day. Every day we discuss taking field notes that will be worth something when we get back to campus. Precise field notes are worth their weight in gold, and are essential because they will form the basis for the individual nature essays. Each day we explore different techniques for becoming an expert on a given plot of ground. We begin a communal plant, insect, and mammal list. One day we mark off a square foot of terrain and make a thorough inventory of it, listing the sounds and smells and textures. I suggest taking a nap and noting any dreams. We keep daily weather notations, comparing the daily differences or noting changes in which plants are in bloom and which aren't. I remind them of the helpful ideas they'll glean from the nature writers they've chosen to report on, and that reading these authors outdoors is a pleasant experience.

Every morning we share some tidbit of writing and technique. In just a few days many of them develop that insatiable curiosity that is the hallmark of a natural history afficionado. I pass on some of the tricks of the trade I've learned as a writer, such as keeping a list of questions to look up later on the back page of my field notebook. While a week seems a miserably short time to get down all that's needed for an essay, I point out that magazine assignments often allow you only one trip to a designated site, so it's wise to address the shortness of time as a positive: You don't waste time, and the intensity of focus enhances what you learn about your haunt.

The initial questions that arise from field work are predominantly those of identification. I insist that writing about "that pretty winged thing" and not knowing it was a *Parnassias* butterfly and that its host plant is stonecrop, or not being aware that that adorable fuzzy flower fly in its larval stage was a fiend feeding on living tissue, making Dracula look like a den mother, is inexcusable and unacceptable. Consequently we spend a lot of time on the skills of identification: how to use a field guide and dichotomous keys. These keys present two notable characteristics (e.g., opposite or alternate leaves) from which you must make a choice; that decision leads to another pair of characteristics, and so on, until by process of elimination you find the correct identification. I encourage two students to work together on a plant or animal they want to identify. It's more fun to work out an identification with a friend, and four eyes are better than two. Careful identification also sharpens observation skills, making students more aware of details. Once you identify something, you have a name, and that name is a key to further information. The best textbook is always the natural world itself, and what one *really* needs is the knowledge of how to enter it, query it, and feel comfortable with it.

A botany professor friend of mine recommends keeping your currently-in-use field guide in the bathroom. Good idea: it's amazing how quickly one, almost unconsciously, builds up a good sense of families and genera. It tickles me that students respond with a surprised satisfaction when they finally nail down what something is, using all the peripheral tricks, including checking the distribution map. In Colorado, if you find that the bird you think you're watching lives only on the Atlantic Coast, *return to go* and start over again! It takes time to learn how to identify quickly and efficiently, and to come to know that in identifying one plant you pick up a lot of peripheral information that helps you to identify the next. Observational and identification skills develop in tandem— such little effort for such tremendous reward.

*   *   *

One of the best techniques I know for fostering good identification is sketching. I encourage students to draw postage-stamp-sized sketches in the margins of their journals or field books. Each sketch needs to indicate the distinctive characteristics of the object under scrutiny. A lupine leaf is a diagnostic giveaway; a cluster of ponderosa needles or a drawing of the bark will help to identify the tree. By keeping the sketches small, I avoid the eternal wail of, "Oh, but I can't dra-aw!" The students must *really* look and really observe, often through a hand lens and in a few minutes of time. Does the leaf have hairs? If so, what kind? How many stamens are there? (Non-botanists learn what stamens are on the instant!) Are there spines?

There are helpful sketching shortcuts to indicate flower shapes (such as the traditional childhood star for a five-petaled flower, etc.) and leaf shapes (simply draw around the leaf if it's small enough). Field treatment is simplistic and will not bring forth fine differences for more sophisticated identification, but sketching does a good job of concentrating the eye, focusing the mind, and limbering the hand. Also a subliminal image forms that may be useful in identification. If any students truly enjoy sketching, I may work with them separately to help them develop their skills; it's amazing to me how quickly skills develop once students concentrate on the natural object at hand and leave behind their fettering preconceptions that what they draw has to "look like something." You can't sit down to the piano and play a Beethoven sonata at first try, either. Patience and practice win the day.

At least once during their fieldwork experience, I ask for half of the students' journals to read overnight (it helps that class is limited to twelve). I take along a laptop (we usually have access to electricity) and write detailed comments keyed to removable numbered tags in their journals. Seeing their journals in the making gives me insights into their orientations and abilities. It also enables me to provide them with direction when and where they need it most. I find a computer essential for this; I could not possibly write or explain as fully by writing longhand. Even so, on these journal review nights, I'm usually up until a bleary-eyed two or three o'clock in the morning.

During the fieldwork, there often comes a change in how a given student views what had been a threatening natural world. I'll never forget one student, who had been afraid of spiders, running to find me late one evening. Thrilled, she showed me a gorgeous, huge spider splayed out on her screen door. She was entranced by its magnificence, fears forgotten. It's these epiphanies that give me joy.

Back on campus, the students concentrate on research for their essays and reports about the nature writers they've been reading. I also block out time for writing. During our last week of class each student gives an oral report on his or her chosen author. For these reports, students need to note how the chosen author has organized their essays, how facts were incorporated, distinctive vocabulary, and use of simile and metaphor. I also ask students to discuss why the author's work was of interest to them, and what they really liked about the writing.

They also read passages aloud, and they *do* need to read well and carefully. Because I believe it's important to do justice to what one reads, I suggest students read their preferred passages out loud by themselves several times before reading them in class, in order to enunciate clearly and do justice to the words. I go through the litany of "sit up straight, take a deep breath, slow down, slow down," etc. Reading also helps students judge their own work. I encourage them to read to each other outside of class, either their own or someone else's work. Most readers usually read out loud in their heads, and unconsciously balk at awkward words and phrases; hearing someone else read your work to you highlights glitches you might otherwise miss.

Reading other nature writers also shows students ways to tackle their own essays. They pick out eye-catching first paragraphs and discuss what makes them "grabbers." The biggest challenge for students is not so much *how* to begin, but *what to begin with*. They may have some dazzling field notes and some intriguing research, but haven't a clue as to how to weave the two together. For a group of eighteen- to twenty-year-olds, using childhood is a powerful place to start an essay, since they are still consciously close to it and generally have not yet had the life experience to open up other pathways. Childhood experiences are typically both universal and unique—evocative, strong, and close to the surface.

The commonality of experience draws readers in, giving them the sense of trust in the writer that's necessary to captivate them and keep them reading. Often a childhood experience will provide the groundwork for the entire essay. Infusing interesting research with their own remembered experience vitalizes many of their essays.

At the same time, students are doing research. Finding the right books and periodicals is essential. At the library they cope with how to do the kind of research that distinguishes nature writing from personal and/or philosophical essay writing. The Colorado College is blessed in having a library with open stacks. We spend time there checking references, discovering that it may not be the initial, obvious book that provides the necessary information, but rather that book one shelf up and four books over that has the "ah-ha!" factor, that contains that surprising fact you never suspected but that gives you a jolt of surprise pleasure. And *that's* what makes nature writing different from any other kind of writing: those wonderful, fascinating tidbits that make it so sprightly, joyous, and satisfying.

Our reference librarians are eternally helpful. Even better is students sharing with each other, for the often esoteric references they stumble across can't be found in typical resource lists. As a class, we develop a bibliography of helpful references that I update regularly.

And when you find that long research article in *Ecology* or *Nature*, what next? Because students' time is limited, I suggest that they read the abstract and the introduction, skip the nuts and bolts of the experiments, and then pick up again with the discussion and conclusion. The meat of the research will be clear without following the complete scientific trail. They will perceive enough from these paragraphs to understand if kangaroo rats hunt on moonlit nights, and if not, why not.

Research is an absolute necessity to good nature writing, and in picking up some shortcuts, students generally find research not onerous but pleasurable—a lot is in the attitude. And yes, on their final paper, they have to provide corroborative evidence—either in the form of notecards or endnotes—to assure me that they have visited the right reference. The natural world is too important to be treated cavalierly, and a "natural history essay" implies a contract with the reader. The writing must be accurate to the fullest extent possible, and the reader must be able to trust the information therein. That trust is a precious commodity, not to be taken lightly.

*   *   *

Writing *is* difficult and, worse, it's isolating. Still, we can reduce those disadvantages by mutual problem-solving. I assure students that writing a first draft is difficult for most authors. It's when I myself grumble most and do most anything to avoid facing my computer. I assure them that they are not alone. To break a bad stretch of work I share some simple stretches that one can do while sitting at the computer, to unstiffen one's neck and free up one's mind. We also talk about the steps in the "creative process" that almost everyone progresses through; for instance, knowing that getting stuck halfway through is not uncommon gives them courage to keep on working.

Saving students from writer's block is the same as not getting stuck in a snowbank: avoid it in the first place. Daily discussions of ways and means, of different approaches, snags (real or imagined), reduce the chance of frustration. And if students do feel thwarted, a good way out is to try writing a letter to a family member or best friend. You begin with "Dear ____," and write as entertaining a letter as you can about where you were for fieldwork and the fabulous project you're involved in. Imagine their faces lighting up at your wit and enthusiasm! When you're all done, sign off with, "Love, Me." Remove the greeting and the salutation and you have an excellent start to an essay, and sometimes the essence of your whole essay. Imagining an audience makes a difference.

* * *

The high quality of the work some of the students produce always delights and reassures me. At the end of a course I sometimes type up a notable paragraph or two from each student, have copies made, and get them simply bound for the whole class. The anthology always bears the title *Excerpts from the Journals of Famous Writers*. When students see their work in the same typeface and same format as everyone else's, they see their work differently because it looks more authoritative and professional. I hope they feel a sense of accomplishment. Here are a few lines, picked at random from several dozen students' essays:

> "My aspen trees lose their yellow wigs from the outside in."
> "The full moon last night . . . made the aspen trees shine white on one side, while they remained black on the other. . . ."
> "The grasses slapped their wet hands against my legs. . . ."
> "Aspens aren't whispering any more—they sound like a dog scratching his ear. . . ."
> "Pausing, then continuing, then pausing again."
> "Complete stillness except for the rustle of my coat and scratch of my pen on this cold page. The sky is gray white and I cannot place where the sun should be."

Once their minds are engaged and they begin to feel at home in the natural world, students begin to write eloquently. I appreciate the ways in which they find a thoughtful context for their subjects and begin to recognize the natural world as an inspiration and guide to good writing. I am reassured, once more, that the natural world is a superb teacher.

At the end of the session, mindful of the class expectations listed on the first day, we review them to see if we got what we wished to out of class. The discussion that follows often indicates a new or more developed awareness of the natural world and an appreciation for the discipline of nature writing. Hopefully, for these college students, exploring natural history has brought an extra dimension to their lives. And that is precisely what college—and nature writing—*ought* to do.

Bibliography

Finch, Robert, and John Elder, editors. *The Norton Book of Nature Writing.* New York: Norton, 1990.

Trimble, Stephen, *Words from the Land.* Salt Lake City, Utah: Gibbs Smith, 1988.

Carolyn Duckworth

Buffalo Journal

Exploring an Animal and an Issue

OVER THE PAST TEN YEARS, I have taught workshops that combine natural history observation, sketching, and creative writing to show students how visual and verbal skills complement each other and to release ideas and expressions that we wouldn't find when practicing just one of these skills. Recently, I developed a special workshop to increase understanding of the buffalo in Yellowstone National Park and of the current threats to these animals.

Gardiner, Montana—the tiny town where I live—sits on the northern edge of Yellowstone National Park. It is one of two places where buffalo emerge from the park when snows cover their grazing lands on the higher plateaus. It is also one of two places where buffalo are killed if they leave the protection of the national park. Some winters they never leave the park. But during the winter of 1996–1997, hundreds poured through. Early deep snows had shut them off from food with three months of winter to go. Eleven hundred animals died, most of them shot in the fields outside of Gardiner.

From January until late March, I could not focus or write. But as spring slowly came, I opened my field journal again and began writing words one by one—*snow, mud, piñon jays, rosy finches*—and then phrase by phrase—*bluebirds on the fenceposts, elk walking the alley.*

In early summer, I began a new journal, one just about the buffalo, which I filled with writing, drawings, observations, questions, and results of research. This field journal led to an idea for a class called "From Bison to Buffalo: Using Field Journals to Explore an Animal and an Issue," which I taught the following summer for the Yellowstone Institute. (I use both names, *bison* and *buffalo*. To me, *bison* is a more objective, scientific word; *buffalo* is a friendlier term, for discussing the animal's behavior and personality.) I envisioned this workshop as teaching the basic skills required for nature writing: the ability to observe the natural world and the ability to record one's experience of it. We would begin by observing buffalo and their environment, recording those observations with words and sketches. Then we would learn about the management issues surrounding bison and explore our own responses to the animal and the issues that surround it. But in the end I decided to keep to the barest of plans for these four days, because I wanted to allow plenty of room for our experiences to shape the class.

The methods described here can be used in other areas of concern, such as wetlands threatened by draining, agricultural land facing development, or city lots filling up with trash instead of gardens. They can also be used simply to build awareness of our natural world, whether your class is in a rural setting or in the center of a metropolitan area.

*　　*　　*

I awoke before dawn the first day. I drove down into Hayden Valley, where I thought we might begin the workshop. Fog hid the river and cloaked the road. Ahead, dark shapes shifted in the mist. Buffalo, crossing the road. Buffalo, grazing beside the road. Hundreds of them. I sat quietly in the car and watched and listened to them until the sun began to burn off the fog, and then I drove back to the cabin where I was staying. I had just enough time for breakfast before meeting the students at 9 A.M.

I knew my class would be small—four adults from Florida, California, Washington, and Montana. Only two showed up on time. While I made calls back to the Yellowstone Institute office to find out where the other two might be, I asked Steve (an educator from California) and Tim (a dairy farmer from Montana) to open their journals and write about why they were taking the class and about their expectations.

Then the three of us began an exploration of the bison's habitat. We drove toward the valley. At our first stop, we followed a faint trail through a wet area and on into some trees. A bison hoofprint. A tree rubbed at horn level. A wallow. We had walked barely one quarter-mile from the road, and already the students were discovering abundant clues about the behavior of buffalo.

As we walked down the hill to the road, the students noticed fringed gentian blooming beside a tiny rivulet. They stopped and asked if we could sketch such an unusual flower. I hesitated—morning was fast moving into afternoon, and if the buffalo were still around, this would be a good time to observe them. But spontaneity was also part of the plan, so I crouched down and showed Tim and Steve how to simplify a complicated object by looking for patterns and basic shapes. Soon they had sketches of gentian with detailed descriptive notes and questions. As they sketched, I studied the nearby grasses. Many of the slender green blades were actually sedges—grasslike plants that make up a large part of the bison's diet. Sedges have a simpler structure than grasses, and thus are easier for buffalo to digest. I told Steve and Tim about sedges, and asked them to compare the two types of plants in writing and drawing.

By the time we arrived in the valley, the buffalo were gone. We followed their tracks to the bank of the river where they had stepped into the water and swum across. I asked Steve and Tim to spend some time writing about what they knew about buffalo and what feelings they had toward them, and add any questions that came to mind. This simple exercise reassured me that my basic lesson plan would take us where we needed to go. The morning's spontaneity had given us a purpose—it was early afternoon, and Tim and Steve wanted to see buffalo.

We pulled out a topographic map and traced the river crossing through a thin band of trees into a series of small clearings. It looked as if a trail led through the area. We drove to the trailhead, loaded up our packs, and began walking.

As we climbed each hill and descended into each draw, I kept looking side to side and ahead for large, dark shapes. This was not only buffalo country—it was also grizzly bear country. From a distance, they look a lot alike.

Less than twenty minutes had passed when I saw, silhouetted on top of a hill, the unmistakable profile of a bull buffalo. Huge hump, massive head, slender hips. We wrote:

He looked in our direction and continued to do so for ten minutes, when it wallowed briefly, sat for five minutes, then rose and walked slowly south into the trees.

Half mile down the Howard Eaton trail, up on a ridge, sighting of our first buffalo—solitary silhouette against the hillside. Five minute stare down; started grazing, turned head. Wallow, then grazed along the adjacent ridge.

He seemed tense at first until we all got down, then he: laid on side, rubbed in dirt.

While we observed the bull buffalo, Tim and Steve sketched or whispered questions to me. I explained about wallowing, and that other buffalo were probably near by. After the bull walked into the trees, we continued along the trail and climbed another hill for a better view.

It's really quiet out here . . . all one can hear is the sound of the breeze—and the constant flies buzzing. The flutter of the wind is wonderful.

As we climbed, I thought I heard a deep rumbling. I motioned for everyone to stop; I cupped my hand to my ear and turned in the direction of the sound. On the hill below us were more than one hundred buffalo—females, calves, and males. The males were making all the noise—their bellows and grunts communicate their readiness to mate and challenge other males.

We spread out on the hill and sat down to observe.

This first day I continued to follow my loose plan: immerse the students in opportunity, observation, and information. Let them scribble notes as they see fit; guide them in simple field sketching techniques.

Steve was using a classic field journal writing technique. He had drawn a line down his page; on the left were his observations, on the right were questions:

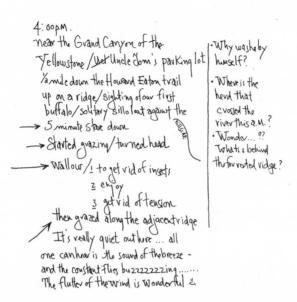

4:00 PM.
near the Grand Canyon of the
Yellowstone / past Uncle Tom's parking lot
½ mile down the Howard Eaton trail
up on a ridge / sighting of our first
buffalo / solitary Sillo'out against the
→ 5 minute stare down
→ Started grazing / turned head
→ Wallow / 1 to get rid of insects
          2 enjoy
          3 get rid of tension
then grazed along the adjacent ridge
It's really quiet out here ... all
one can hear is the sound of the breeze -
and the constant flies buzzzzzzzing.......
The flutter of the wind is wonderful &

• Why was he by
  himself?
• Where is the
  herd that
  crossed the
  river this a.m.?
• Wonder... ??
  What is behind
  the forested ridge?

Tim worked his notes around sketches, sometimes keying the words to the
drawings:

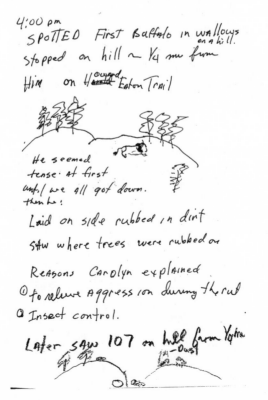

4:00 pm
SPOTTED First Buffalo in wallows
on a hill.
stopped on hill ~ ¼ mi from
Him on Howard Eaton Trail

He seemed
tense at first
until we all got down.
then he:

Laid on side rubbed in dirt

Saw where trees were rubbed on

Reasons Carolyn explained
① to relieve Aggression during the rut
② Insect control.

Later saw 107 on hill from Yↄↄ

By giving the students freedom to work with the blank pages this first day, I learned about their previous experience without the usual round-robin routine of introductions. I also was able to observe their habits, and to consider the directions we could explore in the next three days.

That night, exhausted, I held to the field journal discipline of finishing the notes for the day. I scribbled a one-page narrative of the day's events on the left side of the page, and listed my emotions on the right. I also sketched a plan for the next day. This included the messy necessity of spending time in the morning trying to track down the two missing students. (I found out that the man from Florida had dropped out; he had not been prepared for lengthy walking. The woman from Seattle was having car trouble.)

* * *

The second day's plan was to hike about four miles into Pelican Valley. This grassy, rolling landscape is winter habitat for buffalo; the namesake creek runs free of ice all winter due to hot springs on its banks. Here, in the late 1800s, the last few dozen buffalo survived the slaughter of sixty million of their species. These last buffalo were pursued by poachers; and the capture of one such criminal instigated the first of the laws that continue to protect wildlife and the environment today. Instead of simply telling my two students about this important historic event, I wanted them to walk through the valley to the site, to absorb the atmosphere, and to imagine the day and its activities, one hundred years ago.

We never got there.

Just as we crested the bluff overlooking the valley, and just as I was going to tell the group that we needed to be especially alert for bears, we saw one. It was a huge grizzly, feeding on roots and grubs about a quarter-mile away, across the creek. It looked up; it had heard us.

We held our breaths.

It returned to rooting around in the meadow.

We exhaled. I motioned Steve and Tim to be quiet and to sit still. I felt we were safe to sit and watch, but we definitely could not continue on the trail, which would have brought us directly to the grizzly. We quietly observed the bear for forty-five minutes as it grazed its way across the valley toward the trees. The farther away it went, the more relaxed we became. We began to write and to sketch.

GRIZZLY . . . what a feeling, or should I say feelings—fear, excitement, respect, pride, concern . . .

Grizzly—Rize Hair. Have feelings of delight. No fear yet.

Wonder if it saw/heard us? Was it a male or female? How old was it? What was it finding as it was grazing? Where did it go when it disappeared over the ridge?

The grizzly left our line of vision, perhaps bedding down in the tall grass.

Breaking for lunch, we ate our sandwiches and talked about the bear and the other hikers we could now see coming from the opposite direction. At that point, I told the students why we had come here. We stood and looked northeast, studied the map, and figured out the approximate location of the poacher's capture—where a small creek emerged from the forest into the valley. Although we didn't visit the actual site and didn't complete a writing exercise about it, we did experience Pelican Valley and its inhabitants. Experience to store for later use, the way a writer builds narratives and revisits themes as an essay progresses.

After we hiked out of the valley, we drove to nearby Yellowstone Lake. We found comfortable resting places on the shore, and I assigned a simple writing exercise designed to shift one's focus from the previous scene or event to the present.

The sensory inventory is a basic tool in my teaching kit:

> Find a comfortable place to sit. Close your eyes. Breathe deeply, once, twice, three times. Listen. What do you hear? Sniff. What do you smell? What does your skin tell you? Your hair? For the next five minutes—breathe in a deep rhythm, keep your eyes closed, and constantly inventory your other senses. Open your eyes. What do you see that you didn't see before? List all that you heard, smelled, felt. Link the words together in a narrative. Or draw the scene before you.

This exercise can take five minutes or an hour. I asked Tim and Steve to finish after thirty minutes, because we had another kind of writing to do.

While Tim and Steve wrote by the lake, I visited the ranger station and obtained a form to report the bear sighting. The park scientists appreciate these reports, which aid research and management. When I rejoined Tim and Steve, the three of us filled it out together. We had to describe the sighting location as precisely as we could, so we pulled out the topographic map and figured out exactly where we had been. We compared our field notes to answer questions about the bear's behavior and we had a lively discussion about whether the bear was light brown or medium brown. Each of us was able to augment our own field notes from this discussion: a good lesson in how teamwork can create more detailed field notes, thus leading to more realistic nature writing.

By the time we had completed the bear-sighting report, the afternoon was waning. We headed back to Hayden Valley. We returned to a place that we had visited before: a bridge that swallows nest beneath. I suggested another simple writing exercise: to make notes that compare and contrast the morning with the late-afternoon observations:

> Swallows feeding young under bridge. Constant movement with patterned entry on north and high exit on south and low. Upon reflection: the swallow flies low across the water into the wind probably for better control in starting its flight. And to fly low over the water to get insects.

It's warmer, probably more insects. . . .
The swallows are flying closer to us
They seem more animated
The ducks are still here
The killdeer is gone
Cool breeze; but it's not cold like this A.M.
Constant motion.

We didn't see one buffalo on this day. Tim and Steve didn't mind. Nor did I. We had shifted from buffalo to the entire ecosystem—something I had hoped for, but could not have orchestrated. I simply paid attention to opportunity and opened the way for us to move through it.

The broad scope of this day set the context for the next, third, day of the class, which I wanted to use as a climax of the workshop.

* * *

We began the third day by meeting up with the missing student from Seattle. Frankie had been in one of my previous classes, and I looked forward to the additional energy she would bring to the class. I introduced everyone and then listened as the exchanges of questions and information flowed for the next hour as we drove to the first site for the day.

As I pulled into the parking area, I requested a favor of my three students. We had a half-mile walk to the site, and I asked that we walk quietly. We walked to the scene of many years' field research by Dr. Mary Meagher, Yellowstone Park's retired bison biologist. Her summer research cabin is nestled in a little valley beside Blacktail Deer Creek. After I explained the importance of her work—explicating behavior and social interactions, determining migration routes—I sent everyone off for thirty minutes with instructions to do a sensory inventory for the first five minutes, and then to keep writing until I called them back to the cabin. In this way, I was reinforcing yesterday's introduction to this writing exercise and focusing them on today. The additional instruction was to write continuously—what is sometimes called "stream-of-consciousness writing" or "freewriting"—allows links and connections to appear that otherwise we usually miss in our rush to record and move on. I hoped that everyone would be full of questions, observations, curiosity.

When I called out a half hour later, the students returned from directions I hadn't seen them go: Frankie from the sage, Tim from the sedges, Steve from the copse of trees. We gathered at the cabin porch.

This was the first extended writing time, and I felt everyone had built enough trust to risk reading their writing. The shyness in their voices slowly gave way to surety. In this peaceful, supportive place, they had written about coyotes and creeks, music and God. Tim had entitled his page "Spirit Friend's

Music." He was the shyest of the three, a man who seemed to be bursting with unshared emotion. "The wind whistles like woodwinds . . . the water like violins," he read his description slowly, breathing deeply.

We packed up our gear and walked the half-mile out to the car. The group chatted and laughed during the walk, but as soon as we got back on the road, I quieted them down and shifted the mood. For the next couple of hours, I would be sharing with them what I had experienced in the winter of 1997.

Near the park's northern boundary, we rattled over a gravel road through semi-arid sagebrush habitat. Pronghorn watched us with huge, alert eyes. A coyote paused in hunting to watch us pass. We stopped at the crest of a hill and I set the scene:

> The Yellowstone Plateau had been covered by snow since early December. Then the snows melted, and froze again, and more snow fell on top of the ice. The ice was so thick and hard, you might as well have poured concrete on the ground. Not even the mighty buffalo, with its massive head that can plow through three feet of snow, could break through the ice to food.
>
> Here, in the protected valley around Gardiner, the snow was not so thick, the grass still available. The animals poured off the plateau and into this winter range. Elk and pronghorn and deer moved freely across the park boundary and into the surrounding national forest and private lands. Buffalo were either herded into corrals inside the park or shot as they stepped over the boundary.

"Imagine piles of bodies scattered across the snow of this valley," I told the class. "Imagine walking to the post office in Gardiner and passing flatbeds piled with buffalo. Imagine driving down this road and seeing steaming red gut piles. . . . Imagine living here, watching the slaughter, and being immobilized by horror."

Earlier in the class we had discussed the "official" reasons for the slaughter. Some buffalo carry a bacteria, *Brucella abortus,* which can cause domestic cattle to abort their first pregnancy. The state of Montana contends that buffalo will transmit this disease to livestock. They ignore science and reality: buffalo have never transmitted the bacteria to cattle under natural free-range conditions. But the state insists that buffalo leaving Yellowstone pose a serious health and economic risk to the state's livestock producers, and thus they must be killed.

In 1997, the state of Montana forced National Park Service rangers and other federal employees to round up buffalo. More than five hundred buffalo died before the park's superintendent called a halt to his agency's participation. The state and its hired guns continued killing buffalo. The final count: 1,100 bison.

We turned south onto a narrower gravel road and parked at the corrals. I told the group to take a half hour to explore, to envision the corrals filled with buffalo, to feel the presence of these animals. Then we would move to a nearby site, of equal but very different importance.

Steve, Tim, and Frankie peered through the slats of wood that solidified the corrals. They touched the steel structures and looked up at the catwalk around the perimeter. Tim, the dairy farmer, clambered up the chutes and looked down into the pens.

A silence deeper than wilderness settled over the place, a silence broken only by grasshoppers buzzing away from us as we rustled through the brittle, thigh-high grasses of late summer. The darkness of that winter began to creep through me again; I forced myself to look into the corrals, to run my fingers along the wood and steel until I couldn't look anymore.

At the end of the half-hour, I stood by the car. Tim, Steve, and Frankie walked up, one by one, solemn and quiet. We drove to a field on the other side of the corral. Here I set another scene:

> Fifteen degrees, windless, six inches of new snow, brilliant blue winter sky. We are among fifty other people walking in a slow motion line, in time to the singing of a Lakota spiritual leader.

The students and I walked at that same pace to a spot I will never forget. I led them into a circle, asking everybody to sit and close their eyes. I said to them:

> Imagine you are standing in this circle shoulder to shoulder with people from all around Montana—from Gardiner, from Paradise Valley, from Livingston, from Bozeman. People from three hundred miles away, from Missoula. People who have driven from South Dakota. You are shoulder to shoulder with people you do not know but with whom you share grief. Two Lakota men pace in circles in the center: one chanting in his tribal language; the other speaking in English, as if translating. They speak of the buffalo, of the animal's importance to their lives, of the animal itself, of the slaughter and pain occurring this winter. They sanctify this ground with their prayers; they pass the pipe around the circle; the Indian women, wrapped in their Pendleton blankets, weep; we all have our heads bowed. As the leader's voice soars again in song, several of us glance up and see one bald eagle rising on a wave of heat from the ground. As it circles above our circle, other people lift their heads and see the eagle.

I stopped speaking and let the silence grow. Everybody kept their eyes closed. We sat motionless in this field, during the hottest time of the year, the temperature close to one hundred degrees. Still, I shivered as I had on that cold day, waiting—resisting the urge to break the spell too soon.

Quietly, I asked the students to wait until they were fully ready to open their eyes, and then immediately open their journals and begin to write . . . but in a certain way. They were to begin at the edge of the page and write words that spiraled inward to the center, pause, and then reverse the spiral of words back out to the edge. I opened my journal, doing the exercise with them.

I began with a list of facts—location, date, weather conditions, construction of the corral—and reached the center with "ropes, squeeze, bang, wind, rust, grass," then immediately spiraled back out with a shift to words of mood and emotion—"desolation, sorrow, grief." Reaching the edge touched on my own memory of the prayer ceremony, ending "with the Indians, and the eagle, and the buffalo."

This exercise works on many levels. It provides a specific structure to help ground people and also a solid space to anchor the emerging emotions and thoughts. And because of its confined length, the exercise has a clear beginning and end. As I watched and waited for each student's pen to reach the edge of the

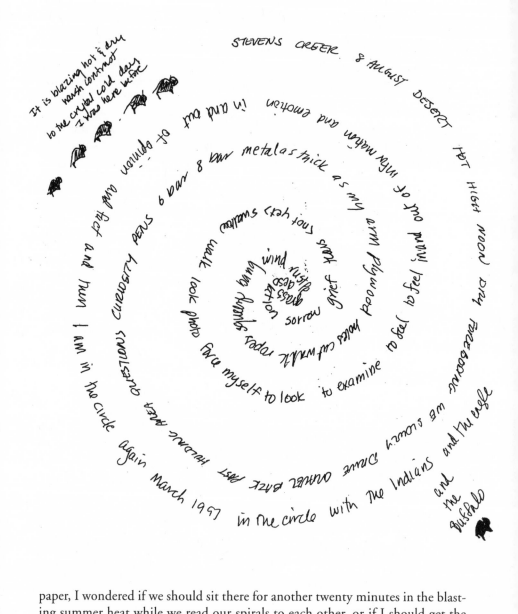

STEVENS CREEK. 8 AUGUST DESERT HOT HIGH NOON our racebooks we crouch Draw arther Back Smell humus in and out of inspiration and emotion out of inspiration to feel inward to feel inward to examine myself to look photo for a look walk radar look past other past HISTORIC QUESTIONS CURIOSITY PENS 6 bar 8 bar metal as thick as my arm physical wire pulled cut walk ropes grief that trees that swallow silver sky arms wind rustle grass desolation sorrow I am in the circle with the Indians and the eagle and the buffalo in the circle again March 1997 I am in the circle again and hurt and but and of opinion wanted to and but in It is blazing hot & a harsh contrast to the crystal cold day I was here before

paper, I wondered if we should sit there for another twenty minutes in the blasting summer heat while we read our spirals to each other, or if I should get the group back to town for water and food. I decided on the latter, but made the transition slowly and as smoothly as I could. When the last student had finished writing, we rose and walked back to the car in silence.

* * *

It was four P.M. when we drove back into the park. We returned to Blacktail, where I had intended to lead the group on a two-mile walk to a site where a Sun Dance had been held during the summer after the slaughter. (Sun Dances are Native American spiritual rites conducted in sacred places; I had been invited as a spectator.) But I had also wanted us to revisit Mary Meagher's cabin, to soak in the peace and balance. I offered the group a choice. They chose to revisit a known place: the cabin.

When we reached the cabin, I placed a few bones on the porch and pulled out my drawing supplies. Everyone quieted down. As we settled into comfortable positions on the porch, I described another classic field sketching technique—contour drawing.

This method of observation disconnects your eye and hand from your overactive brain. You place your pen on the paper, study the object you are to draw, and then slowly begin tracing the object with your eye at the same time that you begin moving the pen. In its classic form, which I always teach first, you don't look at the paper until you are finished. Seldom does the drawing look like the object, but it almost always reveals something about the object you otherwise would have never seen.

The attention and meditation required for this exercise mirrored the atmosphere at the corrals beautifully; its objectivity balanced the emotions that the earlier exercise had evoked. Plus, the students were centered enough to give this exercise the time and trust it requires.

Steve muttered "Impossible!" as he looked at his drawing.

I smiled to myself. *Well, I didn't promise them it would be accurate.*

Then he showed the page to me. I was stunned. He had drawn the bison bone perfectly. We both smiled. He admitted he had tried this exercise just to humor me, figuring it utterly impossible to accomplish.

I sent him off whistling to the creek, with instructions to spend another thirty minutes of quiet time in the same place he had sat this morning. Tim and Frankie followed. I wanted them to inventory their senses, to compare the site now with how they had experienced it that morning, and to freewrite.

When we had regrouped, I decided that the time was right to share the spiral writing. We now had a little distance from the experience of the corrals. To enhance trust, I asked everyone to listen to each other in silence, and to pause between readings. No evaluation, no discussion—just complete attention. Each of us used different words, but they began as facts and spiraled into feelings and back out again. Steve and I ended with *buffalo,* Tim ended with *help,* Frankie ended with *hope.* As a writer, I appreciated the variety. As a teacher, I felt gratified that the experiment had worked. And as a listener, I was moved to tears. The last reader's voice faded in the wind, and we all simply sat in silence.

*   *   *

On the last day, our small group became even smaller. Tim had to leave early; an emergency had occurred on his farm. His departure left us sad, and we discussed how to spend the day.

We decided to spend the morning observing buffalo, looking for them on a wooded slope between the road and a deep canyon. We quietly crept into the trees to a place where we were shielded from view. We pulled out our notebooks and began recording buffalo behavior:

> A huge bull rubs his horns between two trees, then scrapes the points up and down the trunk of one.

> One bull is tending a female: she grazes, he stands beside her; another male comes near, he bellows; she moves, he moves; where she goes, he goes.

> Calves disappear in the deep grass.

> One calf tries to nurse; a male approaches, the mother lunges at the male and then butts away the calf; it looks confused and then turns to graze, milk still on its muzzle.

> A large female moves off into the trees, away from us; the herd gradually follows.

We sat still and listened to the buffalos' grunts and bellows until they were gone from sight.

I packed away my notebook and suggested now would be a good time to go into the meadow and look at the fresh wallows, the rubbings, and the hornings on the tree trunks. As we picked our way over a maze of fallen trees to the wood's edge, suddenly two bulls came charging back into the meadow bellowing and butting heads. Before we could retreat, the entire herd was back in the meadow and walking quickly along the edge of the trees. One huge bull was bellowing away about twenty feet from us; I motioned Frankie and Steve to be absolutely still. The bull looked toward us; so did a female. He snorted; she moved past him. Then he followed her.

Thank god for the lure of sex! I breathed a deep sigh of relief as the animals crossed the road to the broad, open hill.

We waited a few minutes and then began exploring the meadow. In the excitement of the danger we had stopped taking notes to watch and wait. As we bent to examine the slashes on the trunks and run the wallowed soil through our fingers, I reminded everyone to take notes, jot down words, ideas, and information.

I absentmindedly pulled up a blade of grass and noticed that sedges were mixed with the grasses here. An opportunity!

I pulled up three sedge and grass blades. Keeping one set for myself, I gave the others to Frankie and Steve. According to park rules, you can only pick a plant if you eat it on the spot. So I suggested we taste-test the two plants. Were they really different? How so? Was one sweeter than the other? One harder to chew?

This simple experiential exercise brought Steve and me back to the first day of the workshop, when we had stopped to study the gentians and sedges. Steve explained the importance of sedges to Frankie while I thoughtfully chewed the blade. Sedges really are softer, more palatable, and sweeter. I actually chewed and swallowed the sedge; I spit out the grass. Now we knew about the buffalo's food firsthand.

The rest of the day's plan was as loose as that of the first two days—I had hoped to arrive at a field observation site in the morning so that we could complete one more exercise before retreating to the shade for the heat of the day. Our sojourn with the buffalo and sedges foiled those sensible plans. We arrived at the field site when the sun was directly overhead and the heat was almost unbearable. But Steve and Frankie were excited about yet another rare opportunity: one hundred yards from the road lay the carcass of a buffalo. I had seen the carcass four weeks before, and by now all the big scavengers—bears and wolves, for example—were long gone and we could safely approach it.

The only instructions I gave them were to describe the scene with sketches and words:

Redtail hawk overhead, four antelope in distance; very hot, some clouds, thunder clouds; head crushed, hair up to thirty–forty yards from body.

Furs scattered for yards; cause of death unknown, male or female? ribs torn out, decomposed; slight smell/some flies, grasshoppers, crickets.

So much to study here, where to begin? the patterns of fur left on the body? The pattern of bare skin? The splotches of bird droppings white like spilt batter on a dark wood floor?

Together with Steve and Frankie, I sketched the carcass, gagged when the breeze shifted, and settled again upwind to record the presence of beetles, grasshoppers, and butterflies on this pile of bones and skin. We repeated this set of movements and reactions for about an hour. Then we escaped the heat beside a creek where we soaked our toes in icy water as we ate a late lunch. Next we were off to one final observation site: a hill overlooking the Lamar Valley, where we could watch a herd of buffalo.

This time, I instructed Frankie and Steve to study the entire group for a time and describe what they saw. I asked them then to focus on one or two animals and to make detailed notes about the animals' behavior. In this way, we practiced another classic field observation technique: altering points of view. Study the distance, then study the foreground; focus on a group, then focus on individuals. This technique is used for observation, writing, and sketching to exercise your vision, your skills, and your ability to embrace an entire scene.

While the students were practicing these observation skills, I focused on a blade of grass, drawing a series of details with brush pen, fine-line pen, and finally just watercolor pencil. In the corner of the page, I wrote brief notes:

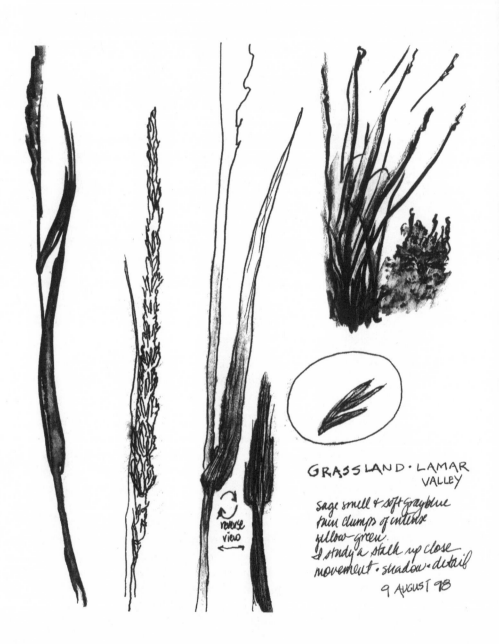

GRASSLAND · LAMAR
VALLEY

sage smell & soft grayblue
thin clumps of intense
yellow-green.
I study a stalk up close
movement · shadow · detail
9 AUGUST 98

reverse
view

Frankie glanced at my page and picked out a selection of watercolor pencils. She transformed her page of writing by adding a map of buffalo movement, a sketch of pines beside the river, a color drawing of a creek meandering through the valley, and a rendering of the shifting light of clouds and sun:

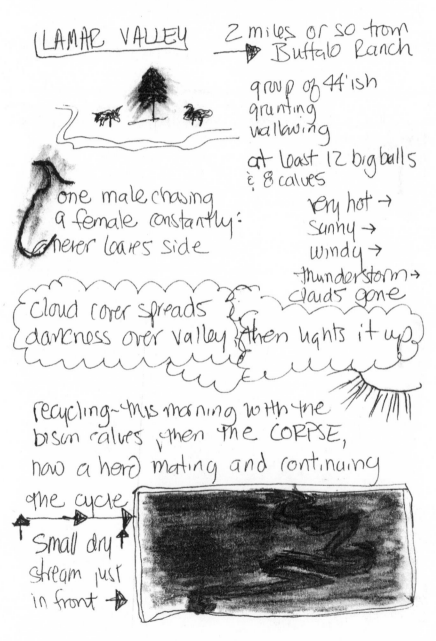

LAMAR VALLEY

2 miles or so from → Buffalo Ranch

grup of 44'ish grunting wallowing

at least 12 big balls & 8 calves

one male chasing a female constantly: never loaves side

very hot →
sunny →
windy →
thunderstorm →
clouds gone

Cloud cover spreads darkness over valley: then lights it up.

recycling~this morning with the bison calves, then the CORPSE, now a herd mating and continuing the cycle

Small dry stream just in front →

We had come a long way, this small class and I, from being strangers to being colleagues writing and painting side by side. In four days, their writing had grown from the rudimentary beginning of lists and facts to an ability to observe, connect, and reflect.

The day and the class ended as Steve and Frankie huddled around a table at the Yellowstone Institute to sort through their journal pages and plan the creation of a group journal. (Tim had generously left his journal with Steve for this project.) Having a group journal was Steve's idea; it would be a gift to each of us.

The soul of this workshop resides between the tattered covers of this group journal—which wasn't even my idea. From time to time, I look through it and see on every page the love and respect for buffalo that Steve, Frankie, and Tim developed during these four days. The journal also conveys their understanding of the land that belongs to these animals. It's in their notes, their drawings, and their quick watercolor sketches, but most of all, in their writing.

INTO THE CLASSROOM

The wild does not have words.
The unwritten pages spread themselves in all directions!
I come across the marks of roe-deers' hooves in the snow.
Language but no words.
  —Tomas Tranströmer

Mary Edwards Wertsch

What Is the Voice That Whispers?

Writing Nature Poems Based on Pablo Neruda's *Book of Questions*

IT WAS THE FIRST DAY at our community's new Green Center, a sprawling old home acquired by the city and rededicated as a community center for activities relating to nature. Ours was the very first class, a small group of fourth graders gathered early on a Saturday morning in May. The amenities were few: a long table and some folding chairs set up in the garage, since the house was still being renovated.

The poetry lesson had been advertised as "Wandering and Wondering," and my intention was to build it around an exploratory walk through a wooded area nearby. The kids had arrived armed with notebooks and pencils, as requested. Before we set out, however, I had them sit around the table in the garage to receive their instructions.

"Can we write about anything we want?" one girl asked, before I had a chance to begin.

"Well, yes and no," I answered. "Yes, you can write about anything in nature that you observe on the walk we're about to take. But no, I don't want you to write it in any way you like; I have some rules for you this morning."

"I know: no rhyming!" a few called out. These kids know me. I discourage them from rhyming their poems, simply because I've found that kids are all too ready to sacrifice the most thrilling lines of thought and the most exciting word combinations, just for the sake of a rhyme. Sometimes we do write poems that rhyme, but in my classes rhyming is confined to those specific lessons.

"Right! No rhyming! But there's another rule, too. Something you've never done before. Your poem is going to be made of questions."

A clamor of disbelief. "Huh? Questions? What kind of poem is that!"

It happens that this group of kids has considerable writing talent. They love writing, and they allow me to teach them, but they are enough at home with their own talents to chafe at restrictions that seem unreasonable.

"Don't worry," I said. "You're going to find that questions are a doorway through which you can grab your readers. Questions are a powerful tool for writers. I'm not talking about questions such as 'How many squirrels are in that tree?' That kind of question has a straightforward answer, and you ordinarily wouldn't dwell on it. I'm talking about questions that are exciting, that get you to think. The kind of questions I mean are wondering questions that spin a bit in your head, perhaps surprise you, and are certainly not easy to answer.

"I have some terrific examples to read to you, by one of the best poets in the world. He's been dead for a while now, but he left many great poems. His name is Pablo Neruda, from the country called Chile in South America. He won the Nobel Prize for Literature."

"And he wrote only in questions?"

"No. But he knew how to write exciting questions, and one of his books, *The Book of Questions,* was a single poem composed entirely of questions. It was one of his last works." Then I read a selection of his lines about nature from that book:

XLVII

In the middle of autumn
do you hear yellow explosions?

By what reason or injustice
does the rain weep its joy?

Which birds lead the way
when the flock takes flight?

From what does the hummingbird hang
its dazzling symmetry?

XLIX

When I see the sea once more
will the sea have seen or not seen me?

Why do the waves ask me
the same questions I ask them?

And why do they strike the rock
with so much wasted passion?

Don't they get tired of repeating
their declaration to the sand?

The fourth graders were listening intently. I began to skip around in the book, each time pausing for them to comment on the questions I'd just read. It wasn't long before they developed a sense of which questions worked best for them. Pretty soon they had decided on a few favorites:

Are they birds or fish
in these nets of moonlight?

Who wakes up the sun when it falls asleep
on its burning bed?

At what does the watermelon laugh
when it's murdered?

Some of the lines made them laugh. Their comments made it clear they were starting to view questions as vehicles for putting together surprising combinations of ideas. The ability to shock, puzzle, and delight through questions appealed to them.

"Okay," I said. "Now let's go outside and get our material." We grabbed notebooks and pencils and set out across the dewy lawn toward the trees. The idea, I told them, was to keep all senses open to what was happening around us and to quietly make lists. "Don't try to write your poem out here," I advised them. "Just make notes of what you find. When we're back at the table, you'll have time to pick and choose among your notes and make your question poem."

The woods themselves were such an unruly tangle that we had to give up on walking through them, but that didn't matter. We found more than enough material around us, just poking through the grass and studying the bushes, vines, and trees along the perimeter. We stopped still every once in a while, just listening. In less than fifteen minutes we all had plenty of notes.

The following is the list of notes made by ten-year-old Anna Shafer-Skelton:

two skinny trees standing together like sisters
rabbits whispering
the song of "birdie, birdie, birdie!"
the wind rattling the trees
the crow calling out in a hoarse voice
a branch snapping behind us
a dark tunnel through the thick, green woods, covered with brown leaves
the questioning, fearful, scared whine of some unknown bird
the overgrown trails unnoticed
the sweet taste of black mulberries

Back at the table in the garage, we talked about the different ways of asking questions. In addition to Who? What? When? Where? How?, there are also Is it true? Does it seem? Have you ever? Will I? And of course many others. We looked again at several lines from the Neruda book, studying his variety of questions.

Anna began to make questions from her notes—and soon discovered that questions inspire other questions. She made a list of them:

Why does a crow choose to talk in a hoarse voice when she can call in a clear,
bell-like voice?
How can a path be truly neglected when it is used all the time by deer and
foxes?

Will this place of wonders be here forever?
When does nature become evil?
Do these animals ever die?
Do the birds ever weep?
Is the greatest place in towering clouds of leaves or loud, noisy cities?
Does nature ever become evil?
Do rabbits die needlessly?
Is the forest ever forgotten?
Are the birds ever envious of one another?
Is there a time when birds do not sing?

Anna played with this list, rewriting lines and moving them around. After struggling with it for a while, she realized that it would work better as two separate poems. Here are her finished versions:

Poem One

Why does a crow talk
in a hoarse, scratchy voice?
Why does a cardinal talk in a clear,
bell-like voice?
Are the birds ever envious
of one another?
Is there a time when birds
do not sing?

Poem Two

Does nature ever become evil?
Do rabbits die needlessly?
Do the birds ever weep?
Is the forest ever forgotten?

We finished the lesson by copying the final versions in permanent fine-point marker into small books created by folding together two pieces of handmade paper from an art store, punching two holes close to the fold, running a piece of raffia-like ribbon through them, and tying a bow. I have learned that when the lesson involves putting the final poem in an attractive booklet or on a pendant or mobile, children have more incentive to do their best, and are more likely to take pleasure in showing off their work afterward.

The students were justifiably proud of their work that Saturday morning, and I was pleased to find the experiment had been successful. It was clear to me that once the kids were exposed to Neruda's poetry, they began to catch on to the powerful effect that is possible when poetic expression is couched in the compelling format of a question. The invitation to the reader to reflect on the words is close to irresistible.

Neruda's *Book of Questions* provides questions on a variety of topics, not just nature. But I think the subject of nature is ideal for a lesson on question-poems. It provides focus. It also forces the student to think in terms of the concrete and observable—and the combination of concrete images and abstract questioning is inherently powerful. Not only do the poems tend to be strong, but the students become excited when they see the unexpected happening on the page before them. Writing about nature in questions is an effective way to unite direct observation and a reflective voice, and it gives the student a sense of power with language, as in the following poem written that same morning by ten-year-old Rebecca Eissenberg:

What Is the Message?

What is the voice
that whispers,
Take me in?

To whom is it that the
prideful cardinal sings?

What does it mean
when the strongest tree
falls to the ground?

Why is it the prettiest flower
always blooms last?

Where is it that the only
sound is the stream
flowing softly?

Why is it that the best place
on earth is always
the most untouched?

Bibliography

Neruda, Pablo. *The Book of Questions.* Translation by William O'Daly. Port Townsend: Copper Canyon Press, 1991.

Michael Morse

The Relative Nature of Nature

Growth and Change in Wallace Stevens's "A Rabbit as King of the Ghosts"

> There is always an analogy between nature and the imagination,
> and possibly poetry is merely the strange rhetoric of that parallel.
>
> —*Wallace Stevens*

I CAN MODESTLY CLAIM that once I was a naturalist of sorts. What I remember best about my two-year stint banding songbirds and conducting field studies on herons and gulls was how good it felt to completely lose track of my "self" and focus on my task—the bird (literally) in my hand. Sometimes, when I'm teaching a lesson, writing a poem, or playing a sport, I am able to reach a similar state. At other times, however, I find that my perceptions of the external world hinge completely on my internal preoccupations: the impending root canal, last night's argument with a friend, or the anticipation of a first date. I could be sitting quietly in a room or riding a barrel over Niagara Falls—it wouldn't matter where I am. In these moments, "nature" serves more as a stage or mirror for internal feelings. As a poet, I am keenly interested in the balance between sensory perception and the filter of thought and feeling—external nature and internal nature, or what's objective and what's subjective—and how that balance is constantly shifting.

This dichotomy echoes a much larger trend in science. To a certain extent, modern physics has revised the way we look at the world. We are more aware of who is doing the looking. Classical physics taught us that the world has an objective existence with immutable laws, but quantum theory champions the notion that "science" is highly subjective.[1] Can the physicist, then, call the poet "cousin"? In some ways, the answer is yes.

One of my favorite poets whose work reflects these relations of "nature," "self," and "world" is Wallace Stevens. While Stevens's poetry is lamentably written off by many teachers as too abstract or philosophical, I consider him a nature poet for our age. Borrowing the term for "physicist" from Isaac Newton's day, I'd call Stevens a "natural philosopher." The joy of reading Stevens lies in how he makes the reader contemplate transformation and change—the relative nature of nature. According to Stevens:

If we were all alike; if we were millions of people saying *do, re, mi* in unison, one poet would be enough. . . . But we are not all alike, and everything needs expounding all the time because, as people live and die, each one perceiving life and death for himself, and mostly by and in himself, there develops a curiosity about the perceptions of others. This is what makes it possible to go on saying new things about old things.[2]

Keen observation and imagination make Stevens's poems exciting and fresh. His ear for music and his baroque spirit of play enhance the reciprocal arrangement of internal nature (feeling, mood, thinking) and external nature (the "outside" world). For Stevens, imagination is a privileged lens, a tool of creation. Objects out in the world are not absolute things; they are the phenomena of perception. Think of the way we vacillate when we choose between appetizers on a menu—wouldn't *this* be good? What about *this*? Think of the way we can look at a boat on the horizon or a bright bird in a high tree. Are our responses physical, emotional, or both? The notion that "nature" is a constant seesaw of presence and absence, of the internal and the external, is something Stevens loved to explore in his poems.

While I was a little wary of teaching Stevens to my youngest students, I was confident that they would "get" Stevens's work if I stressed its imagination and playful language, and had them listen to the music of his words rather than zealously search for "meaning." I wanted my students to experience Stevens's sheer delight with language, his playful side and his eccentric images: horses covered with mice, zithers, angels, mangoes, books being read, snoods, crows that look rusty, tambourines, stars, and people dancing around jars in Tennessee.

While I've had success teaching well-known Stevens poems such as the terrific "Thirteen Ways of Looking at a Blackbird," I chose to use a poem less familiar: "A Rabbit as King of the Ghosts." This poem balances absence, presence, and transformation; it explores the relative nature of nature, both tactile and cognitive. I love how it exalts thinking and feeling and how it chronicles and celebrates change and growth.

Before presenting the poem to my students, I talked about "nature." We talked about the senses, and how verbal images can help reproduce sensory experience; how metaphors and similes and figurative language allow us to define or describe something in a more concrete fashion ("love is a rose"). Then I asked them a series of questions:

Have you ever gone through a transformation or been engaged in an activity and felt as though you "were in a zone" (to use a common sports expression)—or totally at peace in a specific place, or completely confident in your ability to do a task?

The students told me about game-winning goals in hockey or hits in little league baseball, as well as moments of confidence when they prepared well for a test and knew they would "ace it" after merely glancing at the questions.

Have you ever had to overcome a sense of fear to get to this sure, confident place that we just talked about? (This fear might have taken the form of an opponent or an obstacle, human or otherwise—a bully, an aggressive dog, or a fear of heights.)

Some kids discussed their first day of school, which was no easy task for seventh graders entering a school with grades seven through twelve. I asked them if there were any areas in school that they were initially afraid to hang out in, but later could because they eventually overcame their fears. After seeing a few devilish smiles in the room, Jake finally replied, "The senior grass." (This is a patch of lawn that the seniors designate as their own—no underclasspeople allowed! A few bold seventh graders usually work up the gumption to dart across the grass, taunting seniors before speeding off to safety).

How many of you have a place at home where you mark your height on a wall, so that you can go back and see how tall you were, say, five years ago? What's fun about that?

Students comment on how much fun it is to see how far they've come. This visible change—what seemed so high a year ago, now looks low—gives us a new perspective on the world. As we discussed various measurement "systems" from home, other topics cropped up: for instance, how the quarter ride outside the candy store used to be an adventure on a bucking bronco, but now seems a tame "kiddie" ride. Dan mentioned how a mountain he had been afraid to snowboard had become smaller and less intimidating as he grew older, taller, and stronger.

And finally, "What is a nature poem?"

This question got a lot of puzzled looks. I asked them what the term "nature poem" made them think of. Their replies included trees, leaves, grass, animals, sunsets, John Denver, bugs, and peace of mind. One student, Jed, added Mr. Stracke (the school's photography teacher) to the list. Practically everyone turned toward Jed with confused and amused glances, wondering what he meant by the last reference. *Why did you think of the photography teacher?* Jed explained that in art class they were constantly going outside to observe and draw or photograph "nature."

"So where do you fit into a nature poem?" I continued.

Some kids replied that "you" are the one in nature, talking about it . . . or even interacting with it. I then added that we filter nature thorough our own lenses—and discussed how "shutting off the self" to have a more "objective" view of things can seem incomplete. In the same way that sentimental language in poetry excludes our capacity to feel a variety of things in an instant, shutting off the self limits the variety of what it's like to be in a moment in the world.[3]

At this point I felt the students were ready for some Stevens. I read "A Rabbit as King of the Ghosts" aloud, asking them beforehand to be aware of what they noticed.

A Rabbit as King of the Ghosts

The difficulty to think at the end of the day,
When the shapeless shadow covers the sun
And nothing is left except light on your fur—

There was the cat slopping its milk all day,
Fat cat, red tongue, green mind, white milk
And August the most peaceful month.

To be in the grass, in the peacefullest time,
Without that monument of cat,
The cat forgotten in the moon;

And to feel that the light is a rabbit-light,
In which everything is meant for you
And nothing need be explained;

Then there is nothing to think of. It comes of itself;
And east rushes west and west rushes down,
No matter. The grass is full

And full of yourself. The trees around are for you,
The whole of the wideness of night is for you,
A self that touches all edges,

You become a self that fills the four corners of night.
The red cat hides away in the fur-light
And there you are humped high, humped up,

You are humped higher and higher, black as stone—
You sit with your head like a carving in space
And the little green cat is a bug in the grass.

Most noticed the rabbit, light, day into night, and the cat. I then handed out copies of the poem, which we read twice—once silently, and once aloud.

We then began discussing the poem. My students were quick to celebrate the merits of the opening line, asking if we could skip the work and go outside. I laughed but didn't cave in. Kate chimed in about how cool it was that "you" the reader suddenly have fur in line three. Another student pointed out, "Here's where the title comes from," understanding the fur as link to the rabbit of the title. Some kids weren't sure about whom the poem is addressed to—the "you" could be a distinct character—but most wanted to read "you" as a direct address that brings us right into the thick of the poem. It's our fur and our predicament at the end of the day.

We then hit a perplexing question—Who's the cat? A metaphoric "fat cat," as poet Shirley Kaufman suggests in her appraisal of this poem?[4] Perhaps, but I sense two simultaneous possibilities for the cat: on the one hand, it's bloated and lazy; on the other, it's a potential threat to the rabbit, the "you" in the poem. What I love about the cat is the sensory language that comes alive with it—the lively colors; its gluttonous "slopping" its milk; and the musical two-step of the second line in the second stanza, each description a spondee. I asked the students if the cat might be a metaphor of sorts, a warning about laziness or indifference or gluttony. I got lots of blank stares in reply, but continued with a discussion of the two interesting characters that emerge early in the poem—the Cat and the Rabbit.

About the third stanza, Andrew chimed in from the front row about the senior grass and how nice it would be if we could have class there. The students were also quite preoccupied with the term *peacefullest.* Is it a word? They were hesitant to respond but bold Seth exclaimed, "Why not?" I agreed. I love how that one playful word seems newly minted, with a grace foreign to the language of adults.

Then discussion turned to moonlight and monuments. We talked about how the moonlight in the third and fourth stanzas seems to bring with it a feeling of confidence: It not only swallows up the memory of cats past—the gluttonous and superficial cat, the threatening cat—but in turn becomes a part of "you"—it's not just moonlight, it's *rabbit-light.* The last two lines of the fourth stanza tell us this, deftly show us the transformation that's taking place. The other word that intrigued the students was *monument.* One student asked, "Why use some word that sounds like a statue?" Semere thoughtfully responded by saying how statues help us to "remember things, usually positive things," and that they are art that stands for something. I asked the students if the cat stands for something in the poem. We discussed this for a bit, and decided that a monument is sort of like a physical memory—not as intense or "real" as the person or thing being remembered. This "in-between" state is something that Stevens explores in much of his poetry—the fine lines between presence and absence, feeling and thinking, the physical and the abstract. We talked about this and the way that a "ghost" is an intermediary between two worlds, an entity that exists yet only suggests matter, just as a "monument" remains perched between two worlds. To avoid getting sidetracked by ghost stories, I steered the discussion back to the poem. Harley responded that "your" calm feelings of peace and confidence "swallow up" the memory of Cat. How insightful! I added that all of this feeling and change is shown through the natural, physical world—the moonlight becoming rabbit-light.

Stanza five, we decided, brings us to that great place where we feel like we're "in a zone"—the poetic equivalent of what a basketball star feels when he or she can't miss a shot. I love the pattern of iambs and anapests in the second line, followed by the terse music of the confidently dismissive statement, "no matter." In the sixth and seventh stanzas, Rabbit is confident and belongs—even the night becomes a place where he feels fully at home—the "whole" of it "for you." The cat had the spotlight all day, but you—as Rabbit—inhabit the night; it's your "zone," "your own special kingdom." [5]

By poem's end you are, as my students put it, "large and in charge." You have influence over a manageable external world. My kids commented that they love when this happens to them—how they feel "bigger" and in control when with their friends. Part of the wonder of the poem is that it captures a moment of transformation that's often so seamless we don't notice it. We can be Rabbit in the present moment and simultaneously feel and describe the change as we change. We see our old nemesis Cat in a sharp, new light of awareness—now a "bug in the grass"—because imagination and feeling give a new shape to nature. Reading "Rabbit" makes us simultaneously observe and participate as we watch our feelings shift and change from moment to moment. An awareness of the possibility of transformation fills the reader. As readers, we extrapolate to see the promise of change and transformation in our own lives. We see Cat as the equivalent of pencil marks on those growth charts at home—he shows us how much we've grown.

We also briefly discussed the title and "mood" of the poem—both of which suggest something mythical and fairytale-like. The poem's title might suggest that a ghost actually speaks this poem, and that Rabbit's new awareness and transformation serve to "transcend" Cat and the regular world, so that Rabbit can reach some heavenly or spiritual realm. Depending on the class, I'll sometimes talk about how allegory and metaphor work—particularly how metaphor shakes free of direct description or direct imagery in order to discover new relationships through likeness. Seeing the rabbit and the cat as players on a metaphorical stage isn't as fun as simply getting on stage with the characters themselves, but the poem can be read as an extended metaphor on discovery, growth, and change.

At this point, the kids were very much ready to write, ready to re-imagine themselves (or someone or something else), just as the Rabbit does in Stevens's poem. But just before I set my rabbits loose, I gave them a few suggestions:

• Try to write using your senses—literally "get in touch" with your surroundings by letting sight, sound, smell, texture, and even taste bring your environment to life. This "environment" can be a place in nature or it might be your living room.

• Try to show, through the senses, a change or transformation—a change in "you" that is visible and knowable because the relationship changes between you and an obstacle or threat. (To get my point across, I directed their attention back to the poem and how the cat initially seems like a threat, but by poem's end becomes "a bug." The cat hasn't really changed so much as the "you" in the poem has grown: "You . . . are higher and higher." Remember that change is often visible and measurable by the things around us—like those pencil marks on a wall that measure our growth.)

• You might want to try this poem as a dramatic monologue—in the voice of an animal or tree or flower or even an object! Put yourself in the shoes of another being/thing/ghost, and speak in its voice. (What, for example, would it be like to be a butterfly that emerges from a chrysalis, usddenly transformed from a grounded insect to one with the potential and power of flight?)

• Try to imitate the form of the Stevens poem—make it a shortish poem, and if you like, use stanzas of three lines each.

Here are some perceptive and imaginative examples of what my seventh graders came up with:

Prayers and Promises of a Tree

Where the sun kisses the sea on the blind horizon,
and the line between what's real and what's not
is undistinguishable,
where dark knows not if it is light,
or light, the wind,
or wind, the rain.
Where dreams are created
and thoughts become fears,
there are trees.
Tall trees, formed by strength itself.
Their hands rise up and up,
reaching at the sky.
Grabbing at the stars.
I am a tree.
Yet I am no bigger than a shrub.
I am useless.
Why torture me in the land of giants,
where even the ants that crawl
beneath me feel no intimidation
as they trudge on, passing me by.
And then I remember
Father Time shall rise up from his home
within the core of Mother Earth,
and he shall spin the hands on his bronze clock of ages,
And time will push on as it always does.
And I, I will grow and grow.
I will grow past the moon and back again.
My branches, as whips, will be powerful limbs.
I will pass the peaks of majestic mountains
and dust off their snowy caps.
I will twist through the limits of your imagination,
and grow into your mind.

and all will look up to me.
This I promise you.

    —Kyle Beltran

A Pitcher as King of the World

The sheer thought at the end of the day
when the batters dig their feet in.
And what is left is your goosebumped shin
and the small boy standing far from the plate—
small kid, short hair, determined mind, blind eyes
and October is the worst month.

Along with December, January, February, and March.
You see where I'm going.

And to see his scared eyes
and everything is nothing
and your life is depending on this.

There is nothing to do. Have to choose:
high and fast or down and away,
the question of the ages.
You take your time to look up
past the lights and into the
large connect-the-dots game of the world.

The mound gets larger as you shrink
you stand, just another lost dependent clause,
and your little red hat takes the sweat.

    —Ben Kramer

Little Bear

Little bear wants to be fierce,
fierce just like a tiger.

He wants to growl like a lion.
He climbs the trees
and looks around
for something to munch on.

He finds some berries
but no animals.
He can't prey on an animal.
He is just a little bear.

Little bear wants to be fierce,

fierce just like a tiger,
but he is just a little bear
not a tiger or a lion.

Bear wants to be fierce
Thinks about eating tigers
while he eats berries.

—*Cate Weinberg*

Lying face down in the grass with the trees above me
making a little cage
so that I may never get out

an ant crawls onto my finger

it is so tiny and small and little and
it would be so easy to squash
except for the fact that its husband and children and mother and grandfather
are all staring up at
me
begging me to let her go

so I put her down and I let her go and I watch the ants go back and forth
there are millions of them all around
crawling onto a leaf or into a hole where there are even more

they scramble back and forth
to their work or their jobs
and they pace quickly and just all hurry about

and they look down and forward
never once looking up
working and concentrating and never even caring

that maybe there is something bigger
something better
something besides

a job, or food
a blade of grass, an angry boss
or everything that they think that someone said that needs to be done

and I lift my head up
and I look to the sky
and maybe,
we,
like the ants,
do this too

—*Sue Gund*

Notes

1. Peter Stitt, *Uncertainty and Plenitude: Five Contemporary Poets*. Iowa City: University of Iowa Press, 1997. Two groundbreaking theories that have led to this paradigm shift: the principle of complementarity (experimenters unwillingly determine the nature of the thing being measured) and the uncertainty principle (measurements lack absolute accuracy because "measuring" itself interferes with the quantity to be measured).

2. Wallace Stevens, *The Necessary Angel: Essays on Reality and the Imagination*. New York: Vintage Books, 1942.

3. Interview with Dean Young, *Iowa Writers' Workshop Newsletter*, 1998.

4. "On 'A Rabbit as King of the Ghosts,'" by Shirley Kaufman, reprinted in *Poets Reading: The Field Symposia*, ed. by David Walker. Oberlin, Ohio: Oberlin College Press, 1999.

5. Ibid.

Bibliography

Stevens, Wallace. *The Palm at the End of the Mind*. Edited by Holly Stevens. New York: Vintage, 1972. Several other Stevens poems in this collection that might do well in a "nature" format are "Six Significant Landscapes," "Domination of Black," "Autumn Refrain," "A Fading of Sun," and "Evening without Angels."

Penny Harter

A Delicate Web

Writing about Animals

LAST YEAR, THE SEVENTH GRADE TEACHERS at Santa Fe Preparatory School chose "animal issues" as an interdisciplinary topic for Service Learning (community service integrated into the curriculum). Because I had shared some of my own poems with them in my regular English classes, students already knew of my own commitment to animal welfare and to the natural world. In the English segment, we wrote about animals, while in the other disciplines students visited the local animal shelter, saw a movie about wolves, and studied the local news for animal-related stories. We teachers know that seventh grade students feel very close to animals, especially their pets, so we anticipated an enthusiastic response. We got one!

I met with students in four groups of ten or eleven, seeing each group once for an hour and a half as they rotated through the disciplines. When the students entered the room, I listed on the board some categories for writing about animals, verbally elaborating on each as I wrote. These included:

- Personal Relationship with Animals (especially your pets)
- Ceremonies Honoring Animals
- Learning from Animals
- Observing Animals in Their Own Environments (as on camping trips)
- Observing Animals in Man-made Environments (like zoos and water-parks)
- Animal Rights and Abuses (in the news)
- Fantasies about Animals (including dreams)
- Mystical Experiences with Animals

I then spoke with students about effective ways to write about these topics, emphasizing that it is much more important to "show" than to "tell" an experience, and that they should "slow-motion" their descriptions, putting in as many specific details as possible.

Next, I read aloud from Scott McVay's introduction to Stephen R. Kellert and Edward O. Wilson's book *The Biophilia Hypothesis*: "What would happen if every elementary schoolchild chose a creature, whether an ant, a bee, cricket, dragonfly, spider, waterstrider, snake, frog, fly, beetle, or bat, to study and report on repeatedly during his or her first six years of school?" I told them that McVay goes on to say, "The burning center of my own curiosity about nature for thirty years has been the whale." We talked a bit about what it might be like to study an animal for six years—or for thirty. Some students already knew a lot about certain species on McVay's list, especially ants, snakes, and frogs. This led to a few stories about their interactions with those animals.

To warm up the students further, I told them several of my own personal experiences that fit into some of the categories: memories of my childhood dog, Blackberry; long-ago trips to the Staten Island zoo; hearing a great horned owl on a camping trip in Massachusetts; and a dream in which a bat had given me a third ear. I had barely begun when hands shot up around the classroom, as students eagerly chimed in, weaving their own experiences with mine. Here are some the animals and animal-related topics we went on to cover.

Whales

Next I turned to examples, in both poetry and prose, from published writers. I invited the students either to begin writing whenever they heard a phrase, an idea, or anything else that triggered a memory or fantasy for them, or to write after we had talked about the examples a bit. I began with one of my own poems about the whale. I told them that while studying whales, I learned from Diane Ackerman that if a whale is dragged too long through the water after being killed, "its bones will be charred by the heat of its internal decay," a clause that inspired the poem.

Whale Heat

for Scott McVay

Whales dive into frigid waters,
float far beneath the swells,
their great hearts fueling
the heat of their flesh
as they drift
among luminous bottom fish.

In the dark night of the oceans,
in the millions of years before
we were there to hear them,
whale songs lit the Earth
with echoes, arced between
the stars.

When whalers rip their bellies
and drag their gutted bodies
through cold seas,
whales are caves hoarding sun,
for even after death

the heat of their decay
seethes in their bones.

Then I read them a whale poem by the fine nature poet and essayist John Haines. I chose Haines's poem because it is many things at once: surrealistic fantasy, lament, and something of a riddle (the ending).

The Whale in the Blue Washing Machine

There are depths in a household
where a whale can live . . .

His warm bulk swims from room
to room, floating by on the stairway,
searching the drafts, the cold
currents that lap at the sills.

He comes to the surface hungry,
sniffs at the table,
and sinks, his wake rocking the chairs.

His pulsebeat sounds at night
when the washer spins, and the dryer
clanks on stray buttons . . .

Alone in the kitchen darkness,
looking through steamy windows
at the streets draining away in fog;

watching and listening,
for the wail of an unchained buoy,
the steep fall of his wave.

Some students thought the poem was stupid, because a whale couldn't live in a house. I told them it was like a fairytale, and they accepted this. Then I asked them to listen as I read it again. What was the whale feeling? What was it looking for, out the window? And finally, what did the whale's being in a human house have to do with what we humans have done to whales?

The following poem, by Sarah Hamilton, showed her closeness to another mammal of the sea:

Sea Cow–Naty

As I dive into the blue Saratoga Bay,
I swim down into a forest of sea trees.
They brush my face, tenderly caressing.
A sea cow heaves his great bulk
from a sandy bed.
He moves sluggishly towards me.

I am not afraid of this quiet animal.
He pushes his scarred side towards me.
I scratch it like I would my dog.
The manatee makes no objection.
He turns his great round face to me
and pleads with me.
His dark brown melting eyes beg for help.
He is young, no more than a baby,
his mother cut to shreds like cloth
by the roaring boat.
He needs me, as I need him.
I will care for him, help him.
And his name? It will be Naty.

Owls

Another animal we devoted some attention to was the owl. I began this session
by reading the students John Haines's "Prayer to the Snowy Owl":

Prayer to the Snowy Owl

Descend, silent spirit;

you whose golden eyes
pierce the gray
shroud of the world—

Marvelous ghost!

Drifter of the arctic night,
destroyer of those
who gnaw in the dark—

preserver of whiteness.

After hearing this poem, Elizabeth Sobel decided to write about an owl at
night:

Owl Moon

It is midnight on this side of the earth.
All thoughts and outlines are obscured by the net of black that has
    descended.
The pocket of sky reserved for the moon is empty,
And these eastern hills that hail the white moon every night
have seen no marble sphere completing her rounds.
These ghostly unknowing sentinels
hold no leaves now for the still wind to rustle,
and the only light that touches their blind eyes

is that of the stars.
Only one soul moves.
The fingerlike feathers that fan
from its outstretched wings
outline the stars and cut softly
through the silence.

Elizabeth's images are both startling and delicate. I especially like the correspondence between her "net of black" and Haines's "gray / shroud of the world."

Hunting

Because I had only used poems as examples so far, with another group I decided to read the end of Rick Bass' essay "Why We Do It" from his book *The Deer Pasture,* a section about hunting deer in the Texas Hill Country and the one that got away. The passage held the students spellbound:

> I walked up the rock ridge; I walked down it. I looked everywhere, as if I might have just missed him, overlooked him, and he was not gone at all but still on the mountain, right under my gaze, as a set of keys or a pair of scissors are in your desk at work when you really need them, and you rummage back and forth over them several times in the clutter without really seeing them, you are looking for them so hard. That is how I surveyed the woods all around me then. As if the biggest deer in the county had not given me the slip but was indeed still there, hiding camouflaged against a patch of deer-colored boulder, or something, still waiting for me to leave.
>
> I left all right. I was sick.
>
> Also, I never saw him again.
>
> And I never hunted that area again, either.
>
> I've got no truck with that deer anymore; he beat me fair and square and soundly; I know my limitations. . . .

This piece provoked a discussion about hunting. Some of the students abhorred hunting; others thought it was fine, having hunted with family members. I spoke of honoring the hunted animal, and of using all its parts as in the Native American tradition, as opposed to hunting for mere sport. Then I read aloud Mary Oliver's poem "Morning at Great Pond," which celebrates the beauty of wild creatures in their natural habitats. The Bass and Oliver pieces inspired Annalis Clint to write the following:

A Delicate Web

The water slips softly down each soft stone, rolling over them, giving each one a gloss. The clear water stills to a pond as a breeze blows through the world, down each grassy hill, through each tree. The midday sun beats down on each leaf, each twig, each pebble. Blue skies hang above the earth. The sound of life has been silenced as leaves dance across the ground, and on the trees, skipping to the pond and then jumping in and sailing away. The brook bounces on each interruption, making a musical note with each droplet.

A soft step bends down the delicate grass. A doe steps near the brook, checking for harm before taking her next gentle step. She walks, treating the grassy hill like a delicate web. She steps in the pond daintily and stops for a moment, startled by the cold. She lowers her head and begins to take in a cool sip. She hears a sound and lifts her head, realizing she is not alone. She bolts, but the grassy hills are too long, and there is no cover. She looks every which way, but there is nothing. A gunshot pierces the air. The clear water turns to a muddy crimson as the doe drops to the earth.

Experiences with Animals

Wanting to move away from predators and hunting, I reminded students that we can also have beautiful and almost mystical experiences with animals. I read them "A Blessing" by James Wright, asking them to pay special attention to the end of the poem:

A Blessing

Just off the highway to Rochester, Minnesota,
Twilight bounds softly forth on the grass.
And the eyes of those two Indian ponies
Darken with kindness.
They have come gladly out of the willows
To welcome my friend and me.
We step over the barbed wire into the pasture
Where they have been grazing all day, alone.
They ripple tensely, they can hardly contain their happiness
That we have come.
They bow shyly as wet swans. They love each other.
There is no loneliness like theirs.
At home once more,
They begin munching the young tufts of spring in the darkness.
I would like to hold the slenderer one in my arms,
For she has walked over to me
And nuzzled my left hand.
She is black and white,
Her mane falls wild on her forehead,
And the light breeze moves me to caress her long ear
That is delicate as the skin over a girl's wrist.
Suddenly I realize
That if I stepped out of my body I would break
Into blossom.

Some students had trouble with the final metaphor. They asked how one could leave one's body and "blossom." Others, who understood, thought the blossoms were the poet's way of saying that his spirit was joyful. This led Mehera Bonner to describe her encounters with a chipmunk:

Chuckles the Chipmunk

One day just after we had moved into our house, I woke up at exactly 6:30 to a loud clucking noise. I got up and went out to the balcony where I saw a little chipmunk sitting on the railing, watching the sun rise and clucking loudly. I opened the balcony door, trying not to disturb him. Because it was a new house, when I opened it, it made a loud, cracking noise. Instead of running off, the chipmunk turned around and looked at me like I was an intruder. Then he faced the sun and continued clucking. I sat down on the floor to watch the sunrise, and when it had risen, the chipmunk went off to his home.

The same night, I went out to see whether the chipmunk was there watching the sun go down. He was. I watch him every morning and night, and he doesn't seem to mind me. It's really nice because I get to share part of the day with one animal that's not mine.

Being an Animal

With one group, I spoke of how each student could pretend to become an animal and write about life *as that creature.* We talked about what animals they might like to become and why. I told them of a second grader who asked an imaginary rattlesnake why it rattled and the marvelous answer she wrote when she became the snake: "Because it is the only music I have." In response to the idea of taking on the persona of an animal, Darcy Lyons chose to become a pacifist puffin watching others that she saw fighting in the zoo; she also managed to comment on harmful effects of confinement. Her invention of the word *dartly,* to describe the human stares, is certainly effective.

The Prison

I stand there with guilt running through my veins. I watch my fellow puffins fight carelessly. They remind me of trees blowing in the harsh wind, getting stuck on each other's scrawny branches. Strange figures of all different sizes of humans, their wide eyes glistening with admiration, stare dartly at the ferocious animals of my kind. The prison surrounds my body in a limited habitat. I stand there on a rock with water flowing upon it. I stand in silence with my eyes facing shamefully at my cousins. I have longed for the day of my freedom which might never come.

Suddenly, all is dead silent, and the fighting has stopped. I look down to see the blood flowing out of one weak dead body while the other flexes his feathers, feeling proud of what he has done to his sibling. Once more, I dart my eyes fiercely and shamefully at my most obnoxious cousin.

Yes, Even Pets

Of course, nearly all children love to write about the family pet, with everything from humor to the grief of loss. When I brought up the subject of pets with one group, we easily could have spent an hour trading pet stories. At the peak of excitement, I commanded, "Don't tell it, write it!" Noga Landau delighted us all with a poem about her cat:

Adina, the Cat

Adina likes to watch TV.
She likes the nature shows
with flat birds she pounces on.
She always wonders why
the birds don't react.

She pounces on the newscaster's head and meows
at him when he says something she doesn't like.
She rubs against the TV set
when she likes the show,
but yells at it when she doesn't.

When we watch operas she sings along,
and when we watch comedy, she sits contentedly
staring at the screen, looking like she knows
more about everything than we do.

Whenever a TV set goes on
she prances into the room like a queen,
casually rubbing against us,
and finally settling herself
in front of the screen, contented
to stay there until the show ends.

Chris White expressed his sorrow at the death of his dog Dopey. The class noted the power of the simple repetition, "I loved that dog."

Dopey

I had a dog named Dopey. That dog was the greatest dog you could have. I loved that dog. Her fur all twisted and wound. The golden hair of that dog shined up the sadness of my day. The eyes of that dog made me just want to start crying with joy. Her floppy ears swung gently in the wind. She was a great dog. I loved that dog. She never bit or growled at me. She didn't say much, but I could tell somehow she wanted to talk. I sometimes saw tears in her eyes, glowing with sorrow or happiness. She died two years ago at the age of 18. I loved that dog.

Conclusion

The lessons I have described can be adapted for students between fourth and twelfth grades. Asking elementary or middle school students to write about animals, without providing a variety of strong examples, can sometimes result only in rhymed poems about the family pet. There is room for some of these, but students can write much more insightful pieces about their relationship with the animal world. My seventh grade students and I were often moved by their writing when they read it aloud at the end of each session. It typically showed sensitivity, maturity, and a deep concern for the welfare of the fellow beings we live with on this planet.

I'd like to give the last word to student writer Anna Merlan, who states clearly a relationship she sees between animals in their habitats, and us in ours.

Captive

We are all captive here
Though we don't like to think it.
Humans trap themselves,
But animals are free.

We weave a delicate cage,
A cage for ourselves,
Out of things we don't want to do
And places we should not be.
But we do,
And we are.

Animals move
Like the wind
The rain
The sun.
A simple life.
Hard.
But it is where they want to be
What they want to do.

We could live like that.
If we wanted.
If we could just break free.

Bibliography

Ackerman, Diane. *The Moon by Whale Light.* New York: Vintage, 1992.
Bass, Rick. *The Deer Pasture.* New York: Norton, 1985.
Haines, John. *The Owl in the Mask of the Dreamer: Collected Poems.* St. Paul, Minn.: Graywolf, 1996.

Harter, Penny. *Lizard Light: Poems from the Earth.* Santa Fe: Sherman Asher, 1998.

Kellert, Stephen R. and Edward O. Wilson, editors. *The Biophilia Hypothesis.* Washington, D.C.: Island Press, 1993.

Oliver, Mary. *New and Selected Poems.* Boston: Beacon Press, 1992.

Wright, James. *Above the River: The Collected Poems of James Wright.* New York: Farrar, Straus & Giroux, 1990.

William J. Higginson

To Clean the Mind

Haiku, Linked Poems, and the Seasons

DENNIS DUTTON INVITED poet-teacher Penny Harter and me to join the leadership of a bookmaking workshop at the El Rito Public Library in rural northern New Mexico. Dennis, a haiku poet and assistant director of the library, explained that participants in the workshop were to create texts and incorporate them into books that they would later make by hand. For our two sessions, Dennis, Penny, and I decided on a sequence moving from haiku to "pass-around linking" to a final linked poem in the Japanese style called *renku*. We were to lead two one-and-a-half-hour sessions.

Session One

We met the first evening with nine participants, who ranged from age seven to adults in their sixties. Since the workshop had already been going for a few weeks, everyone knew everyone else. We sat at a long table, arranged so that the children could talk to each other easily, but were seated next to adults in case they needed help.

Dennis had already introduced the group to haiku, so we talked a bit about the use of nature in haiku, how most haiku in Japan and many in America have special "season words" in them to help the reader recognize the larger natural context of each poem. Season words do not necessarily name the season outright, but present phenomena that typically occur at a particular time of year or have become traditionally associated with a specific season.

A season word often brings a rich set of physical and literary associations to a poem. The rest of the poem, if it is a good haiku, connects these associations with a specific momentary event in the present. In the words of Bashō, the great seventeenth-century master of haiku and linked poems, we must strive to incorporate "the unchanging and the ever-changing" into our poems. The unchanging represents the tradition as embodied in the great literature of the past, while the ever-changing is provided by the events of the moment. Our response to this combination of past and present, tradition and sensation, is what gives haiku its special power.

To give an example by Bashō, here is one of his most famous poems:

hototogisu   there where
kie yuku kata ya   *hototogisu* disappears:
shima hitotsu   a lone island

The *hototogisu* or "little cuckoo" is a bird of summer, more often heard than
seen. Its name represents the sound it makes, a five-note whistling call, quite
unlike the "cuc-koo" of its larger cousin. Here the sound of the unseen bird disappears. Japanese poets often pair something seen with the *hototogisu,* thus recre-
ating its legendary invisibility. With the word *hitotsu* (lone), Bashō both repeats
sounds in *hototogisu* and deepens the sense of aloneness already suggested by the
bird's disappearing cry.

Through the literary associations of its season word, even the simplest-seem-
ing haiku may contain a deeper meaning, as in this poem by Bashō:

cho no tobu   just a butterfly
bakari nonaka no   flying—out in the field
hikage kana   this sunshine

For the East Asian reader, this poem echoes the famous story in which the
Chinese philosopher Chuang-tzu dreamt he was a butterfly. On waking, he did
not know whether he was really a man who had dreamt he was a butterfly, or a
butterfly now dreaming he was a man. This literary association adds a dreamy
quality to the spring field. (In haiku, the single word *butterfly* represents a white
butterfly of spring; a swallowtail butterfly indicates summer, and so on.)

By using season words, Japanese haiku poets anchor their poems in the cycles
of nature and in the world of literature at the same time. The skillful poet can
deepen that relationship by adding a few carefully chosen details from present
experience.

The Japanese have books called *haiku saijiki* (haiku almanacs) that guide
them to the natural and literary associations of the season words. In English, my
book *Haiku World: An International Poetry Almanac* serves a similar purpose. I
read the workshop members a few passages from it, including poems by today's
haiku poets, to give them a sense of how the seasonal background can provide
the foundation for appreciating a poem on several levels. If a specific phenom-
enon is unfamiliar, a season-word guide like *Haiku World* can help, as in:

SKYLARK, *hibari* [the Japanese word]. . . (all spring). One of the most joyous of
birds, skylarks have long been noted for their brimming songs in flight, to which
poems about them typically refer. . . .

kakete kuru   I catch
ko o uketomete   my kid come running—
hibari no no   skylark field
   —*Soshi Chihara*

Such background information gives us a deeper sense of the Japanese haiku poets' feelings springing from their actual encounters with the phenomena named in the season words.

We quickly followed these Japanese examples by reading aloud highly imagistic and often amusing poems from Cor van den Heuvel's *Haiku Anthology*. After a few minutes discussing the poems and noting that they are mostly in three lines, that they appeal to the senses, and that most of them connect with nature or the seasons, we invited everyone to write their own. We suggested that they each write one from here-and-now experience, one from memory, and one from an imagined experience made to seem real. We suggested that, as is usual in haiku, all the poems be written in the present tense, so that they seem like something happening right now, regardless of their origin. Some fine examples came out of that first forty-five minutes or so. Here are a few:

gray rain
your absence
fills the room

    —Louise Grunewald

Bear bells jingle
Branches break off the path
Sing loud!

    —Judith Shotwell

singing
to an empty nest
the oriole

    —Dennis H. Dutton

cicada shells
crunch
the smell of pine

    —Julie Wagner

These got us off to a good start, and we asked everyone to pick their best haiku, write it neatly at the top of a fresh sheet, and put their initials to the right of it. Then everyone passed their papers one person to the right, and Penny and I explained the basics of linking in traditional Japanese-style linked poetry. Briefly, linking involves expanding on some aspect of the previous verse, often by one of the following methods:

Linking through Words: Give a twist to a key word or phrase in the previous verse; pun; complete a familiar phrase; relate sounds or striking grammatical patterns; allude to or briefly quote a piece of well-known literature that seems related.

Linking through Things: Continue an action or a description; invent an action for the previous setting or a setting for the previous action; reverse an action (if something goes up in the previous verse, present something coming down in the next, etc.); suddenly shift locale or focus, or move from large to small, close to distant, darkness to light, and so on—like cutting from scene to scene in a movie.

Linking through Scent: Echo the mood or tone of the previous stanza, but use different contents. (This more subtle style of linking, called *nioizuke* in Japanese, was invented by Bashō.)

We suggested that participants draft a few possible stanzas on scrap paper, and add theirs to the preceding verse only after they had fully revised it to fit. To get them ready for more formal linked-verse writing later, we suggested that their responses be in two lines added to the previous three. And we reminded them to add their initials to the right of their stanzas. Here are two of the linked pairs that resulted:

March wind
dust devils
the screen door sings   *Ginger Legato*

ragweed
grey haze on brown earth   *Julie Wagner*

    *   *   *

I saw
a red-headed bird
in a book   *Shaynae Vasquez*

hollow tree
loud   *Gloria McFarland*

After these first two stanzas, we explained the way that linked poems move: A renku should not be a continuous narrative, but rather be like an oriental scroll painting, shifting from place to place, close to distant, people to landscape, and season to season. While narrative segments may occur, they must not last more than two stanzas. The most important value in renku is variety.

A poet must be especially careful not to make the third of three consecutive verses similar to the first of the three. Such an *a-b-a* pattern creates a triptych effect and stops the forward motion. Any unwanted repetition between two verses with one in the middle is called a *throwback*—one of the most common reasons for rejecting a proposed verse.

Passing the papers one person to the right again, everyone then added one stanza in three lines to the previous two stanzas. With reminders to draft on scrap paper, to write neatly on the passing sheets, and to add their initials to the right, we soon had four to six verses on each sheet. In some cases, when people were taking their time over their responses, we allowed sheets to be passed more than one place, to find a person ready to write. All this, and we had time enough to read the results back to the whole group. Here are two:

strange
empty house
my chair   *Gloria McFarland*

curtainless window
opens to spring wind   *Louise Grunewald*

she steps
naked
from the shower   *Judith Shotwell*

apple petals
in my hair   *W. J. Higginson*

blossoms
i can already taste
the pies   *Louise Grunewald*

    *   *   *

coffeepots bubbling
what happens
a year later?   *Angela W. Dapp-Graves*

her belly swells
the bed smaller now   *Dennis H. Dutton*

a snake is crawling
through the grass   *Bianca C. Vasquez*

salt blocks
horses snuffle
hot tongues   *Ginger Legato*

We were flexible in our application of any of the "rules," treating them more as guidelines. But the essence of what we were doing was not lost on anyone. We found out how deeply these short poems and the process sunk in when Dennis told us of a brief conversation he had with a participant. Here is an extract from his notes:

> While haiku were being passed around for linking, Bianca Vasquez, a third grader, looked up at me with her big, brown eyes, and asked, "Dennis, can doing this clean the mind?"
>
> Amazing question—amazing too that it could come from a nine-year-old. It could have come from nowhere but Bianca's own experience; there was nothing in

the handouts she'd been given that took up the therapeutic effects of haiku, and nothing in the discussion.

I told Bianca, "That's a very good question, and yes, it can. In fact, that's one reason people write haiku."

"I have a friend who needs her mind cleaned," she added. "Can she come next week?"

"Of course," I answered.

Session Two

While focusing on nature and writing haiku may clean the mind, the mind-cleaning that comes with writing linked poems probably derives from the concentration necessary to remember the various guidelines and the specific requirements for the particular verse one is working on. Penny and I agreed that for a first, short session of formal renku, the simplest and briefest twelve-stanza format would be best, though there is a variety of accepted lengths.

We wanted to make it easy for participants to shift their previously held concepts of the seasons into the seasons of haiku and renku. Beginners also need help in achieving variety. How easy it is to expand something your colleague has said, rather than striking out in a new direction! To help overcome these problems, I prepared two one-page handouts summarizing many of the factors that would go into our writing. (They are reproduced at the end of this chapter.) I modeled ours loosely on similar handouts used by one of my teachers, Master Meiga Higashi of the Nekomino Renku Club in Tokyo. Necessarily, I added material that Japanese renku poets would already know, but I tried to keep the handouts brief. Also, I made a few copies of the lists of season words from *Haiku World,* to have available for those who wanted the added stimulation while we were writing.

Apparently word had spread, for a dozen people gathered for the second of our two sessions. We arranged the tables so that we all could see one another. I plunged directly into the seasonal issue, using the "Renku Topics" handout and the season-word lists to help us all shift to a world in which spring starts in February, summer begins in May, autumn in August, and winter in November. This led to some discussion of "early signs of spring" and the other seasons.

Next, I pointed out the variety of phenomena listed in the "Renku Topics" handout, and the seasons (or the period of months) in which one might find them. Those phenomena without such time-related notations are called "non-seasonal" or "all-year" topics, and may be used with others or in verses that are not supposed to include a season. The renku topics list helps us make a renku with references to many different kinds of phenomena.

The simple rule is that a renku must contain verses on all four of the seasons and on love. The deeper concept is that a renku is like a mandala: a diagram of the physical and spiritual universe, with all its good and bad, bright and dark objects, events, and feelings.

Turning to the handout labeled "Format for a Twelve-Stanza Renku," I described how we would use the seasonal information in writing the renku. The opening stanza of a renku must reflect the season in which the poem is composed—this is where haiku, which derives from such opening stanzas, gets it emphasis on the here-and-now. The second verse is usually in the same season as the first. (In a twelve-stanza renku written in summer or winter it need not be, but it always is in longer forms.) After that, the seasons appear in an aesthetic order governed by tradition and rules, rather than by the usual order of the seasons. And there are rules about where the moon and blossoms go. I pointed out that the word *blossoms* in Japanese linked poems, when unspecified, refers to cherry blossoms, but that American poets frequently take it to refer to any spring-flowering tree, and often name a tree specific to their area.

I also told them that although many verses might speak of nature, half of the verses would use season words, half not. In a longer format, this is adhered to approximately, and may vary a bit from renku to renku. As the chart shows, autumn and spring are the dominant seasons in renku, because they are considered more aesthetically pleasing.

We also briefly reviewed the kinds of linking from stanza to stanza discussed in the first session. Such linking frequently moves from one natural setting or event to another, or may shift from less to more involvement with nature or vice-versa.

Regarding form, I mentioned the alternation of three- and two-line stanzas, indicated in the second column of the handout. Ideally, the three-line stanzas have a middle line a bit longer than the other two, and the two-line stanzas have lines more or less equal in length to the longer lines of the three-line stanzas. For this session we worked pretty much with free-form stanzas, simply alternating three and two lines.

One of the most striking features of renku is its fictional aspect. True, the opening verse must be grounded in the circumstances of composition (locale and season). But after that, it's off and running. Renku poets draw on their personal experience, but often they project themselves into another time and space quite beyond anything actually experienced. The main requirement is that the fiction seem real—the poet avoids wildly surreal or fantastic images and occurrences. But the world of renku is hardly the real world in minute detail. Like good fiction, it is the whole picture that forms a simulacrum for reality, for nature in its broadest sense, not a picayune adherence to "truth."

To be fun, a renku must be written in a spirit of collaboration, and rules may be set aside occasionally to make way for some especially interesting accident of composition or exciting turn of the collective mind. Our point here was not to enforce all the rules, but to have a good time and focus mainly on the content and the linking, the interweaving of the seasonal and other kinds of experiences that would naturally arise from the interactions of group composition.

Next, I explained that we were going to run this session more like a traditional renku session in Japan. Instead of automatically passing verses around, as we had in the previous session, we would ask everyone to try to write "the next verse"; then we would pick the best one, perhaps revising it a little, and add it to the poem. We encouraged participants to keep all their drafts, even if they were not included in the renku on a particular turn, for such independent verses later might be rewritten to fit into the renku, or to become good haiku on their own.

All of this background took close to an hour, so we were pressed for time when we actually began writing. But we quickly had a strong opening stanza, and with a group already somewhat used to working together, we made rapid progress through the first six stanzas. Penny, Dennis, and I floated around to help participants who had not attended the previous session.

At each turn, we collected the drafts proposed for the next stanza and briefly discussed them. For those that did not fit the conditions (wrong season, wrong number of lines, too much like something that had already appeared, and so on), we explained what was wrong and returned them to their authors. If a verse seemed very apt but needed some slight revision, we proposed the revision and sought the author's approval. With the field narrowed to the two or three that actually met all the conditions, everyone voted for a favorite verse. This process—stating the conditions to be met, writing, sifting and discussing, and voting—took about ten minutes per verse, on average, though some verses fell into place quickly while others took longer to decide on.

With the workshop running overtime, we gathered up everyone's loose verses that had not fit in for one reason or another, and Dennis took them home to work into a collective whole and fill out the twelve-stanza pattern. Part of his mandate was to include as many different authors as possible. Because we had not gotten to verses with summer and autumn season words, some editing had to be done to fill out the pattern. It would have been good to have another half hour to work on the poem as a group. With a little tinkering, though, Dennis, Penny, and I came up with a final version, which later was typed up and approved by the participants. Here is the result:

On the Old Tree

Apricot blossoms
on the old tree
by grandma's house   *Frances Herrera*

the neighbor's cow
misses her calf   *Lisa Schwartzberg*

i sing
music everywhere
today   *Shaynae Vasquez*

winter wind rushing
through the bell tower   *Ginger Legato*

icicles stab
the blue sky—
he's alone   *Judith Shotwell*

on the side of the road
a yellow bike   *Dennis H. Dutton*

prints in the mud
the dog days
of summer   *Julie Wagner*

a bad dream
turns the sky gray   *Angela W. Dapp-Graves*

a halo
around the moon
what worlds beyond?   *Anonymous*

a light dew
drifts from the roof   *Ginger Legato*

deep in the woods
we come upon
a meadow   *Daniel Archuleta*

the old caretaker
points the way to the shrine   *Penny Harter*

This may be the kind of poem that we need to be writing more often to make our way forward in the new millennium. In such a poem, we all contribute some small part of our experience of the natural world—a world that includes us. And, just as our lives are not lived outside of nature and nature is not outside of us, the poem reflects a natural rhythm of human concerns, focusing now inward, now outward, through both seasonal and nonseasonal verses. Renku depends on an understanding of the natural world. But more than that, renku requires a willingness to give and take with one's fellow poets, a collegiality that could serve as a model for our relationships, both individual and societal, with the others who inhabit nature with us. If we can get along with each other in writing a poem, perhaps we can learn a little more about how to get along with everything else that contributes to the poem that is the world.

Renku Topics*

Besides the seasons and love, there are many other topics that can appear in a renku. We should use as wide a variety of topics as possible; to make this easier, the table below lists several.

At least one topic from each category must appear in the renku. So as the renku progresses, cross off topics as they are used and try to write verses that use topics from fresh categories. (Some verses may include two or more topics.) The phenomena in this list that are special to particular seasons are indicated by month(s).

The seasons of haiku and renku come earlier than we're used to: Spring (February–April), Summer (May–July), Autumn (August–October), and Winter (November–January). People throughout the north temperate zone used to think of the seasons as earlier, which is why the solstices are also called "midsummer" and "midwinter" in English, though today we commonly think of the solstices as beginning their respective seasons. Haiku and renku retain the older usage.

WEATHER	EARTH	ANIMALS	PEOPLE
rain	mountain	bird	clothing
snow (Jan.)	sea/ocean	robin (Feb.–April)	house
hail (May-July)	river	beast (mammal)	food
snow pellets	lake	horse	beverage
(Nov.-Jan.)	meadow	colt (Feb.–April)	
dew (Aug.-Oct.)		fish	writing
mist (Aug.-Oct.)	crop	amphibian	painting
haze (Feb.-April)	field	frog (March–April)	music
smoke	garden	insects	sport
cloud	grasses	butterfly	study
wind	wildflowers	(March–April)	work
	(Aug.–Oct.)	swallowtail	entertainment
	trees	(May–July)	
		other	travel
			boat
			train
			car
GOOD THINGS	BAD THINGS		bike
			road
graduation	sickness		
promotion	accident		
new job	calamity		
health	conflagration		
	transience		

If something you want to use normally appears in a season different from the season you want to use it in, such as butterfly (spring) or mist (autumn), for example, you can put the name of the season in front of it. So if you're talking about mist in April, say "spring mist" or "April mist." And so on.

If in doubt, ask one of the workshop leaders. (Note to workshop leaders: Greatly expanded seasonal topic lists will be found in *Haiku World*.)

Format for a Twelve-Stanza Renku*

This format lists some rules for a renku written in April, and will help writers keep track of where they are in the poem and what to do next. (A different starting month will change some rules.) These rules were adapted from general renku guidelines specifically for this workshop, and do not have to be followed exactly.

verse #	# of lines	Special Topics	Seasonal Phenomena	Other Considerations
1	3	Tree Blossoms	Late Spring: April	Complimentary
2	2		Late or All Spring: April	
3	3		none	
4	2		Winter: Nov.-Dec.-Jan.	(Love can move up to this position.)
5	3	Love	none	
6	2	(Love)	none	Summer can be in any *one* of these verses but no more than one verse.
7	3		Summer: May–June–July	
8	2		none	
9	3	Moon	Autumn: Aug.-Sep.-Oct.	Moon can be in either this verse or the next.
10	2		Autumn: Aug.-Sep.-Oct.	
11	3		none	peaceful
12	2		none	optimistic

NOTE: Within the three-month periods, you cannot "back up"—that is, if you mention apple blossoms, which typically come out in April, you cannot talk about "spring snow" in the next verse, because that is most common to March. The seasons indicated on the list of renku topics will help you avoid problems like this. Note that half of the verses are not seasonal—they don't relate to any particular month. In those non-seasonal verses, you may mention natural things, but not things that "belong" to one time of the year only.

For a renku beginning in another season, the two spring verses will come at the end. A Japanese renku poet has suggested the following sequence of seasons, stanza by stanza, for a renku starting in summer: 1, summer; 2, nonseasonal; 3, nonseasonal; 4, autumn; 5, autumn (moon in one of these two); 6, nonseasonal/love; 7, nonseasonal (love); 8, winter; 9, nonseasonal; 10, nonseasonal; 11, spring (blossoms); 12, spring. Charts for 36-stanza renku appear in *The Haiku Seasons.*

Bibliography

Blyth, R. H. *Haiku, Vol. 1, Eastern Culture.* Tokyo: Hokuseido Press, 1949. Includes a good chapter on renku with a complete, annotated translation of "The Kite's Feathers"—an important renku led by Bashō.

Finch, Annie, and Katherine Varnes, editors. *An Exaltation of Forms, Chosen and Introduced by Contemporary Poets.* Ann Arbor: University of Michigan Press, in preparation. Includes an article on writing renku, with examples.

Higginson, William J. *The Haiku Seasons: Poetry of the Natural World.* Tokyo: Kodansha International, 1996. Stresses the nature content of haikai poetry from before Bashō to contemporary renku. The chapter on linked poetry has annotated examples in translation and a chart showing the organization of the seasons in typical 36-stanza renku composed at different times of the year.

———. *Haiku World: An International Poetry Almanac.* Tokyo: Kodansha International, 1996. Expands the cosncept of the Japanese *saijiki,* or poetry almanac. Over 600 seasonal and nonseasonal topics are presented, with 1,000 poems by 650 contemporary poets from 50 countries.

Higginson, William J., with Penny Harter. *The Haiku Handbook: How to Write, Share, and Teach Haiku.* New York: McGraw-Hill, 1985; reissued Tokyo: Kodansha International, 1989. Includes sections on nature in haiku and on linked poetry with a thirty-six-stanza renku in English.

Mayhew, Lenore, translator. *Monkey's Raincoat: Linked Poetry of the Bashō School with Haiku Selections.* Rutland, Vt. and Tokyo: Charles E. Tuttle Co., 1985. Contains the most readable translations available of all four renku and selected haiku from the original Japanese collection *Sarumino,* by Bashō and his colleagues.

Padgett, Ron, editor. *The Teachers & Writers Handbook of Poetic Forms.* New York: Teachers & Writers Collaborative, 2000. Includes an article on students writing *renga* (an alternative name for linked poetry), with several examples.

Reichhold, Jane. *Narrow Road to Renga.* Gualala, Calif.: Aha Books, 1989. The first, and so far only, substantial collection of linked poems by non-Japanese poets. It demonstrates the range of interest in linked poetry in English before the 1990s, which brought with them an expanded knowledge of the Japanese tradition.

Sato, Hiroaki. *One Hundred Frogs: From Renga to Haiku to English.* New York and Tokyo: Weatherhill, 1983. Excellent discussion and translations of Japanese linked poems; includes some haiku and linked poems by American poets.

Shirane, Haruo. *Traces of Dreams: Landscape, Cultural Memory, and the Poetry of Bashō.* Stanford, Calif.: Stanford University Press, 1998. Extended discussion of the interaction of tradition and immediate environment in the hokku (haiku), renku, and prose of Bashō.

Ueda, Makoto. *Literary and Art Theories in Japan.* Cleveland, Ohio: Press of Western Reserve University, 1967. Has valuable chapters on linked poetry and on Bashō's poetics.

―――. *Matsuo Bashō.* New York: Twayne Publishers, 1970; reissued Tokyo and New York: Kodansha International, 1982. This is the standard literary biography in English of the greatest Japanese renku master, with many fine translations, including two fully annotated renku.

―――. *Bashō and His Interpreters: Selected Hokku with Commentary.* Stanford, Calif.: Stanford University Press, 1991. Features excellent translations of almost 300 of Bashō's haiku, with excerpts from many poets' and scholars' comments on the poems and notes on the immediate contexts in which the poems were written. Arranged chronologically, interspersed with a narrative of the poet's life.

van den Heuvel, Cor, editor. *The Haiku Anthology: Haiku and Senryu in English,* expanded edition. New York: Norton, 1999. This is the most comprehensive anthology of English-language haiku available, with some 850 poems by almost 90 poets. The two prior editions (Doubleday, 1974, and Simon & Schuster, 1986) are also generous and useful.

Cynde Gregory

Gardens of Earthy Delights

IT'S ANOTHER BLECHY DAY. The skies pour down a deadening light the same gray as in a subway station, turning everything into blurs. It's cold again, the sixth day in a row; the kind of cold that crawls into your bones and gnaws them from the inside out. Parents have buried their offspring in layers of sweaters and leggings and flannel shirts and pullovers and thick socks and jackets before sending them off this morning. Of course, the classroom furnace is compensating for the cold with undulating waves of damp heat. The fifth graders are draped across their desks, eyes rolling, tongues hanging out. After a quick consultation, the teacher and I let them kick off their shoes, unpeel their socks, and wiggle out of excess layers. We shove aside the desks and pile everybody's extras into the middle of the room. The kids sprawl across the impromptu nest, yawning and blinking sleepily. Great. The final day of my week-long residency and I'm going to lose them for sure. Time to tap-dance.

"Where do cows come from?"

The kids yawn. Who cares? A couple of youngsters shoot me a look that says, *We're city kids, so don't even* think *about talking to us about cows.*

"From a garden," I answer my own question. "You have to plant a glass of milk and then wait for a long time. First a vine sprouts and twines up the garden fence, then it gets covered with soft red flowers that look kind of like barns."

Several of the kids sit up and look at me suspiciously.

"When the flowers drop off, you find tiny hooves, the size of your little fingernail."

A few more kids sit up and examine their nails to see just how small the hooves could be.

"The hooves grow bigger, and pretty soon, four black-and-white cow-legs appear."

Two or three kids start to giggle.

"Then those milk-bag things pop out," someone hollers.

"You mean udders!" somebody else corrects.

Ah. In spite of the tropical heat in the room, it looks like I just might be able to get these kids to write.

Or maybe not. A girl with forty gazillion braids crosses her arms and glares. "Cows don't grow in gardens," she informs everyone crisply. Uh-oh. A realist. If I don't act fast, she'll infect the others with the deadly disease, anti-humor. It might be possible to distract her with an important job.

"Ah," I say with admiration. "You know about gardens." I call her to the board and give her chalk. "Your job is to write the responses to my questions on the board."

The realist starts to protest. This isn't an important job, it's taking dictation!

"But," I add, "you know about gardens, so if somebody says something that isn't true about gardens, tell us."

Ah, her look tells me, that's more like it.

"What do you need to make a real garden?" I ask the kids.

Silence. Many of these kids, I'm sure, have never even seen a garden.

"Well, seeds," begins my helper. She writes down her own answer. "And fertilizer," she adds that to the list.

I'm getting nervous. If I can't get the others involved, they won't be willing to write later on. If I don't stop her, my helper will supply all the answers to all my questions while the others fall asleep on the floor.

"Don't forget about sunlight," sighs a freckle-faced boy, gazing sadly out the window at the gray sky.

"And water," adds his buddy, a kid with a chipped tooth.

"But not too much water," Little Miss Realist announces authoritatively. "Or the plants will suffocate."

Several kids protest—that doesn't make sense. Wouldn't the plants drown? Suffocating is when you can't breathe. Plants don't have mouths, so how can they suffocate?

Their classroom teacher leaps into action. She finds a page in the encyclopedia that explains what over-watering does to a plant, then shoots me a grin. The class is about to start a unit on plants and the environment, so this is a good introduction.

"Not too much sun, either," mumbles a girl with adorable, poky-out ears.

"Plants *can* sunburn," my assistant adds firmly. A couple of kids look about ready to argue with that, but the teacher nods in agreement.

"That's true," she says. "Different plants have different needs. Some plants can't tolerate a lot of sunlight."

Most of the kids are tuned in by now, trying to think of more garden information to add to the board. Somebody remembers the two tiny leaves that emerged in her Dixie cup in kindergarten. Another remembers how the avocado pit split open when it sprouted.

My stern helper soon has the board covered with gardening needs:

seeds
fertilizer
enough water and sunlight
not too much water and sunlight
rich soil

a fence
a wheelbarrow
a shovel
wire cages or stakes
a tool to dig out weeds
a watering can
watch out for bad bugs
you should plant in rows
garden gloves
wear old clothes
a baseball cap or straw hat

Next question: What do vegetables and flowers grow on? This one is relatively easy:

vines
stalks
bushes
trees
stems
in the ground, like potatoes

"But I want to talk about that cow garden," a voice rises out of the kid-heap. "Yeah!" several others chime in, "let's talk about those cows!"

"The cow garden isn't nearly as interesting as the garden of acrobats," I tell them. That gets their attention. Before they can start yakking again, I add, "But first we've got to make two more lists. What are some verbs that people might use when talking about gardens?"

After the first few (and more obvious) offerings, the teacher and I toss out some hints. How do you move a heavy wheelbarrow? What's it called when the flower opens? What are some words that mean "too wet"? What's it called when the garden is ready to be picked? With a little effort, the class manages to come up with a fairly comprehensive list of garden-related verbs:

dig
plant
bury
haul
weed
water
blossom
bloom
twine
twist
wrap
brace

drench
soak
peel
shuck
drag
shove
pinch
pick
gather
harvest

By now, everybody's in a good mood. Even Little Miss Realism grins as she scribbles on the board. For the moment, the heat indoors and the cold outdoors are forgotten. Time for the final question:

"Things that absolutely, positively, do not grow in gardens?"

"Pianos!"

"Catcher's mitts!"

"Giraffes!"

"Greyhound buses filled with tourists!"

"Game show hosts!"

Everybody answers at once, waving their arms, jumping to their feet, trying to out-yelp each other. The classroom teacher gets them calmed down, and my beaming helper scribbles their ideas on the board:

grandfather clocks
kittens
dentures
substitute teachers
books
opera singers
manicurists
tutus
floor lamps
babies
firecrackers
bagpipes

Money, gold, lottery tickets, guns, knives, and all things related to bucks or blood get erased. A couple of kids protest, but I point out that those things are so obvious and boring, nobody will be interested in their stories.

The teacher hands out paper while I give instructions and prompts:

• Choose one thing to grow in your garden. You can use an item from the board, or think up your own, original idea.

• What could you use for seeds? (E.g., plant lost teeth to grow dentures.)

- What kind of weather conditions are required?
- What must the soil be like?
- What would make a good fertilizer? (E.g., toothpaste for the dentures.)
- What does this thing grow on? Vine? Stem? Tree? Stalk? The ground?
- What emerges first?
- What is its growing cycle?
- What insect or disease must you watch for? (E.g., the cavity beetle.)
- How do you know it's time to harvest?
- What happens if you don't harvest in time?

A few kids decide to clarify their ideas by drawing first, but most students dive right into writing. I don't need to remind the kids to describe things in detail; the topic is so amusing to them that they aren't about to let any details go undescribed. As the students compose, I remind them to use garden verbs, and to include sounds, smells, and touch details, as well as what they see happening in the garden.

The children's gardens unfold like time-lapse photography: gardens of lifeguards, baby shoes, pencil stubs, Frisbees, helium balloons, tattoo artists, motorcycles, thugs, cops, pots and pans, and kitchen sinks sprout up across the room. Vines wind out of pages, stalks shoot up from sentences, bushes blossom from words. Soon the classroom has transformed into the best kind of garden—a wildly fecund one, budding with young writers.

A Garden of Babies

I change into a bright flowery spring dress and visit my garden. When I approach the gate, the smell of baby powder tickles my nose. As I walk in, a baby starts giggling. She is wrapped in flower petals. I wander around, touching soft baby skin, sprinkling baby powder, watering the baby flowers with milk. They smile happily. A boy wrapped in leaves starts to cry. I know it's time to harvest. I hold him in my arms and carefully unwrap the leaves. Then I put him in a soft pink blanket. I swing him on the baby swing in the middle of the garden, and I name him Michael. A three-year-old girl comes into the garden. I, myself, grew her. Her name is Rachel. She runs round joyfully in the garden. . . . She has silky brown hair with a touch of gold sunlight, white milky skin, and you can see the ocean waves in her aqua blue eyes. I love her dearly. I brush her long hair and braid it. Mike starts to laugh. Rachel laughs with him. Soon the garden is full of laughter. A cool breeze comes and wakes the baby flowers. The babies are surprised. The sun goes down, and the moon starts coming up. Oh, the stars. One star is falling. I make a wish that my garden of baby flowers stays beautiful forever.

—*Lucy Eom, fifth grade*

Jordan Clary

Beowulf Rides the Range

Using the Nature Imagery in Old and Middle English Poetry

WHEN I THINK ABOUT the poet who has most influenced me, the answer is usually: Anonymous. The first time I remember coming across Anonymous was in the Middle English lyric:

Westron wind, where wilt thou blow,
The small rains down shall rain.
Christ, that my love were in my arms,
And I in my bed again.

Anonymous intrigued me. Who had he been? A lover? A traveling bard? A young man, vital or dying? I believed that the writer of "Western Wind" was male, just as later I would read lyrics that would speak to me in a female voice. Part storyteller, part lyricist, Anonymous had many faces, many voices. Old and Middle English poetry led me into an ancient world of adventure and travel where waves battered rocky cliffs and monsters devoured warriors. I believe it was this poetry that also first inspired my love of the sea.

Last fall I was asked to do a series of poetry workshops for Janesville Elementary School in Janesville, California, for the River of Words art and poetry contest there coordinated by Becky Thompson. Former poet laureate Robert Hass originated River of Words (a nationwide project) as a way for communities to learn about their local watersheds. It's an idea I am especially attracted to because it connects poetry to the tangible world of nature, and also teaches students about the biology, ecology, and history of their area.

I had recently been re-reading poems from *The Exeter Book* and decided to use some of these poems and *Beowulf* as a springboard for nature writing. *The Exeter Book* contains the largest extant collection of Old English poetry and is believed to have been copied circa 970–90. The original manuscript is still housed in the Exeter Cathedral Library. Nature images permeate Old English poetry. To the wanderer on the sea, the only sound the wind carries is the cry of a lone seagull. The waves are violent and the weather is always cold. Anglo-Saxon England was a landscape defined by the elements. Yet I found the poetry challenging as well. Our modern concept of nature writing would have likely seemed strange to an Old English poet. It wasn't until much later, with the Romantics, that nature began to be personified and idealized. Old English poetry generally presents nature as a challenge to be overcome rather than an idyllic symbol of beauty.

I also wasn't sure how the two worlds of Old England and the contemporary American West would merge. Janesville is located in the high desert, a dry land where rocks crack in the summer sun and strong winds blow tumbleweed across the lawn in front of the school. Would the misty seacoast of "The Seafarer" and "The Wanderer" inspire these students to create their own landscape images?

At the time, I was a writer-in-residence at two other local schools, Credence Continuation High School and The Community Day School, a small school for boys on probation. I decided to try out Old English poetry and nature writing on the teenagers first.

We began by discussing the area's main watershed, Honey Lake. During dry years, Honey Lake exists only as mud flat, but in its current state, after several winters of heavy rains, it appears as a pristine lake stretching nearly twenty miles from Highway 395 to the base of the Skedaddle Mountains. Local legend has it that a tall person can practically walk across it without going under. Honey Lake was once part of Lake Lahotan, a huge inland sea stretching from Oregon and California through much of Nevada and Utah. It's a watershed with a rich history: petroglyphs and artifacts abound, and legends from the Paiute and Modoc peoples of the area tell of battles fought and civilizations that have come and gone on its shores. The first settlement of Europeans was on the shores of Honey Lake, until dry years sent them farther north, to the Susan River.

I passed out a copy of my own translation of "The Wanderer" and a copy of Ezra Pound's translation of "The Seafarer." My treatment of "The Wanderer" is a fairly literal, rough rendition of the poem. I sacrificed much of the alliteration and rhythm that define Old English poetry. Pound's marvelous translation, on the other hand, captures the essence of the poem while incorporating the alliteration and "feel" of the poet's voice. The students first read through the translations on their own. Next I read aloud certain verses that emphasize the natural world, such as:

> . . . Storms battered the stony slope,
> Falling snow storm binds the earth,
> The tumult of winter
> When the dark one comes.
> The shadow of night grows dark,
> Sends from the north a fierce hail storm
> To the vexation of men.
> All the kingdom of earth is full of hardship.
> The ordained course of events changes the world under the heavens.

I then read the beginning of Pound's translation of "The Seafarer":

May I for my own self song's truth reckon.
Journey's jargon, how I in harsh days
Hardship endured oft.
Bitter breast-cares have I abided,
Known on my keel many a care's hold,
And dire sea-surge, and there I oft spent
Narrow nightwatch nigh the ship's head
While she tossed close to cliffs. Coldly afflicted,
My feet were by frost benumbed.
Chill its chains are; chafing sighs
Hew my heart round and hunger begot
Mere-weary mood. Lest man know not
That he on dry land loveliest liveth,
List how I, care-wretched, on ice-cold sea,
Weathered the winter, wretched outcast
Deprived of my kinsmen;
Hung with hard ice-flakes where hail-scur flew,
There I heard naught save the harsh sea
And ice-cold wave, at whiles the swan cries,
Did for my games the gannet's clamor,
Sea-fowls' loudness was for me laughter,
The mews' singing all my mead-drink.
Storms, on the stone-cliffs beaten, fell on the stern
In icy feathers; full oft the eagle screamed
With spray on his pinion.

For those of us who have been enchanted by these works, the poems' technicalities are only one part of the spell cast by Old English poetry. The poems create places where myth and history blend. They come from a time when poetry was spoken rather than written. For a glimpse into contemporary spoken poetry, I questioned James, a young Mexican-Native American from the Community Day School who hated writing but who could invent a spontaneous two-to-three-minute rap on nearly any subject. "They call me 'Music' in my group home," James had told me earlier. "I'm who they come to if they want somethin' real said, whether it be a love poem for their girlfriend or an admonition to a little brother. They know I can do it 'cause I'm Music."

"So where do you get your words," I asked him in class, "when someone asks you to rap something for them?"

James shrugged. "I don't know how to explain it. It's like I get a sense of the person and the words just come to me."

"Do you know that if you'd been born in a different time you would have held an honored place in your community? This would have been your job, creating stories and poems and telling them to your people."

"My uncle does it, too," James said. "Only his is different. He don't do rap. It's more story-like."

This led to a discussion of how poetry is memorized and rendered from one telling to another. Rap is held in memory by its rhyme; Old English by alliteration and patterns of stressed and unstressed syllables. Each line of poetry is divided into two half-lines with three or four stressed syllables and several unstressed syllables.

For the writing assignment I told students to choose an emotion and, without naming it, to write a description of nature that would express that feeling. I told them to incorporate alliteration if they wanted to. Rick Baker, a young man who had been in my classes for two years and who usually wrote pieces with lines such as "dark shadows plague my sleep, running my mind ragged with their incessant jabbering," wrote:

> The setting sun rested blissfully on the soft silky horizon
> The colors flowed across the sky like the graceful brush strokes
> of a talented painter.
> The gentle wind whispered and caressed the clouds into colorful cotton
> moving gently across the evening sky.
> Oranges and reds, purples and pinks all faded fast
> into deep blue shadows, silky and sensuous
> danced across the mountains and valleys.
> The land was drenched deliriously in colorful bliss
> then it faded, all of it, into deep blue and purple.

Tandi LaRae wrote:

> The leaves swirl
> at a ferocious speed.
> The wind picks up,
> strangling you,
> gnawing at your face.
> Your eyes water
> and your breath catches
> your throat.

One of the great rewards of teaching is the surprises that it offers, the quiet student who creates magic or the hostile one who suddenly finds she has something to say. James's raps were among those rewards, although he always pointedly refused to commit anything to paper. That day, the magic came from Amanda Harlow, a new student most of the kids shunned. Amanda wore thick glasses and had long hair that hung over her face. Sometimes she made strange verbal outbursts or would ramble on about unrelated topics. She lived in one of the group homes out in the desert far from town, and was not destined for popularity. She usually sat by herself near the front of the room, often sketching in a spiral-bound notebook. That day, Amanda wrote the following poem:

A tree, a desert
An image in water, pure
Shimmering and cool.
The sky high above
Favors a ruddy color
Like death
Humbled tree branches
Bare, pale under the sky's view
Bent in its defeat
Yet held just above
The water-tree position
Favored but beaten
Knowing no sorrow
The tree holds its withered place
For time yet to come.

That poem brought attention to Amanda, which inspired her to create more fine pieces throughout the year. I made a broadside of it and hung it in the hall. A few weeks later when the performers for the Poetry Alive! group came to the school, they asked her to autograph a copy.

The next week two students, Tandi LaRae and Rob Brocksen, accompanied me to a fourth grade class in Janesville. We read short selections from "The Wanderer" and "The Seafarer." I also paraphrased the story of *Beowulf*, the Old English epic about the life and death of the Geatish warrior called Beowulf, who traveled across the sea to help the Danish king rid himself of a monster. I focused on Beowulf's fight with the monsters Grendel and Grendel's mother, reading the description of the mere where they lived (a *mere* can be a pond, a lake, a marsh, or an arm of the sea):

They occupied the secret land, the wolf slopes, the windy headlands, the terrible fen passage where the mountain stream goes downwards under the dark cliff, under the torrent of earth. It is not far hence in miles that the mere stands, over which hangs the rime-covered grove. The wood, firm in roots, overshadows the water.

(trans. Jordan Clary)

We talked about alliteration and brainstormed a list of descriptive words and alliterative pairs, which I wrote on the board. I asked the students to choose a body of water they were familiar with. This could be the area's main watershed, Honey Lake, or one of the other local lakes or streams that run through the high desert. If they still could not get started, I told them to imagine themselves as a body of water, or as an animal who used the water, and then to write from that perspective. Personification came easily to these students. I was surprised at the large number of them who chose to become the object they wrote about, as in:

> In the spring, the smell of fragrant tulips all around me.
> Colors of the rainbow on me after it rains—purple, blue and red.
> The fish in me splashing and playing.
> Trees and flowers whisper in the wind.
> The deer and antelope drink from me.
> Rain hits me like a thousand little rocks.
> I am the Susan River flowing in the wind.
>
> —*Nichol Shaver*

> In the spring the rain falls. My red berries smell ever so sweet in the morning. Rain drops still on the red berries with their sweet fragrance. The rain tingles the berries all over. The berries are talking to each other asking when will the next rain fall? Then the rain comes again. The berries cheer and laugh. When the rain ends, birds eat my berries. What am I? I am a bush, a green luscious bush.
>
> —*Chelsea Harmon*

Water holds a special place in the high desert. Nearly all the students had vivid memories of driving into the nearby mountains to swim or fish in one of the area's lakes. Eagle Lake, a pristine alkaline lake surrounded by pine-covered mountains, is equal in beauty and nearly equal in size to its more famous neighbor Lake Tahoe, 150 miles to the southwest. Eagle Lake was a favorite topic for many of the students, including Kelli Hallam:

> Eagle Lake is like a bowl of soup to animals. It has green leaves like vegetables. Animals come and drink from it. It's surrounded with flowers. When it rains, it smells like wet grass. When the waters run the animals bathe in it. The trees sway when the wind blows. The animals love to swim in the shade. The animals love the colors of the leaves: red, green, and orange. After the long day they lie down on the grass and rest.

Later that spring I discovered another dimension to Old English poetry, through an unexpected channel—cowboy poetry. As part of my residency, I invited a local cowboy poet, Russ Collier, to do a performance at Credence High School and at the Community Day School. I wasn't sure how the students would react to Russ. Most of them had cultivated tough exterior personae. Many lived in group homes or foster homes. A high percentage had been sent to this rural area by courts in Oakland or San Francisco, to "straighten them out." Their music was rap, heavy metal, Goth. Most scorned country music and cowboys— those were for the kids who went to the "real" high school down the road. Yet within a matter of minutes Russ, with his easy manner and off-color jokes, had these city kids laughing and participating in the performance. Russ and James

(Music) formed an instant connection with their love of wordplay and rhyming poetry. "A cowboy rapper" is what James called Russ.

During his introduction, Russ spoke of the way poetry travels, and about how many traditional cowboy poems could be traced to the sailors and pirates who came to the New World. Russ recited cowboy poems and old seafaring songs. Some poems were in fact nearly identical to the old seafaring songs, the only difference being the words *desert* or *prairie* were substituted for *ocean*. As he spoke, verses from "The Wanderer" and "The Seafarer" flitted through my mind. I realized that I had considered the career of Anonymous to have ended hundreds of years ago, when in fact he or she was alive and well in isolated pockets of folk arts around the world.

That afternoon I bought a collection of cowboy poetry that Russ had recommended. Like Old English poetry, many cowboy poems tell of isolation and long nights alone with the elements while longing for some ephemeral comfort only half-remembered. The following verses from the poem "The Blizzard" by Eugene Ware, who is said to have written it "way back in the 1860s," carry some of the flavor of Old English seafaring poems:

> It was midnight at the Cimarron
> Not many a year ago;
> The blizzard was whirling pebbles and sand
> And billows of frozen snow.
>
> He sat on a bale of harness,
> In a dugout roofed with clay;
> The wolves overhead bewailed
> In a dismal protracted way;
>
> They peeped down the adobe chimney,
> And quarreled and sniffed and clawed,
> But the fiddler kept on with his music
> As the blizzard stalked abroad;
>
> And time and again, that strange refrain
> Came forth in a minor key:
> "No matter how long the river,
> The river will reach the sea!"

From there it was an easy leap to imagine Beowulf as a cowboy. He rode a ship instead of a bronco, but the swaggering attitude, the love of adventure for adventure's sake, and the strict codes of honor all had correlatives in the American West. Perhaps the Old West was not so far removed from the concept of the blood feud as we are today. Dragons and monsters such as Grendel seldom show up in cowboy poetry, but giant oxen, whirlwinds of mythic proportions, and talking animals that lead lonely cowboys astray are all common fare—as is the devil, who appears in this anonymous rendition called "Hell in Texas":

> The devil in Hades we're told was chained,
> And there for a thousand years remained.
> He did not grumble nor did he groan.
> But determined to make a hell of his own
> Where he could torture the souls of men
> Without being chained in that poisoned pen. . . .
>
> He put thorns on the cactus and horns on the toads
> And scattered tarantulas along the road.
> He gave spiral springs to the bronco steed
> And a thousand legs to the centipede.
>
> And all will be mavericks unless they bore
> Thorns and scratches and bites by the score.
> The sand burrs prevail and so do the ants,
> And those who sit down need half soles on their pants.
> Oh, the wild boar roams the black chaparral.
> It's a hell of a place he's got for hell.

(This rendition recited by Roy Green of Shandon, California)

Even the concept of fate, in Old English poetry called *wyrd*, shows up frequently in cowboy poems. In one called "Like It or Not," contemporary cowboy poet Bill Simpson tells of an old buckaroo who talks "About drinkin' and fightin'! / An' ridin' em hard! / About fate he called luck! / In the turn of a card." Like Old English poetry, cowboy poetry uses the harsh elements of the natural world to provide a backdrop for its lyrics and narratives. In both, the natural world is often in opposition to the characters in it. Authors in both genres use natural images to speak of loneliness, struggle, and isolation. The forlorn wail of the wind, whether blowing across the empty prairie or the open sea, echoes through them both.

Bibliography

Abrams, M. H., editor. *The Norton Anthology of English Literature, Sixth Edition, Volume 1.* New York: Norton, 1993. (Incudes excerpts from *Beowulf,* "The Seafarer," and "The Wanderer.")

Cannon, Hal, editor. *Cowboy Poetry: A Gathering.* Layton, Utah: Gibbs Smith, Inc., 1985.

Cassidy, F. J. and Richard Ringler, editors. *Brights Old English Grammar & Reader.* New York: Holt, Rinehart and Winston, 1971.

Jack Collom

An Ecosystem of Writing Ideas

FOR TEN YEARS I've taught a graduate writing course called "Eco-Lit" (Ecology Literature) at Naropa University in Boulder, Colorado. Eco-Lit is offered by Naropa's Writing & Poetics Department, but welcomes students in other departments and local citizens at large.

In Eco-Lit I strive to be expansive, to suggest far more than we can thoroughly cover. We use a 400-page coursebook as well as many supplements (especially now that nature writing is gathering steam and becoming more than isolated "cries in the wilderness"). Such a hefty load may confuse students at first, but eventually makes sense to them—sometimes long past the end of the course. We read and discuss (as literature, as representations of nature) poems and essays by recognized luminaries of the field, the writings of Thoreau and after—John Muir, Rachel Carson, Aldo Leopold, Leslie Marmon Silko, Gary Snyder, Edward Abbey, Barry Lopez, Gretel Ehrlich, Susan Griffin, Loren Eiseley, Annie Dillard, Robinson Jeffers, et al. We also go back in time—to Boethius, Thomas Nashe, Gilbert White—and around the world—to Issa, Coyote and Jataka Tales, Orpingalik the Eskimo songmaker, //kabbo the Bushman, and others. Beyond these "nature people," we read fine poets of all subjects in the belief that a good poem, in being intensely relational within itself, is an ecosystem whatever it's nominally about. Writers of scope inevitably include—are included in—nature. We seek that sense, too, in comic strips, diaries, songs, lists, letters, slang, politics, slogans, definitions, fables, rebuses, jokes, and science jargon. And we touch on perhaps the greatest nature book, *Moby-Dick*.

Looking at a wide variety of forms allows us to keep up with, and even help to lead, the profound and rapid changes going on in humanity's knowledge of and attitudes toward nature. In my view, the word *nature* is peculiarly misunderstood by most of us. It's seen as something pretty one might sniff in passing, or as something disastrous such as a flood—in any case, as something secondary to the world and culture of *Homo sapiens*. It's something, in fact, that we're busy replacing with pavement, hydroponics, genetic engineering, zoos, animation, tree farms, and virtual waterways. It's something too dumb for irony.

In truth, *nature is everything*. It gains breadth from its subsidiary, limited meanings: beauty, wildness, source-of-life, and all their specifics. It gains poignancy through its contradictions. It's the big matrix; we're a few dots not only in it but *of it*. The "of" is what we forget. "Of" is identity of processes. Recognizing "of" is the springboard of love, without which there's only destruction, of ourselves and others. Jackson Pollock's remark, "I am nature," still has the ring of an outrageous cry—although it's just an overdue recognition. The word *ecology* means literally "knowledge of the house." In the sense that our house is now the entire world, the study of ecology has come to be a comprehensive study of the relational—the spreading interdependence of all things.

I encourage my Eco-Lit students to bring in their own favorite writers, variant viewpoints, and new facts. I continually hear about new, dynamic writing ideas from them. The more the merrier; I'd rather we struggle with bewilderment than oversimplify the possible links between writing and nature. In addition to our varied classwork, we go on a couple of fieldtrips each semester. These can simply be nature walks with writing, in the mountains or plains. Typically and inevitably, however, they take place in settings that include people-generated stuff; in this and other ways we learn that no separation between nature and humanity is possible. At the end of the semester we assemble a class anthology, for which each student contributes a certain number of pages. Many (but not all) of the included pieces reflect the class assignments. What follows is a sampling from those anthologies (keep in mind that these are writing students, mostly new to "nature writing"). It's also a walk through the many forms of writing I have my students experiment with.

* * *

The prime act that must precede writing—or talking—about nature is observation. Since pure perception cannot remain unaltered by language and our human psychology, the class discusses this question of phenomenology and we write with it in mind. We strive to approach, with our very limited senses, a fairly accurate take on a "leaf of grass."

Direct Observation Poem

mind
between
me
and
mountain

   —*Jeff Grimes*

Rhubarb red like a starched erect sinew sticking out of
the dirt: the Stem

Ending in triangular formations sharp drooping like
floppy garrisons: the leaves

Margarine yellow starting to melt on a skillet pan
intricate like doily patterns: the Head

One tarnished copper green leaf the tip of it starting to
change into rhubarb red like rusting plate mail

The most important part a wrinkled dried-out sun-scorched

leaf like a wet walnut brown sock left twisted upon
itself after being wrung out

This burnt potatochip leaf is barely connected to the
stem.

—*Aaron Hoge*

Another basic of nature writing is the sense of place. I urge students to write about place in any or all of several ways: by cataloguing what's there; by focusing on one or more of the senses; by narrating themselves into the picture; by writing acrostic poems about the place; or by making a small portion of a place stand for the whole (synecdoche). Poet and writer Merrill Gilfillan put it this way:

Look closely. Make notes on all the particulars you can In-place—sketch shapes, colors, sounds, aromas—and when you think you've done that, give it five minutes more; the summoning and staking of details leads, of course, to details-in-configuration, in context, i.e , to *relations*, root of all esthetics (and ethics). The same goes for a barrier reef or a freightyard or Gary, Indiana.

Ultimately, the poet finds his or her own way to depict the here and there:

a place called here (excerpt)

> *The days are stacked against what we think they are.*—Jim Harrison

stacked against what we know we are while wet flakes flower on the hoods of red volvos and drape aspen branches like lace. we know we were in love but the snow came too late. flouncing in on the tail of red robes layered against dusk. at the mercy of turnings, squinting to catch a stack of metered time rolling off slope of moon or the bridge of a nose that reminds you who you were. your own sweating breasts against a killing dream . . .

the earth stacked in favor of a bird's wings, ladder of plates grunting their way from hell to blue. in streams water whistles like air. dispersed falling, who we think we are. fallen. . . .

—*Shanley Rhodes*

Enviropoem

I am in my
body wrapped in skin
skin clothed in cotton
in a room with florescent light
and slightly stuffy air
in a building with classrooms
offices and library books
on a patch of ground with other buildings
making a school
surrounded by streets

stoplights and cars
in the middle of Boulder
full of random or purposeful human activity
dependent on electricity and gas
connected by telephones and computers
under the mountains
where goldseekers from the east
thought it looked like a good place to winter
one hundred thirty-one years ago
and never left
end of plains beginning of mountains
end of Arapahoe when the Americans came
only the statue of Niwot left
squatting by the creek west of 9th St.
staring at downtown Boulder
with its restaurants and banks
the creek by which he sits
comes down a canyon
drops 3000 feet in fifteen miles
is fed by other creeks
going back to lakes and glacier
if you keep walking up
you can see a good deal of it all at once
to the east, Boulder, Denver, brown cloud
pollution now makes its own horizon
a dingy line in the sky
and there are always airplanes
flying over all of it
and there are always satellites
orbiting above them
always a moon
always a sun
they always return
and the earth
so far
remains

  —*Chuck Pirtle*

The journal is an I-remember of the present: it always encourages us to notice our surroundings and our five or six senses. Here's one that displays a rocky compaction:

Grand Teton (excerpts)

August 1st

0300—Dark and cold. Wind blowing from the west. Very little sleep. Shared the cave at 10,500 feet with pikas. Up, already dressed. Headlamp on. Find Wesley and Bob. Quick breakfast—oatmeal and coffee. No one talking. Grunts.

0415—Start down through boulders and talus. Wesley leading. Down about 1000 feet then up to the Lower Saddle. Headlamps catch pikas. Occasional bird noises....

0600—On the saddle between the Middle and Grand Teton—glow to the east. Predawn. Still cold. North through long boulderfield. Smells of human shit. Exum Guides must still be dragging pack-trains of tourists up the ridge. Purchase an experience. No one around. Breathing hard. Look west into Idaho. Almost light now. To the east Signal Mountain, Jackson Lake, the Snake River, Alpine Lakes. . . .

0915—On the summit—very small place. Only other people there two crazy Brits—one chain-smoking. Sun beginning to warm, but not much. Take a few pictures. Look north to Cascade Canyon and all around. Still very clear.

　—*Bill Campbell*

The Portrait, or Sketch, is also one of our staples. It's a natural with animals. As always, details rather than generalizations make the reality:

The Magpie

Mulling and clucking under its breath
like the tanned and stained
homeless man downtown.
Huge and black and white
gloriously white, like rabbits' fur.
Breast feathers pristine
without benefit of a rasping,
rough cat tongue.
It mewed and whispered,
rolled its small obsidian eyes,
tail flashing blue pearls upon liftoff.
The branch vibrating
seconds after
the last huff of a wingbeat
pushed the air away.

　—*Deborah Crooks*

Inspired by Charles Simic's poem "Stone," in which the poet whisks our imaginations inside a plain rock and finds magic there, "Going-Inside" poems aim for the active empathy with "the other" so basic to an ecological sense:

Tripping in Cell

Stuck in sticky cell jam
my hands clasp the walls and
　　Martha Graham did a dance like this
　　using an elastic bag as
　　elastic plasma membrane containing
　　slurpy elastic blob blopping cytosol.

I bounce against altochondria
climb twisted DNA into a Jungian mansion
up is down into
ancient rooms
can't breathe for the dust
I'm an ape! no . . .
     a whale . . .
am I a whale or an ape or a
     whale of an ape!
         amoeba   pear   viking . . . . can't decipher this
         genetic code caught between a chicken and its egg.

Whatever . . . . . I'm stuck in this lethargic liquid
bang my head on a nucleus
feels like I've got a rock in my shoe.

    —*Karin Rathert*

Concrete poetry emphasizes the visual (sometimes sound) aspects of letters and words. Writing has always had a pictorial component (we can still see it in present-day Chinese), just as language has always had a musical component. In the Middle Ages, poems were constructed in the shapes of crosses or angel's wings, and so forth. Here are two contemporary works from my Eco-Lit classes:

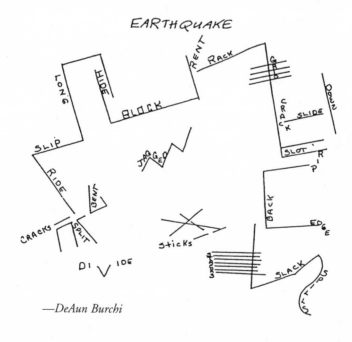

    —*DeAun Burchi*

My Faucet My Faucet My Faucet My Faucet My Faucet My Faucet My Faucet
The water treatment devices listed on this certificate have met the
following requirements pursuant to section 4057.i of the Health and
Safety Code for
the following
health related
contaminants:

Lead
Asbestos
(Protozoan)
2,4 D, Lindane
Benzene, Bromoform
Lead, p-Dichlorobenzene
Chloroform, Chlorobenzene
CarbonTetrachloride, Ethylbenzene
1,1- and 1,2-Dichloroethane, Toluene
Dibromodichloromethane, Dichlorobenzine
Hexachlorobutadiene, Tetrachloroethylenes
trans-1,2-Dicholroethene, Trichloroethylene
Tetrachloroethylene, Lindane, Lead, o-xylene
1,1,1-Trichloroethane, o-xylene, Bromoform, 1-
cls-1,3-Dichloropropene, Ethylbenzine, Chloroform
Ethylbenzene, Dibromodichloroethene, Cysts, Cysts
Turbidity, Asbestos, Lead, Lead, Bromoform, Lindane
Carbon tetrachloride, Hexachlorobutadiene, Trihalo-
methane H$_2$O trans-1,2-Tetrachloroethane, o-xylene
Trihalomethanes, Chlorobenzene, Cysts(Protozoans)
Dibromodichloroethene, Dichloroethane, Asbestos
Lindane, Lead, cls-1,3-Dichloropropene, 1,1-
Hexachlorobutadiene, Tetrachloroethylenes,
Chlorobnezene, Lindane, Bromoform
Chloroform, o-xylene
Lead

—*Suzanne Keith*

I encourage experimental approaches (following Mother Nature's lead). My Eco-Lit students have often, I think, invented new forms, or at least new formal modes:

With Their Voices They Are Calling You

                Whales ivory walrus
        coral *phylum coelenterata* cult
        scleractinia   gorgonia
          brain   star   fire
                    nematocyst
      black fin fan   tube   sponge   basket   *porifera*
          seals black sea cream
            tea leaves in teal stream
        millions of minnows in silver
                  negligees
          royal ribbon morays
                anemone
      lemon   lilac   lily
                    emerald   sapphire   jade
          interleafing coral cables in diamond lattice
                angels in striped pajamas
            French   butterfly   queens
        rosequartz candy in yellow cellophane wrapper
        Tahiti starfish   seaworms   lions
                cucumbers   elephants
            squirrel fish   wild wedding veil
                  noble brandy gold
      yolks — sun and moon — flounder globes
                seams   sugar sand
          porpoise saxophones patterns   around
              nurse shark tabernacles
              inset — vestibule for
                    snapper   grouper   jacks
        pisaster star
                little feather sister
          sea urchins with *pedicellariae*
                        Caribbean buttercups
            celestial kelp
                    duster worms
                      hermit crabs and scallops
            Rays - round   butterfly   bat   true

—*Resa Register*

"Silent Eyes"

—

Ghost Smile

"The words have no meaning,
but the song means,
Take it, I give it to you."
                    —Navajo

   Soft
      Footsteps

                          Light
                      Howl

            Coyohohohohehehe
            heyaheyaOhohohoh
            eheheyaheyaOhoho
            hheheDANCEheyahe
            yaohohohohhehehe
            yaheyaOhohohohhe
            heheyaheyaOhohTE

On
   Dirt

                Earthen
                    Ground
       Deep
     River

      Dry
        Tears

            CROhohohohhehehe
            heyaheya0hohohoh
            heheheSOAKyaheya
            Ohohohohheheheya
            heyaOhohohohhehe
            heyaheya0hohohoW

In
   Dirt
                Earthen
            Ground

—Mike Lees

Loomings

The sky
is the color of
split

cantaloupe
and it is
raining

seeds big
as Santa Fe
boxcars on

the heaven
of the human
tongue.

—*Randy Klutts*

Yet another basic of nature writing is the question mode. Nothing else stirs information about or turns it over like a question:

Is Nature Moral? (excerpt)

How can I think well enough to answer that question when the beauty of the sunlight on the pine needles keeps catching me? When there are blue jays eating berries from the vine on the side of my house? When some new magpies just moved in to the tree next door? When I'm kept up at night by the shuffling and scuffling and growling and chattering and lip-smacking of all ages of raccoons outside my bedroom window? When the singing of coyotes awakens me at three? When the stars are so bright I linger for too long beneath them? When there's a pulling in my chest at the way the wind and sun are making everything look at this moment?

—*Sarah Brennan*

Wallace Stevens's great poem "Thirteen Ways of Looking at a Blackbird" gives us the perfect form for looking into multiple truths:

seven ways of looking at a cloud

1   i, a disappointed child
     when told that clouds weren't solid

2   clouds gathering into massive anvil fist
     muttering over the silent desert
     spitting rain onto cracked red ground

3   the rain-giving clouds are distinctive
     with their countless pouchy buttocks
     mooning the earth below

4   Lenny the lenticular was a
    mean machine, leaning out across the sky
    a speeding ellipse against the blue

5   cumulette puffs of white dropped like wads of cookie dough
    their cloudbottoms dark and flat against an unseen nonstick pan

6   a cloud is the ultimate philanthropist
    poor in his youth, he becomes generous
    with age and girth
    sharing his water-horde at last

7   in ancient days a man was turned into a cloud
    forever banned from the earth
    but at night his form loosened into mist
    and he touched the face of his love as she slumbered

—*Chris Burk*

One of the most colorful formats is the recipe. Recipes show how elements can be combined to create new elements. They have a distinct vocabulary that is familiar to everyone. Recipe poems encourage wild imaginative leaps—but no food allowed!

Boulder Valley Surprise

boil igneous rock for millions of years
let stand until cool
when inland seas subside
uplift red sandstone, crimp edges
grind soil with glaciers
boil off glaciers
decorate with trees, evergreen and deciduous
then add large mammals, fish and birds
transfer humans with stone weapons
across the Bering Strait
convert large mammals
to food clothing and shelter
now add other humans from the east
sprinkle liberally with iron and gunpowder
in a large well-wooded valley
sift for gold dust
construct wooden buildings, then add brick
steam railroads, a shot of whiskey
then, with a large spatula
smooth out even layers of concrete
on any possible surface
sauté in carbon monoxide

bake with electromagnetic waves until saturated
in a large sealed container
cook plutonium until doomsday
garnish with shopping malls, tanning salons
takeout chicken, video arcades and massage parlors
set blender on purée
bring to a boil
run from the kitchen

—*John Wright*

The acrostic poem has been practiced for thousands of years: basically, a word is set vertically, and lines of a poem "spill out" of the letters. Acrostics serve any topic with great structural readiness, since the "spine word" resonates through the poem. Here's one with the whole alphabet, for that inclusive effect:

All together now, longer lives are special, longer lives are
Better. Because one gets to learn a lot,
Cuz one has the opportunity to learn from mistakes,
Dumb mistakes, dumb stupid mistakes like
Environmental disasters, like
Flooding lowlands for recreation, like
Giant dams that hold back water, like
Habitat destroyed in name of progress, like
Incan ruins unearthed and shattered, like
Jays being shot because they're too loud.
Kill, kill, why not kill? this globe this planet this
Land that bustles on its own much noisier than the
Moon. Oh, opal light, eclipse and mountain—
Now is the time to strike back, reform the earth,
Our knowledge unleashed for centuries without
Prior thought, without consideration of the side effects, without
Questioning the start of what once begun will take lifetimes to
Reverse. There is a
Sweet trickle of clear water, there is a tiny stream
Trapped beneath the underbrush, singing beneath the
Unborn ferns, where all the fiddleheads pop up like
Violins and accompany the stream.
Where has it all gone and why are these places now named "treasures"
eXactly where a small valley was, not far from where
Yellow poppies battle with winds, their skinny stems the strings of
Zithers still playing for us, still playing for us, can you hear them?

—*Stan Rudstrom*

"Everybody has a water story," exulted poet Sheryl Noethe. Here is an example of the form from Eco-Lit:

Water Autobiography

3 A.M. Longs Peak Trailhead: I strap two liters of water to my pack.

2 P.M. Fredericksted: Hot, very hot. I roll off the raft and into the cooling Caribbean Sea, and bob like a cork.

11 A.M. San Juan River, Utah: A wave catches me. I'm pulled under and am embraced by the current.

10 P.M. New York: We took long hot shower together, saving water in the 60s drought.

8 A.M. Lyons: A dead battery on cold winter morning I was late, late for school, late for work—the battery needed water.

4 P.M. Taj Mahal: Two naked children's bodies lie lifeless by the Ganges, their innocence swept away by the lapping holy waters.

11 P.M. Tip of Long Island: With our toes in the icy waters, we sent our spirits to Kohotec to become One with the Universe.

1 P.M. Hesperus: Very pregnant with my own, I break the water sack of a *cria* (baby llama) and help him emerge, feeling my own child move within me.

5 A.M. Hesperus: The warm soothing bathwater eases the labor pains as I wait for the midwife to arrive.

2 A.M. Lyons: "Maaaaaaaaam . . . Maaaaaaaaam, I want some water."

5 P.M. Mediterranean: The sea is calm, eerily calm, not a ripple, just the slightest telling whisper from the north.

9 A.M. Top Longs Peak: The first liter of water was drunk on the way up—now with the second we toast our success.

6 A.M. Outside New Delhi: "Water is running." I slipped from my tent wrapped in a lungi with my towel, soap, and cup in hand to perform our morning ablutions with the women in the irrigation ditch.

8 P.M. Lyons: What it was specifically I don't remember, except perhaps that impish look, but we started to laugh and giggle, the three of us together laughing, laughing so hard that the tears rolled down our cheeks. We embraced with contagious giggles, my girls and I.

6 P.M. Bedminster: Old Tom and I sat on the river bank fishing and drinking beer and talking of life. He was 72 and I was $7^1/_2$.

3 P.M. Fredericksted: It hadn't rained for weeks, the cisterns were empty. A crack of thunder the skies opened and we ran about dancing and shouting and tried to drink the sky.

7 A.M. Wherever: I splash the marvelously cold water on my face—Good Morning!

9 P.M. Far Hills: The rains just didn't stop, the water rose and rose, it was brown and muddy, it took the old cow, the footbridge, and the willow, then it stopped and slowly receded.

12 P.M. Kabul: The fact that he said it was the water gave me little consolation as I lay there bathed in sweat, folded in agony and praying for relief or death.

4 A.M. Mediterranean: The waves buffeted the *Eostra* about, the skipper yelled orders, the jib was in shreds: Poseidon had definitely lost his cool.

1 A.M. Amsterdam: The subtle movement of the houseboat lulled me into a deep sensuous sleep and dreams of Eros.

7 A.M. Blair's Lake: We scattered his ashes as he had wished—void of emotion.
10 A.M. High Time Farm: Dressed in a long white gown, my tiny bald head
sprinkled with water, I received my name.
12 A.M. 12th Street: It was some movie, she said goodbye and I let go like a
tropical storm, the tears flowing for every goodbye I ever said or that was said
to me.

—*Suki Dewey*

As I noted earlier, this is only a sampling of the writing forms my Eco-Lit
students try. We also do field notes, list poems, imitations, chant poems, definitions, haiku, haibun, lunes, letters, phrase-based acrostics, speeches, sonnets,
plays, sestinas, and prose narratives. (You can find detailed descriptions of these
in *Poetry Everywhere,* a book I wrote with Sheryl Noethe; see Bibliography at the
end of this chapter.)

We also experiment with different types of collaborations. Writing collaborations can be as myriad in form as writing itself. Collaboration by its essence
(multiple causation) exemplifies the spirit that moves ecology. It's also a lot of
fun, and can help escort a reluctant group into the joys of writing. And it helps
free up student minds to a wider range of connections.

My students swrite essays throughout the course. Some are critical responses
to readings. One is to research a local (Colorado-wide) eco-situation and write
about it. The final paper is an essay on Eco-Lit—what's happened, what's happening, what will or should happen. One student, for example, traced ecology
themes in music and song.

Some might argue that we should master one or two forms (styles, genres),
but I believe that generally in creative writing, as in learning different languages,
the more variety you undertake, the more mastery you achieve. When language
exemplifies its subject, the impact is considerably strengthened and diversified.
Obvious examples would be a poem about the sea having line-lengths that
resemble waves or a poem about emotional upset moving zigzag on the page.
When poetry discusses nature as if from a great height then nature seems both
bounded and lowered. Sometimes, nature is only allowed to be a blank screen on
which we project our emotions. But the realization that we are part of nature is
growing. Our human culture—truly amazing though it is—may be less complex than the legs of a spider, or than our own cellular existence. What better
way to use our indeed unprecedented cultural gifts than to build bridges back to
our larger selves?

I think both older styles of nature writing and the currently accepted ones
are fine; I have no desire to replace them, only to add to them. Language works
as a field, a geometry, in which anything can take place, and the definition of
nature should be something like "that within which we bob and swim." Were
someone to argue that depth is more important than breadth, I'd say that depth
consists of variation even more than breadth does.

*   *   *

I have also taught poetry to elementary, junior high, and high school students. For over twenty-five years, I have borrowed, stolen, been given, adapted, and made up well over sixty writing exercises for schoolchildren (see *Poetry Everywhere*). *All* of them, I believe, are good for teaching nature writing. And, in their variety, they resemble an ecosystem. Here are a few of my favorite ones for younger students (but not exclusively), with notes on how they physically relate to nature:

ANATOMY POEMS—personifications of body parts (the bones strike up a conversation with the heart, for example).

BUMPERSTICKERS—inventing these (e.g., REMEMBER WATER?) is fun and helps wean us from as sanctimonious reverence for nature.

"CAPTURED TALK" (students pull language from all around them: signs, books, overheard chat, TV, etc.)—a gleaning, like berry-picking; the rhythm and comedy of language tend to stand out in such collections.

CHANT POEMS—emphasis on rhythm and repetition, both of which operate abundantly in nature.

COLLAGE—grafting, hybridization.

COLLABORATIVE POEMS—exemplify the multiple truths and relational emphases that energize all of nature.

COMPOST-BASED POEMS (after Walt Whitman's "This Compost")—rot, and how life is fed by it.

CONCRETE POETRY—language forming aural or visual patterns, even recapitulating natural shapes.

CREATIVE REWRITES—personifications (or other adaptations) derived from science texts, resulting in such creations as talking winds or volcanoes.

"HOW-I-WRITE" PIECES—process-oriented, breaking habits down into physical details, bringing out the connections between writing and the most homely particulars in your life.

"I REMEMBERS"—list poems composed of lines each beginning "I remember . . ." can release hundreds of intricate memories, making nature immediate.

LIST POEMS— an expansive way to talk about anything.

METAPHORS—I see exercises in metaphor as objective correlatives of the relational.

NO-WARMUP DELIVERIES—not only spontaneous but unguided, as sudden events in nature seem.

ON POETRY—"a slow flash of light that comes to you piece by piece" (by a sixth grader).

ORIGINS (after Jacques Prévert's poem, "Pages from a Notebook")—playful little reverse creation myths ("The music teacher turns back to music," wrote one first grader).

OUTDOORS POEMS—being outdoors and writing a circle or path of observations.

PANTOUMS (Southeast Asian form with a weave of repeated lines)—like the cycles of nature.

PICTURE-INSPIRED WRITINGS—for example, one student wrote from a closeup of a cabbage leaf, describing it as a faraway galaxy.

POLITICAL POEMS—compassionate noise.

PROCESS POEMS—letting language be subject to mathematical processes, as nature is.

QUESTIONS WITHOUT ANSWERS—"Where do all the noises go?" The poem is a response (but not closure) to the question posed.

SPANISH/ENGLISH POEMS—students can write poems in which the two languages are mixed, as in a garden.

TALKING TO ANIMALS—"Tyger, tyger, burning bright" and other possible conversations.

THINGS TO DO IN . . . —another way to project the mind outward (into the Brain of a Bumblebee, the Bottom of the Sea—or one's own kitchen).

USED-TO-BE-BUT-NOW . . . POEMS—(I used to be . . . , but now . . .) playing with and against cause and effect.

WALL-OF-WORDS—distributed objects, announced words, and readings-aloud during writing time all help emphasize *scene* as source, so that nature writing not only discusses, but also *models*, nature's processes.

I've saved my favorite nature writing idea for last.

The first time I asked some of my elementary students to respond directly to the idea of Nature, using creative writing, was one Earth Day years ago. First I spoke of list poems: lists, or catalogues, have been a common element of both poetry and practical life for millennia. They are packed with information and encourage students to use surprise, to play with odd or wide-ranging juxtapositions. List poems tend to be rhythmic and full of energy.

I suggested that we make list poems from the idea "Things to Save." To give the word *save* the right context, I said a little about the looming ecological problems facing the world, but I didn't want to preach to the students. I also let the students know that they didn't have to feel restricted to "nature items" for their things to save; they should feel free to include personal things and favorite things—little sisters, books, or the teddy bear with a missing arm and its eye pulled out on a rusty spring. In this way, we could indicate that nature and civilization are interconnected.

The usual precautions about what helps make good poetry were appropriate at this point, so I told them that details are better than generalities. (Don't simply save "trees, animals, and water," save the lopsided old sycamore by Salt

Creek where the gray-cheeked thrushes sing.) It takes imagination not only to create fantasies, but just to see what's in front of you, to go beyond a "bird" or a "bush." I also tried to show the students that it's both fun and necessary to create *variety* in their "things to save" writings, variety not only in the items listed but also in the *kinds* of items ("wild horses, acorns, smiles"). I asked them also to vary syntax in their pieces—not to get into the rut of "Save the blank / save the blink / save the blonk."

Here is a selection of these "Things to Save" pieces by younger students:

I'd like to save the sweet chocolaty chewy candy bars
that melt in your mouth, the warm cozy pillow that you
can't wait to sleep on, I'd like to save green meadows
that you run barefoot across running and running until
you collapse on the wet soft grass, the hot days when
you try to eat ice cream but it melts and plops on your
foot, I'd like to save the amusement parks where you go
on a twisty ride and throw up all over yourself but that's
just what you thought would happen, I'd like to save the
little green bug my big brother viciously killed six
months ago, I'd like to save the world all green and blue
and beautiful, I'd like to save the little things that
everyone enjoys.

   —*Juli Koski, fifth grade*

clouds, white shadows in the sky, cotton candy white as the lining of
silk, soil black as coal, koala gray as rain clouds, trees tall as
the sky, polar bears white as ever, dolphins swimming in the sea.

   —*Jessica Flodine, fifth grade*

The darkness of shadow-like wolves
darting across the night like
black bullets, and the moon
shimmering like a sphere of glowing mass.
Let us save lush grass, green as green
can be, but, best of all,
imagination glowing with joy aha,
images it is composed of, it is this
that is making the earth grow
with flavor and destination.

   —*Fletcher Williams, fifth grade*

Poem #1
Save the Earth

Poem #2
Save the red fox, the white-tailed deer, the blue whale, the bald eagle,
    the black bear, the spotted owl
and animals not discovered yet . . .
Save the black and white lily bug
Save the striped toad
Save the bunga-bird
Save the Galápagos hare
Save the green ten-legged spider
Save the rock troll
Save the hairy lizard
Save the Antarctic elephant
Save the Asian fire squirrel
Save the yellow-tailed nonkey
Save the snow otter
Save the white-eyed dog

    —*Marco Barreo, junior high*

I would like to save the colors on Earth

White as the snow
Blue as the sky
Night

Sunlight
Yellow as the sun, daffodil and bees
White as snow, whiteout and gems
Red as blood, flowers and your heart also hair
Orange as the fruit, gold earrings I see around
Green grass and shrubs
Darkness
The Black at night, in your eyes and in your hair
The Purple flowers and Purple polka-dot pencil you see
The Blue tears and Blue book covers
Gray we see in dreams.

    —*Shannon Foley, fifth grade*

And finally—proving that this exercise can work at all levels—here is a
poem by one of my Eco-Lit students:

Save pearly everlasting dried broken at the roadside.
The sound of Arenal at night. Lava
and parakeets in flocks, and storms.
Save hills and high cliffs, save
animal teeth, save

fur and claws and tendons and bones.
Save stars but change the constellations if you want.
Save baobab trees,
llamas, rusty old meat grinders,
the organ grinder's monkey. Save
old shoes and hair.
Save caterpillars, nasturtiums,
grass-of-parnassus.
Save chokecherries
and phosphorescence,
sea horses, flies.
Save stone walls for walking,
and drift wood on beaches.
Save things that live in the Indian Ocean.
And things that swim in the South China Seas.
Save sand.
Save music and humming and whistling through teeth.
Save people on streets, but don't save the streets.
Then sumacs, and fescue and fenugreek seeds,
and ladybugs, aphids, paper-birch, leaves.
Touch-me-nots. Cockroaches.
Carnivores. Herbivores. Omnivores. Fields. Save
seed shadows. Leaf litter. And marshes. Save
duff.
Sea shrimp and squid ink and
octopus feet, and
hurricanes. And 80-knot winds. And
sailboats thrown onto high cliff roads.
And slugs and snails and scallops and scarabs.
Kestrels and nightshades. Vipers and honey.
Save blue things. Save bower birds.
Devil's club, mulch.
Save sea otters, ospreys and
things the color of stone.

—*Saskia Wolsak*

Bibliography

Collom, Jack, and Sheryl Noethe. *Poetry Everywhere: Teaching Poetry Writing in School and in the Community.* New York: Teachers & Writers Collaborative, 1994.

Simic, Charles. "Stone." From *Selected Poems.* New York: Braziller, 1985.

The Web of Life

When we try to pick out anything in Nature,
We find it hitched to everything else in the universe.

—*John Muir*

Terry Hermsen

Earth Water Air Fire

An Exercise in Creative Memory

DANCER-CHOREOGRAPHER Shawn Womak and I were walking back to her apartment in a neighborhood lined with brick streets and century-old trees after a long day at a conference on "integrating the arts into the curriculum." We breathed a sigh of gratitude for the breeze and the gracious way the neighborhood's park invited us to wander further than we'd planned. At age forty and pregnant for the first time, Shawn told me how her changing body had changed her thinking about her dancing, her choreography, and her work with students in state arts council residencies. Maybe it was the watery world in which her baby was growing, she speculated, or the increasingly computerized world of the classrooms and offices she saw around her, but something was pulling her to explore the "lost elements" of earth, water, fire, and air.

This led Shawn to invent a series of exercises for her dance company members in which they "entered the memory," as she put it, to see in what ways they were still connected to these four basic yet increasingly distant aspects of our environment. First they traced their own childhoods for images of one of the elements, then they sought movements growing out of that early imagery. Shawn wanted her dancers to bring what might be called the ancient knowledge of the earth into their dancing. How did they visualize ground and dirt and soil? Where within their bodies was the essential touch of water? How could they translate a memory of sleeping as a child in a frigid cabin? Such was the essential stuff of life for humans for centuries—and still is in so many parts of the world. But what do the four elements mean for us, in contemporary, sanitized, plasticized America? Shawn's questions led to a series of performances, and since her own work as a dancer and choreographer usually translates directly into new work with students, she was finding that non-professional dancers also hungered for this resubmergence in a gritty world of earth, water, fire, and air.

I drove home that evening quite inspired. Why couldn't poets take on these same elemental challenges? The following week I found myself leading a workshop based on Shawn's to a group of high school dance students, only I wanted them to do it with words. I began by giving them the following poem by William Stafford:

Evening News

That one great window puts forth
its own scene, the whole world
alive in glass. In it a war happens,
only an eighth of an inch thick.
Some of our friends have leaped
through, disappeared, become unknown
voices and rumors of crowds.

In our thick house, every evening
I turn from that world,
and room by room I walk, to
enjoy space. At the sink I start
a faucet; water from far is
immediate in my hand. I open our
door, to check where we live.
In the yard I pray birds,
wind, unscheduled grass,
that they please help to make
everything go deep again.

> —*William Stafford*

After reading the Stafford poem, we talked about how simple, but how essential, water is. We discussed some of Shawn's ideas. I showed the students a poster I had brought in entitled "Creative Amnesia," which depicts an editor asking for works of all kinds that recall what we humans have forgotten. I quoted from the poster: "The true artists will be those who pick the cogent pieces from all times and gather them in a tidal wave of awareness toward the twenty-first century." We can do this with our bodies—using the methods Shawn developed—or we can do it with words. Here are a few of examples of what my students wrote. (Many of them had little prior experience with poetry.)

The waves roll in—forcing me
down
Salt in my eyes—on my skin
pulling me under—out
leaving craters under my feet

> —*Kate Hutchison*

I breathe hot air into my hands
& it echoes back onto my face,
warming it for too short a time. . . .

> —*Callie Wilson*

Thick dust rises devilishly
in delicate swirls.
Shining big broncos
are carted by.
Smell of pigs and putrid stalls
and black polish drying on horses' hooves...

—*Emily Smith*

*   *   *

The assignment continues to grow for me. Each time I have adapted it for a new class, it has been like entering a forgotten world. Here is how I usually do it.

I begin by asking students to think about ways in which we were more closely involved with earth, water, air, and fire than, say, 100 years ago. Whether they're in fifth grade or high school seniors, my students seem fascinated by such questions as: How did people on a daily basis touch earth, water, fire, or air in a very direct way? (As, again, much of the world still does.) The answers proliferate: carrying water from the well, digging a new well, damming rivers, plowing and harvesting by hand, building cooking fires, hanging iron pots over the fire, feeling heat from the flames, fighting forest or brush fires, crossing rivers on horseback or in canoes or rafts, plowing soil, panning for gold, fishing, dredging swamps, walking to a neighbor's or riding in a wagon or open-air buggy, warming their feet on a long ride with wrapped bricks from the fire. . . . Then we shift the question: How do we experience these four elements now? Where is the fire in *our* lives? Hidden under the hood of the car powered by oil pumped from Saudi wells? Where does our water come from? When do we ever feel its weight or its power? (I tell them that more and more summer camps are building chlorinated pools because young people refuse to swim in lakes with sandy bottoms and weeds.) The ensuing discussion covers a lot of ground. I suggest to students that maybe one of the tasks of poetry—and all art—is to re-engage us with what we know in some distant way, but find ourselves increasingly estranged from.

I ask my students to jot down memories of their own, dividing the paper into quadrants and listing whatever experiences arise for them concerning the four elements. Some memories, of course, will cross boundaries: for instance, I might put the time when it rained on a camping trip and my father and I used a garbage can lid as a "hood" for our cooking fire under either "fire" or "water." But what does it matter which category it fills? One element leads to another, and the important thing is to tap back into the experience itself.

After the students have generated lists of memories, I ask them to set their pages aside for a while. I want their memories to percolate. For me, a memory will often hang around for a few days before it finds its way into a poem. Rushing the process might make it more mechanical. Besides, I want them to look at how some other poets have approached these topics. I pass out some pages with poems by various writers:

Spanish Dancer

As on all its sides a kitchen-match darts white
flickering tongues before it bursts into flame:
with the audience around her, quickened, hot,
her dance begins to flicker in the dark room.

And all at once it is completely fire.

One upward glance and she ignites her hair
and, whirling faster and faster, fans her dress
into passionate flames, till it becomes a furnace
from which, like startled rattlesnakes, the long
naked arms uncoil, aroused and clicking.

And then: as if the fire were too tight
around her body, she takes and flings it out
haughtily, with an imperious gesture,
and watches: it lies raging on the floor,
still blazing up, and the flames refuse to die—.
Till, moving with total confidence and a sweet
exultant smile, she looks up finally
and stamps it out with powerful small feet.

—Rainer Maria Rilke (translated by Stephen Mitchell)

Mid-August at Sourdough Mountain Lookout

Down valley a smoke haze
Three days heat, after five days rain
Pitch glows on the fir-cones
Across rocks and meadows
Swarms of new flies.

I cannot remember things I once read
A few friends, but they are in cities.
Drinking cold snow-water from a tin cup
Looking down for miles
Through high still air.

—Gary Snyder

"Take the next fifteen minutes or so and let the lines wash over you, noticing where your attention or your ear is caught," I suggest. I prefer that the pace of the reading be casual, more attuned to the way reading happens when we're off by ourselves, free to love a line or image without understanding the whole poem, rather than the way we read in a classroom. This freer kind of reading can be as helpful to the process of writing as any direct instruction.

Then we talk. "Which poems should we discuss?" I ask them. Often there is a consensus—a consensus that varies from group to group. If one class just *has* to talk about "Spanish Dancer" for its intense imagery, another will be more attuned to the airiness of "Mid-August. . . ." We look at the ways the poet shaped a line or a phrase—or broke the rules, as Snyder does. What students mostly need at this point, I believe, is to experience the poem, as in James Wright's short prose poem "Saying Dante Aloud":

> You can feel the muscles and veins rippling in widening and rising circles, like a bird in flight under your tongue.

That's the type of reading experiences I want my students to have. I'm not so concerned with discussing meaning as with noticing the sounds and shapes of these poems. I want students to see how the four elements enter the poems, and to look for the lines that make our bodies want to move or our heads turn, for the physical presence within the words.

Then I give three choices for writing, though of course there could be many more:

1) Re-create a memory in the form of a poem that focuses on one of the elements. No need to tell us the whole story—stay within one particular moment that conveys the physical sense of being there. Theodore Roethke's "Big Wind" or Ann Stanford's "The Blackberry Thicket" are good models here, especially for the way they accumulate detail. (So is Roethke's "Child on Top of a Greenhouse.")

2) Write your "dream" of one of the four elements, evoking images of it through metaphor and visualization. This could be a dream you've actually had, or a dream the element itself might have if it were a person. Again, you don't need to tell a story. Focus instead on the physical sensation of a particular manifestation of water, fire, earth, or air. What ways can you find to evoke the feeling of it coming alive within the dream? Mary Oliver's "Sleeping in the Forest" or Carol Muske's "Found" are be good examples here.

3) Mix and match: Try a series of memories that spill into fantasy, or a series of images that evoke these elements. Daryl Chinn has a poem called "Silences" that investigates those silences that hang in the air. Harley Elliott's "Whales" is another good example here, especially for shifting from reality into fantasy.

Here are some examples of poems by high school students. All are first drafts written during one session.

Dirtbike

My legs were on fire as I peddled faster and faster
The wind whipping by my ears as I turned the
corner of South 7th and the road that went to the hills
Pulling into the open field harboring mounds of dirt piled high
I breathed in the air of competition and the scent of success
It was here at this little insignificant place I learned
the world expected you to beat the dirt hills.
Each time I fell to the earth from my metal throne
it received me softly and filled me with endurance
The endurance I need to prove myself to the mountains
of tiny men who camped in Spiderman houses
and hunted Chef-Boyardee.

    —Mary Beth Beraun

The Meal

The fool sits around me with legs
stretched to the max. I lick his toes.
He crawls back to the gnarly bale
of hay. I look up and get kicked in the
face when the short one tries to fly over
me. The ugly one feeds me.
Wind passes through me and I say hello.
The fools moved their thrones of hay
back, for the fear I may get a tasty
snack I do not deserve. Ah, but the

lanky one missed some. I hop
from one morsel of appetizer to another,
until finally I reach my main course.
Next, some barn for dessert.

    —Heather Nightwine

Earth and Air

I remember this plane, I remember sitting in it.
I remember trying to see my family for a last time
behind those windows, but I didn't succeed.
I remember praying to stop this plane, but it
didn't listen to me. It just flew without stopping.
I was in the air, admiring my French earth.
I tried to remember every single detail: a car,
a road, some colors, some blue spot that was
nothing else than some swimming pool.

And the air was here surrounding me, with
those clouds that didn't have anything to do
covering home. I was breathing this French air for
a few more minutes. And I was offering more tears
to show my earth and my French air how
I loved them.

    —Emilie Descamps (exchange student)

The assignment could end here, with students taking time to revise and read their work aloud, but if there's time, I often move directly into "mixing the elements" in a group revision exercise. I pass out four slips of paper to each student, saying, "We'll read our own individual poems in a little bit. For now, write out four of your best lines on each one of these pieces of paper. Vary the tone of each, maybe putting your best metaphor or simile on one piece of paper, and adapting one of your lines into a question for another. Perhaps make one a fragment, and another a command." When they're done, we collect the lines into a box, stir well, and pair up, each pair taking out eight of the lines at random.

The next step is for the pairs of students to re-order their random lines into a new poem. They should feel free to cut lines where needed, perhaps splitting them in half, using the first half at the beginning of the poem and the second half in the middle somewhere. Pronouns might need to be adjusted, as might verb tenses. They are also "allowed" to drop one line—or to use it as a title. The process is invariably fun—and surprising. Although the lines come from many different people, the students begin to see how they can be molded together nonetheless, into fresh poems, by making expansive leaps and connections.

Here are two examples of student poems constructed from gathered lines:

I am ocean
waiting fifty laps before a word
Brownish, green, salty with tiny bodies
A blue sky gulping
a distant moon
A windmill set on stuck
For in my dreams the air will
cool my still body

    —Leah and Cody

Flying over mountains and trees, a plane.
As if I had grown wings.
Pressed to their edges
Never at rest, always at work
Surrender
Roll with huge thunderous waves
Words melt and bubble
Starting to think, why walk around

Like a lost child
Why not swim

   —Amy and Holly

*   *   *

Back in the early 1960s, W. S. Merwin wrote:

> Among my peculiar failings is an inability to believe that the experience of being human, that gave rise to the arts in the first place, can continue to be nourished in a world contrived and populated by nothing but humans.

And around the same time, Edith Cobb wrote:

> As the environment crumbles and steel and concrete take the place of earth, the spirit may crumble as well. Without the element of spirit, man becomes sheer animal while retaining the cunning of intellect.

Little has changed since then, in terms of our basic needs. Kids still need to walk in rivers, to dip down skeins for a stream study and raise up multi-colored fish in order to know what goes on under the surface of the rivers which they may walk by every day. They need to stand at the edge of a meadow at dusk and watch the fog roll in or lie and watch the stars create their own elusive pictographs. We need reminders of the richer world we have left behind. Maybe we can begin, as William Stafford says in "Evening News," by just walking room to room, opening the door to "check where we live," and touching "water from far" close in our hands. Or we can start with poems. They too can be a way to "help to make / everything go deep again."

Bibliography

Cobb, Edith. *The Ecology of Imagination in Childhood.* Dallas, Texas: Spring Publications, 1993.

Martz, William. *The Distinctive Voice.* Edited by William Martz. New York: Scott Foresman, 1966. (Source of quotation from W. S. Merwin.)

Merwin, W. S. "Witness." In *The Forgotten Language: Contemporary Poets on Nature.* Edited by Christopher Merrill. Logan, Utah: Gibbs Smith, 1991.

Rilke, Rainer Maria. "Spanish Dancer." From *The Selected Poetry of Rainer Maria Rilke.* Translated by Stephen Mitchell. New York: Random House, 1982.

Snyder, Gary. *Riprap.* San Francisco: Four Seasons Foundation, 1969.

Stafford, William. *Allegiances.* New York: Harper & Row, 1970.

Wright, James. *Above the River: Collected Poems.* New York: Noonday Press, 1990.

Other Poems about Earth, Water, Air, and Fire

Earth

Louise Gluck, "The Wild Iris." From *The Wild Iris.* Hopewell, N.J.: Ecco Press, 1992.

Mary Oliver, "Sleeping in the Forest." From *Twelve Moons.* Boston: Little, Brown, 1979.

Ann Stanford, "The Blackberry Thicket." From *Selected Poems.* New York: Viking Press, 1965.

Water

Harley Elliott, "Whales." From *Animals That Stand in Dreams.* Brooklyn, N.Y.: Hanging Loose Press, 1976.

Li-Young Lee, "I Ask My Mother To Sing." From *Rose.* Brockport, N.Y.: BOA Editions, 1986.

Carol Muske, "Found." From *Camouflage.* Pittsburgh, Pa.: University of Pittsburgh Press, 1975.

Air

Daryl Chinn, "Silences." From *The Soft Part of the Shoulder.* Orlando, Fl.: University of Central Florida Press, 1989.

Robert Francis, "Polevaulter." From *The Orb Weaver.* Middletown, Ct.: Wesleyan University Press, 1960.

Theodore Roethke, "Big Wind." From *Words for the Wind.* Bloomington: University of Indiana Press, 1961.

Fire

Osip Mandelstam, "How dark it gets along the Kama (#310)." From *Selected Poems,* translated by W.S. Merwin. New York: Atheneum, 1974.

Margot Fortunato Galt

Nature as Teacher and Guide

Two Interlocking Poetry Writing Exercises

TURNING TO NATURE as a guide for human life is as old as the Greeks and Romans and as contemporary as writers Mary Oliver and N. Scott Momaday. These days, even urban young people encounter environmental studies and become alert to the relations between humans and other parts of the natural world. To translate such awareness into poems, however, students may need guidance from good literary and ecological models.

Older poems from the Euro-American tradition, such as Tennyson's "Flower in a crannied wall," emphasize human agency and dominance: The poet plucks a flower and holds it up to learn "what God and man is." When I teach nature poems to students from upper-elementary age to adulthood, I start from a different attitude: namely, that humans and other forms of natural life are equal and complementary. We don't have to pluck the flower to understand how alike our lives are.

To convey this distinction in the classroom, I often begin by drawing a pyramid on the board. Then I draw a circle beside it. My pre-writing discussion with students begins by considering these two forms as symbolic of different views of natural—including human—life.

Step One: Pyramid and Circle

"Many Native American cultures," I tell the students, "conceive of the world as a circle, and not just because it's a globe. On the other hand, many of our ancestors from Europe considered that the value of all living things could be charted in the form of a pyramid. Let's imagine that we are ranking our world's things on a pyramid. What would go at the top?"

Inevitably a student or two will say "God." I don't dismiss this: the Renaissance "Great Chain of Being," my prototype for the pyramid, did place God over all. But in secular schools today, I feel uncomfortable writing God on the board, so I say, "We'll imagine the word there. What comes next?"

Gradually the class will fill in the top ranks with humans beings, ranging from the U.S. president to movie stars and athletes, to family and friends.

"What about plants and animals?" I ask.

Pets win lots of approval, as do dolphins and monkeys. Then come animals used for food, food plants, flowers we love.

"What about insects and reptiles?" I ask. By this time the students' environmental education often exerts itself; students insist we have to put water on the pyramid, and air too. They are willing to consider insects and reptiles. Butterflies are highly ranked (some Native American tribes consider butterflies to be fragments of the Great Spirit). Ticks and mosquitoes are low. Fish are low. Snakes low. Dirt and rock are underneath it all. By this time, the students' environmental consciousness has nearly derailed the activity. "But how can you put cats above water? We all have to have water?" I ask. This slows them down; otherwise, the class pyramid might turn out like this:

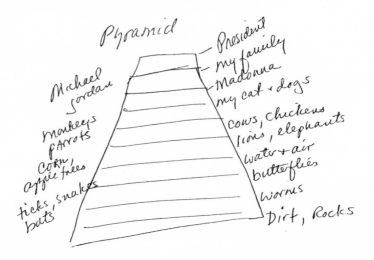

Next, we turn to the circle. "Draw a circle in the middle of your large sheet of paper," I tell the students. (I like to use unlined newsprint folded to around 14" x 17", with a crease down the middle. This gives students one side for drawing and brainstorming, and one side for writing.) "On the circle, every place is equal and every place is important and every place is the same," I suggest. "When we think of living things on a circle, we see that they are all connected, all related. Lose one and the connection to all is broken."

Now that we have circles, we place living things on them. I begin: "Let's start by putting a tree on our circle, any particular type of tree you know. You can write it anywhere because every place is equal and every place is important and every place is connected." Then we read our choices aloud: "*Beech, oak, birch, maple, pine, ginkgo, ash, apple tree.*"

Soon we have a game going. Someone calls out a category and everyone writes a familiar or beloved example on some part of the circle: Birds, then

Flowers, then Animals (I change Animals to Mammals to make sure we don't forget Reptiles and Amphibians). Then I say, "A form of water," which provokes a flurry of discussion about what forms water takes: *ponds, rivers, rain, hail, snow, ice, waterfalls, oceans, lakes, deltas, steams.* We go back and list reptiles, amphibians, insects, things in the sky. "A landform," I suggest, and we talk about what that means: *beach, mountain, valley, prairie, mesa, canyon, island, peninsula, archipelago.*

It's important for people to be represented on the circle, but I want to circumvent rock stars or other media figures. I insist that the human be "someone related to you, a grandmother, friend, uncle, cousin, father, sister, brother, or mother." "Don't write the name of the person," I tell them, "write the relation."

Here is an example of what a circle might look like. You don't have to include every possible category; in this one, for instance, we missed rocks and forms of fire.

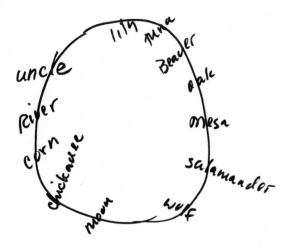

Step Two: Presenting Some Models

Next, I read them two poems. The first was written by seventeen-year-old Darrel Daniel St. Clair, of the Alaskan Tlingit tribe:

> My school the earth
> My teachers,
> The sky, the clouds, the sun, the moon,
> The trees, the bushes, the grass,
> The birds, the bears, the wolves,
> The rivers, whom I claim to be
> My mad genius.
> Once I missed a day
> Because they tried to make

Me learn it from the books
In a little room
That was really too stuffy.
I hope my teachers don't
Put me on the absent list.
I enjoy going to that school
Where the air is fresh.
Where nothing is said and I learn
From the sounds.
From the things I touch,
From all that I see.
Joy to the world and
I've fallen in love with my teachers

The speaker's affection and reverence for the natural world are so evident that I rarely say much about the poem, although I will ask younger students, "Does anyone here feel the same way?"

The second poem I read is incorporated in Step Three below.

Step Three: Writing a Circle Poem in the Native American Spirit

N. Scott Momaday, of the Kiowa tribe from Oklahoma, is well known for his Pulitzer-prize-winning novel *A House Made of Dawn*. He has also written a number of beautiful poems. The one I use is called "The Delight Song of Tsoai-Talee."[1]

"This is a chant," I say, "a spoken song. The poem has many repetitions like choruses in songs. Listen for what is repeated."

I am a feather on the bright sky
I am the blue horse that runs in the plain
I am the fish that rolls, shining, in the water
I am the shadow that follows a child
I am the evening light, the luster of meadows
I am an eagle playing with the wind
I am a cluster of bright beads
I am the farthest star
I am the cold of the dawn
I am the roaring of the rain
I am the glitter on the crust of the snow
I am the long track of the moon in a lake
I am a flame of four colors
I am a deer standing away in the dusk
I am a field of sumac and the pomme blanche
I am an angle of geese in the winter sky
I am the hunger of a young wolf
I am the whole dream of these things

You see, I am alive, I am alive
I stand in good relation to the earth
I stand in good relation to the gods
I stand in good relation to all that is beautiful
I stand in good relation to the daughter of *Tsen-tainte*
You see, I am alive, I am alive.

We talk about our favorite images—children remember precise language as well as older readers do. We identify the repeating parts; we discuss what it means to "stand in good relation." I tell the class that in the South where I grew up, we discussed our friends and relations. Relations are family. "How would you like your family to treat you?" I ask. They answer, "With love, with respect, with honesty and care." Momaday suggests that we treat the earth in the same way: like family—with kindness, consideration, care, attention, love, and respect. With older students, I remark that the poem is a love song, not just to the daughter of Tsen-tainte, but to the earth.

Next we go back to our circles. I tell the students we're going to write our own songs of good relation. Then I choose one of the several ways I've discovered to nudge students into their poems. The first is to have them write poems that describe how one part of the circle teaches something to another part. This approach was inspired by a rural Minnesota fourth grade class who had just visited a pig farm. They were full of what pigs had taught them about being pigs. It was easy to ask next what they had learned from other creatures, and from water, air, wind, and then to have them move from there to a poem depicting nature as guide.

"Pick up your pencils," I say next, "and draw a line between any two items on your circles; it doesn't matter which two because everything is related, everything is equal and everything is connected."

The first two words I connect on my chalkboard circle are *beaver* and *moon*. Then I write my first line on the board as an example: "The brown beaver leaps in the stream and shows the silver moon how to fill with rain."

We brainstorm other words for teach, like *preach, demonstrate, educate, show, display, learn, understand, prove.* As we write each line, I encourage students to think of particular skills and beauties for each member of their pairs.

After they write their first lines, students make a second connection and write a second line, and so forth. Here is a poem from fourth grader Heidi Bakken:

The goat teaches
the mountain how to sing.
The moon told
the people how to be quiet.
The old woman made

the elm tree come alive
and he liked that.
The hail was in the sky, so
he told the star to come too.
The deer told
the old man, I like you.
The goat got shaped
like a cloud because
he looked at it.

A second way to help students along is to suggest that they borrow the "I am" beginning from Scott Momaday's poem and use it to start each line in their own poems. After the students have connected two things on their circles, I say, "Now write a line that shows these two in relation. This can mean being in a scene together. Or it can mean that one is above, below, beside, behind, around, or in the other." To demonstrate, I write the line: "I am a brown beaver gnawing wood under the new moon."

It's important—especially with young students who enjoy reading their writing aloud—to give them time to do that. Hearing the lines aloud also subtly emphasizes our connection with each other, as well as our individuality. "Now connect two more items on your circle," I say. "In your next line, add a color." I have found that offering these specific literary suggestions focuses students on making vivid description, and becomes another element in the pattern they are creating. So for the third line I suggest they use a vivid verb. We brainstorm a few together: *flying, diving, squatting, slithering, ambling, throwing, twisting, singing*. For the fourth line, I suggest that they use an emotional or interior state to describe one of their creatures: *angry, sad, happy, irritated, hungry, lonely*.

To help students with their endings, we return to Momaday's poem and notice how it shifts. In the final lines of the Momaday poem, the speaker identifies with the earth and offers a pledge to "stand in good relation" to all that is beautiful. The students and I talk about what a pledge means, and what we can do to help sustain the earth. We also look at the design that their connecting lines have made within the circles; these look like webs or nests or—as some students notice—an Ojibway Dream Catcher. "Use these ideas in your endings," I urge.

When the students have completed their writing, I ask them to put a star beside their favorite line. Later, at home, I assemble a group poem from these favorite lines and from selected endings. The next day in class, I hand out xeroxed copies of this class poem and we read it aloud, the authors reading their own lines. It is like a chant with students joining their voices to create another kind of circle, with its own equality and identity and charm.

Here is a fourth grade "Circle Poem in the Native American Spirit," by students at Adams Spanish-Immersion Elementary School in St. Paul, Minnesota:

I am a bear in a garden of daisies (Brianna R.)
I am the apple tree waiting for the sun (Madeline N.)
I am the moon at night and a bird (Benny F.)
I am the mountain that makes the snow fall at night (Adam V.)
I am the okapi eating the eggplant (Neal W.)
I am a hawk that flies in a rain storm (Paul J.)
I am a lemon tree rustling in the wind at dawn (Ezra S.)
I am a father going to the beach (Jesse V.)
I am the forest, the bluest blue jay makes his home in me (Amalia)
I am the pine that hit the oriole and made him cry (John H.)
I am glowing white snow falling on your best friend (Kenzie)
I am flying like a blue jay looking at a bear (Matthew C.)
I am the red rose by the birch (Carissa)
I am the black horse who rules the planets (Jasmin M.)
I am the pale grandma falling off the hill (Lydia)
I am the tulip that grew on the island (Benjamin R.)
I am the wheat that grows on the mountain (Caleb)
I am the sad mountain with snow on my top (Zavari A.)
I am a dog smelling a rose (Johnny K.)
I am a happy dad under an oak tree (Leo O.)
I am the shiny moon reflecting in a puddle (Anna R.)
I am the soft rabbit looking at the bluejay (?)
I am the sparrow on the red rose (Zach.)
I am the wolf creeping at night (Brooks)
I am a very sad eagle falling from the sky (Alexis)

I am a child who lives in turning circles (Alexis)
I am the life of the earth and will never leave you (Anna R.)
I am all these things in the circle of life (Lydia)
I am part of all these things and much more (Kenzie)
I am the boy who lives in this world (Adam V.)
I feel that the circle of life has made me proud (John H.)
I am glad I am living in the circle of life (Brianna R.)
I am all these things and more but my favorite thing is being a kid (Amalia)
I am all these things. I have colors, feelings and endings (Zavari A.)

Note that I typed each student's name after their lines: this allows each student to identify the line and read it aloud in a group reading. (The line with the question mark was identified in class by the student who forgot to put his name on his paper.)

Teachers often mount the students' individual circle poems and the class group poem—along with the brainstorming circles—on posterboard. The art and writing, individual and collaborative, makes for lively visual and literary displays. It is also wonderful to have classes perform their group poems for other classes, parents, or the community—the different voices speaking the song-like lines express the students' homage to their place in the natural world.

Step Four: A Journey into Nature toward a Mentor

With students junior high age and older, I often use next another exercise in writing nature poems, one that builds on the same attitude toward nature as the Circle Poem exercise. This second exercise is based on a poem by the Chinese poet Tu Fu (712–770). To introduce Chinese poetry, I sometimes show students landscapes by Chinese artists and point out the relation between the huge mountains and the tiny human figures. I also mention the Chinese reverence for philosophers and poets who withdrew from business to contemplate nature, to partake of a tea ceremony, to play meditative games like chess, or to write poems. Such pursuits were available to an educated elite, it is true, but many Chinese landscapes also convey an appreciation and knowledge of crows, say, or plum trees, which were available to all observers, regardless of education or status.

I began by summarizing Tu Fu's life.[2] Tu Fu served at the court of the emperor Ming Huang, the Bright Emperor, but in the struggle to bring the "associated peoples of the inner Asian frontiers to a share of power and a measure of autonomy," he went to live in the remote province of Szechuan. Tu Fu's son died of starvation (or disease), and he himself perished on a houseboat on which he lived in his final years. Tu Fu had adequate means to survive, but sometimes just barely. The reverence for life in his poetry also suggests that he enjoyed his years of retirement from the glitter and intrigue of the court.

Tu Fu's method of presenting images—essentially one to a line—has had an enormous impact on contemporary American poets like James Wright and Robert Bly, as has the fluid manner in which Tu Fu moves us through a landscape or experience to what is often a startling conclusion. Because of this influence—and Kenneth Rexroth's beautiful translations—Tu Fu's poetry strikes us as having a contemporary sound. It seems to belongs to our age.

The Tu Fu poem I use with students is "Written on the Wall at Chang's Hermitage." The students and I pause to discuss the meaning of *hermit* and *hermitage*, then I read the poem:

> It is Spring in the mountains.
> I come alone seeking you.
> The sound of chopping wood echoes
> between the silent peaks.
> The streams are still icy.
> There is snow on the trail.
> At sunset I reach your grove
> In the stony mountain pass.
> You want nothing, although at night
> You can see the aura of gold
> and silver ore all around you.
> You have learned to be gentle
> as the mountain deer you have tamed.
> The way back forgotten, hidden

Away, I become like you,
An empty boat, floating, adrift.

First I ask the students what season it is in the poem. After they answer, "Spring," I ask, "Early, middle, or late spring, almost summer?" This question sends us back to the first six lines, with their specific details of early spring: icy streams, snow on the trail, the sound of chopping that suggests firewood needed to heat cold houses.

Next we discuss what Chang teaches the speaker. "What qualities does it take to tame a mountain deer?" I ask. Students answer: patience, attention to the deer's habits and needs, and willingness to blend into the natural world and to follow its rhythms. I also ask them to explain what the lines "You can see the aura of gold / and silver ore all around you" suggest about Chang. We consider if mining is going on in the mountains or if "aura" suggests rather human greed which Chang sees but has put aside.

Finally we consider the final three lines, the hardest lines in the poem. Not only is there a shift in focus—from season and mountain in lines 1–8, to Chang and his life in lines 9–13, and then to the concluding effect of this visit on the speaker—but there is also the first obvious use of a comparison in the poem: "I become like you, / An empty boat, floating, adrift." The comparison itself and the words Tu Fu uses to describe the way back ("forgotten, hidden away") create a sense of ambivalence: Has the speaker forgotten the way back on purpose, or has he been so changed that he can't find it? Does "hidden away" suggest he can't go back the same way, because he's been changed? And what about the comparison?

I ask the students, "If I said to you, 'My life has become like an empty boat, floating, adrift,' what would you think I meant?" The answers are always interesting: "That you've lost direction, are drifting with the current." Or, "You're lonely and afraid." I admit such interpretations are possible, but I also suggest that there's a freedom in letting one's life into the current, empty of expectations and goals, willing to go where the river takes you. However we interpret the speaker's attitude at the end, we all agree that the visit to Chang's hermitage has changed him. And that Chang himself exemplifies many qualities of respect and attention to the natural world that are found in Scott Momaday's "Delight Song." Both poems indicate how to "stand in good relation" to the natural world.

Step Five: Brainstorming Landscape, Season, and Mentor, then Drafting a Poem

Using the big newsprint I prefer, I ask students to use one-half of their folded sheets for creating "word maps" (sometimes called "word webs"), with a central theme in the center and related words and phrases radiating around it. "We're going to brainstorm a season and landscape where you would like to go," I tell them. If the class has shown interest in drawing, I suggest that students draw the landscape. "You don't have to have been there," I say, "but you should know something about it. Decide also what season you would like around you. And remember that early autumn is very different from late autumn, harvest versus snow showers; ditto with early summer and later summer, cool nights full of stars versus thunderstorms with crackling thunder." We talk about different landscapes, and I try to mention a few that my Minnesota students may not immediately consider, such as the desert plateaus in New Mexico's pueblo country or bogs in Michigan, rich with pitcher plants, floating mats of sphagnum moss, and islands of black spruce. The goal is to have students begin to envision a landscape in large and small features—with particular insects, toads, hawks, pocket gophers, plants, mosses, trees, landscape, and soil, as well as a particular type of weather.

I have to admit that many times these landscapes become somewhat generalized, like idealized places of tourism. I don't fight this because Tu Fu's poem, used as a model, takes the students into the landscape as observers and helps to make the generalizations more specific. This exercise would make a wonderful addition, by the way, to a unit on particular ecological zones—local, regional, or global.

Selecting or creating a mentor to encounter is often harder for students than selecting and describing a landscape. I try to enlarge their notions of mentor to include animals or elements of the natural world itself. If students have written Circle Poems, they are already attuned the the idea that we learn from nature. I suggest that they add their mentors to their word maps, along with some notes about how the mentor guides them, what habits of its mind or character are worthy. I also ask students to write down how they feel in the presence of their mentors.

Now we're ready to draft our poems. I remind the students of Tu Fu's model: Keep the lines simple, with only one or two main details per line, and divide the poem into three parts—approach and observation, encounter and lesson, and transformation and comparison. If they have trouble getting started, I suggest that they borrow and adapt Tu Fu's first line, "It is Spring in the mountains."

Students often do beautiful writing with no further prompting from me, but if I sense that the students are having trouble with endings, I interrupt them maybe five minutes from the end of class and read them Tu Fu's conclusion. Once again I bring their attention to the "boat" comparison, emphasizing its ambiguity and strong visual quality.

Here are two student poems from the seventh grade at St. Paul Academy.

The Mountain

It is midwinter, gray, cold
and snowy.
Bare trees and evergreens
cover the beautiful mountain

pass.
Bears and rabbits are the
only ones to live in
the loud quietness.
I am there for it,
but it is not there
for me.
I am there for nature.
I am there for the full nothingness
of it all.
I'm there for the trip.
I am one and it is many.
The mountain holds many,
I hold one.
The mountain helps others to survive.
I only help myself.
Afterward I am like a grain of sand rolling
down a vast boulder.

—*Arne Gjelten*

Alone

I am tired of it all.
I didn't want all of the pressure.
That is why I left.
I took only what I needed.
With luck, they will not miss me until morning.
I may return.
But they cannot make me.
Only if I want to.
I told no one of my plans,
not even my best friends.
They will miss me,
but this was for the better.
Now here I am on the beach.
The waves silenced by ice
And the trees' leaves gone.
All that moves is me.
There are tracks beside me in the snow.
I will become one with nature.
I am free as a bird in the gray sky.
I will return when I am ready.

—*Sam McVeety*

I am happy when I am able to use both exercises, because they convey an underlying message of unity that cuts across borders and eras. Ecological concerns have no borders, and one of the greatest challenges facing us is finding ways to respect the differences in our attitudes toward nature and at the same time protect the natural world. Tu Fu's poem, though more challenging than the Circle Poem, can also work with younger students: I've used it with fourth graders—but only after I'm familiar with their writing and level of maturity. Conversely, I have used the Circle Poem with older students, including adults, who seem to enjoy it as much as the elementary students. The Circle Poem strikes a chord in almost everyone who encounters it; both its process and the variety of written results have an integrity and transparent relation to the whole that make it a joy to teach and write. It is, for me, our era's version of Tennyson's "flower in the crannied wall."

Notes

1. For younger students I shorten the title to "The Delight Song," and ask them what *delight* means. I also shorten the concluding stanza, dropping the lines "I stand in good relation to the gods" and "I stand in good relation to the daughter of *Tsen-tainte.*" I have encountered students who object to poems that mention a god or gods. I also don't want the element of romance implied which sometimes leads to comments or questions from younger students.

2. My information about Tu Fu comes from his accomplished translator Kenneth Rexroth in *One Hundred Poems from the Chinese* and from contemporary Tu Fu scholar and translator David Hinton.

Bibliography

Bakken, Heidi, "The goat teaches. . . ." From *Three Magics.* Edited by John Caddy. St. Paul, Minn.: COMPAS, 1987.

Momaday, N. Scott, "The Delight Song of Tsoai-Talee." From *Carriers of the Dream Wheel: Contemporary Native American Poetry.* Edited by Duane Niatum. New York: Harper & Row, 1975.

St. Clair, Darrell Daniel, "My school the earth. . . ." From *The Belly of the Shark: A New Anthology of Native Americans.* Edited by Walter Lowenfels. New York: Random House, 1973.

Tu Fu, "Written on the Wall at Chang's Hermitage." From *One Hundred Poems from the Chinese.* Translated by Kenneth Rexroth. New York: New Directions, 1971.

Janine Pommy Vega

The Spirit Voice in Nature

I TELL MY STUDENTS that traditional Native Americans believe that everything alive is part of a circle, and in the circle we are all people—rock people, tree people, coyote people, people people—and that we talk to each other across the circle. Native Americans believe that everything in nature has a voice and a spirit. I tell my students that today we'll be tapping into the spirit of a particular thing in nature, and speaking with its voice. This does not mean your dog or your hamster. This is bigger, more mysterious, and wilder than that.

I write the word *persona* on the board, and say it out loud. Does anyone see a word in it? Person. I explain that when we speak for something in nature, we take on the personality of that thing—an animal, a mountain, a star —and speak with its voice. So in a persona poem it's important to pick something you like or can identify with. (Sometimes as a homework assignment the night before, I ask the students to think about what they would like to speak for in nature.) You can say you're anything—a lion, the north wind—but to be believable you have to get into character, as in a play. If you pick a mountain, you have to think with mountain mind, feel the universe around you with mountain heart. You have to *be* the mountain.

"Who can tell me a short short version of what happened to the *Titanic*?" I ask, looking around the class. Several people raise their hands. I pick Vanessa.

"A big ship floated out into the Atlantic," she says. "It hit an iceberg and sank."

Exactly. On the blackboard I draw a craggy iceberg about two feet wide and eight inches high. Underneath it I draw a wide line of continuous *w*s for the water. "This is the iceberg, this is the sea." I see nods around the classroom.

"But have you ever heard the expression, 'That's just the tip of the iceberg'?"

If no one has, I'll explain. "It means that what we can see is just a little part of all there is. So even if the people on the huge *Titanic* saw this little floating piece of ice, they kept on coming. What they failed it see was its enormous bulk underneath the water." I draw the underwater part of the iceberg until it stretches across the entire blackboard and down to the bottom. The people on the *Titanic* saw only the tip of the iceberg.

"So," I point to the iceberg visible above the waves, "this part is like you and me in this room, visible to each other. I'm waving my hands around, you're playing with your pencil, you're leaning on your hand. This is the physical universe we experience through our senses." I write *see, smell, taste, touch,* and *hear* like rays coming out of the iceberg. "But the real person we are is this vast area right here, under the water."

There's usually the slightest stirring, especially among elementary school kids: here we all are with our faces hanging out, each with his or her unseen universe within.

"In the real world of yourself," I tap the part of the iceberg that is underwater, "you have your feelings, your thoughts, your secrets, your memories, and a lot more, and it's completely private, unless you invite us in." I list these inner faculties on the submerged iceberg. "No one knows how you feel, unless you tell us. We can't read your thoughts. Your secret is completely your own until you reveal it. Your memories make you a unique individual with your own history. This is all hidden.

"So when you pick something in nature to speak for, you have to identify with it enough to describe both the inner and outer worlds. From what you already know about the thing or animal, from what you already feel, you have to make a leap of imagination to take on its life, and picture how that would be, right down to the details."

Next we read Diane DiPrima's "The Ruses: A Coyote Tale":

Sometimes you take up the trap &
run with the metal between yr teeth,
At times it is better to chew off
your leg.
You have in this case to consider
the trail of blood.
Sometimes for weeks it is better
not to eat, the meat is poisoned, but
you wait it out
knowing the creatures are not
consistent, they forget. Or they will
move on. It is hard to explain this
to the cubs.
You keep downwind, stick to
the water; journey in thick mist
or at the dark of the moon.

There come the safe times when
we congregate in the snow,
under large barren trees & each
of us is a flame,
an offering to the moon.
At such times it is unnecessary
to sing.

I explain how coyotes, after being nearly eliminated, are coming back all over America. Because of the increase of deer and other game, there are more coyotes now in the East than there ever were, and they've grown stronger and healthier than their cousins in the West. If I'm working in a rural or suburban setting, the class might already know this. If it's a city school, I tell them coyotes have been seen inside Denver and Los Angeles; they've even been sighted in the Bronx! Though human beings are not generous to them, coyotes are survivors.

If the poem feels like it was actually written by a coyote, as Diane di Prima's does, it's a success. Anyone can give us facts about an animal or something in nature, but it takes a leap of imagination to actually feel yourself in a cave and see the first rays of the sun hit the top of the mountain across the way, or feel the cubs roll away from you as they play, or smell the sap coming out of your leaves in the heat of summer. You have to get into character. Get into what you know your thing or animal does and imagine how that feels. We pick out which senses Diane DiPrima used in the poem, which inner faculties.

Where is the mystery in it? Someone points to the end of the poem. The coyotes are together, the ones that have survived. The moon is out, and no one makes a sound. Sometimes, when we are with people we love, there is a moment when we feel the togetherness, and no one says a word. We feel our connection with each other, with something bigger than ourselves. In nature the feeling of connectedness is apparent to anyone who has stood quietly in the woods, or observed a storm move through the trees, or noticed how seagulls squabble and fly about in the rays of sunset before settling down.

An additional poem I use to illustrate the power of a particular being in nature is Pablo Neruda's "The Condor":

> I am the condor. I fly
> over you who are walking
> and suddenly in a whirlwind
> of feathers and claws
> I attack you and carry you
> in a whistling cyclone
> of hurricane cold
>
> And to my tower of snow,
> to my black lair
> I carry you, and you live alone
> and you fill out with feathers
> and you fly over the world
> motionless, in the heights.
>
> Female condor,
> we jump on our red prize,
> we rip out the life
> that passes throbbing,

and we take up together
our savage flight.

This is straightforward. The condor is a raptor. I ask what the red prize might be. Ten hands go up. No one has trouble identifying it as meat. We can suggest the mystery that our lives contain by using metaphors or similes. DiPrima says each of the coyotes is a flame, an offering to the moon. The meat is a red prize. In the student poem below the field calls itself a father. We read aloud one or two more poems by students to illustrate the idea. Here is one:

Field

I am a field
of dry grasses, in
the summer the children
roll over me
while the old apple tree
laughs—I don't care.
People walk through
my paths, every day
it tickles. I am well
cared for. My grasses
are cut to keep me
from looking shaggy.
I am a father to
the children, they
lie on my belly
to soak in the sun.
That makes me feel
so warm.

   —*Taima Smith, fifth grade*

We now have all the tools we need: description through the senses and the inner faculties, and the use of metaphor and simile. The only thing left is making the leap: becoming the part of nature we have chosen. If there is still hesitancy, I elicit a collaborative poem on the board.

Here are some examples of the students' persona poems:

Cougar

I am strong, but I am gentle.
I do not harm man, but man
harms me. He tries to trap me.
He tries to hunt me. He kills me.
Man takes my food. He wants
my skin. He destroys my home.
I do not bother man.

He kills off my brothers who only
want to live.
Is this the way of the wisest animal?
Or doesn't he know the truth?
Does he think he's so great?
A rock is wiser.

    —*Jim Michaelides, twelfth grade*

Storm Wind

You can't see me
my anger hides and when
you least expect it,
I knock you down

I think about it
by myself
why I am angry.
It doesn't matter
I'll never tell you, never
tell anyone

I hide in the dark corners
by the beach
waiting for the sea to call me
to join the hurricane
waiting to let loose everything
I contain
and knock down
everything in my way.

    —*Tamara Wilson, eighth grade*

The Life of a Tree

I'm a tree in Jamaica
I'm forty-one years old.
I have seen the lightness
And the darkness.
In the warm sun
The children sit next to me.
They like the shade I give.
I like the short Jamaican songs
That they sing.
I listen
And I memorize them all,
I even sing along
But they can't hear me.

When the little kids start to leave
I try to go with them
But my roots hold me back
Come back, come back! I shout
But they still don't hear.
I guess I have to wait for
Another day.

  —*Nikki Thomas, seventh grade*

Panda

Up on the cool mountains I live,
Feeding on bamboo and leaves.
With my masked eyes, I stalk
the farmer's honey like a cat
stalking a mouse.
In the winter time I slide down
the mountain side like a fat
pine cone falling to the ground.
Spring brings hunters. The sound
of guns like a bell
through the silent countryside.

  —*Karen Carmody, fifth grade*

A Kitten

I am a kitten with
black-and-white fur.
I have glittering eyes that
shine in the moonlight.
I walk like a sly fox
though the woods
on a stormy night.
My fur is fluffy
like an overstuffed pillow.
When I'm in a playful mood,
I run around the house
and bite somebody's ankle.

When it's dark at night
and no one is awake
the mischief inside me
just comes out and shines
like the sun, and I
knock down all the garbage cans.

Then I hide in the closet
for protection.

  —Iesha Cain, fourth grade

Even though city kids may be cut off from what we think of as nature, their faculties of perception, observation, and memory are alive and well nonetheless. Below are two poems written in different schools in the Bronx:

Sand

I am a grain of sand
the sea carries me
to all the countries
of the world.
Travel is my life.
I hear the waves
in the night,
it seems like they are
calling my name,
inviting me to go with them.
The waves touch me
so soft
like the hands of my mother.

Arena

Soy un grano de arena
El mar me lleva
a todos los paìses
del mundo.
Mi vida es viajar.
Oígo las olas
en la noche, me parece
que estan llamando mi nombre,
invitándome a viajar.
Las olas me tocan
tan suave
como las manos de mi mamá.

  —Sonia Martinez, sixth grade
  (Translation by Janine Pommy Vega)

El Sol

Soy el sol que da luz
a todo el mundo
Soy como la nieve que cae
del cielo azul
brillo como la luna

en el firmamento
sobre el valle del río
Oígo el sonido de los pájaros
del monte, toco las olas
del mar azul.
Sueño contigo
cuando estoy despierto.
Siento que estás conmigo
cuando estoy sólo.
Memorizo las cosas lindas
que piensas de mì.

The Sun

I am the sun that gives light
to everyone
I am like the snow that falls
from the blue sky
I shine like the moon
in the firmament
over the river valley
I hear the sound of the mountain
birds, I touch the waves
of the blue ocean.
I dream with you
when I am awake.
I feel that you are with me
when I am alone.
I memorize the pretty things
you think about me.

   —*Ana Estrella, fifth grade*
   (Translation by Janine Pommy Vega)

These examples work well with students of most ages. Younger kids have no problem pretending they're a lizard or a lightning bolt. Even kindergarteners can do it. If they can read, I hand out written examples, and we read them out loud. If they are not reading yet, I read to them. Then we do a collaborative poem on the board, and I read it back to them. Here are two examples from beginning grades:

Cobra

When the man plays
the flute I come out of
the basket.
I'm a deadly snake
and very dangerous.

My colors are brown
and black diamonds.
I make a sound
like a car
getting a flat tire.

    —Ah-Kimm, second grade

Volcano

I am the volcano. I grew
from the sea to an island.
The lava bubbling in my stomach.
The smell of ash coming out
of me. When my lava
touches the ground
it feels like I'm
hugging my parents.

    —Norberto Martinez, third grade

Bibliography

DiPrima, Diane. *Loba.* New York: Penguin, 1998.

Neruda, Pablo. Source unknown.

Barry Gilmore

The Naming of Things

Being Specific in Nature Writing

ALL SAINTS' DAY SCHOOL is perched on the bank of the Carmel River a few miles from the ocean in Carmel Valley, California. It's a far cry from the city schools where I've done most of my teaching. Here, students take nature for granted. Outside the classrooms are picnic tables on lush grass where classes can do group work. The front walk of the school is always manicured and flowers are always in bloom.

Still, the natural setting didn't automatically inspire creativity. My seventh and eighth grade students had been trained to be more concerned with academics and grade point averages than with self-expression. In many ways, it was far more difficult to get these kids to open themselves up to imaginative writing than those students in less bucolic environments.

I decided to teach a unit on writing about the specific names of things in nature because I figured the first step was to get the students simply to notice the world around them. Close observation, I hoped, would accomplish two goals. First, the students would be forced to examine physical objects, establishing the basis for a "show, don't tell" approach to writing. Second, after spending the time and effort it takes to examine an object closely, students would sense a closer connection to a part of nature and *want* to write about it.

I. Observation and Names in *Walden*

We started in the classroom, with one of the greatest close observers of nature ever to put pen to paper. Thoreau himself valued this role, and strove to describe Walden Pond and its surroundings in minute detail and exact terms:

> In my front yard grew the strawberry, blackberry, and life-ever-lasting, johnswort and goldenrod, shrub-oaks, and sand-cherry, blueberry, and ground-nut. Near the end of May, the sand-cherry, (*cerasus pumila*), adorned the sides of the path with its delicate flowers arranged in umbels cylindrically around its short stems, which last, in the fall, weighed down with good sized and handsome cherries, fell over in wreaths like rays on every side . . . the sumach, (*rhus glabra*), grew luxuriantly about the house, pushing up through the embankment which I had made, growing five or six feet in the first season.

The twenty-four students in my eighth grade English class had been studying American Literature, and Thoreau fit right in. The class was made up of both accomplished and struggling readers and writers, but I thought that close observation would offer a challenge to every student.

The excerpt from *Walden* above, though brief, opened several avenues for discussion. First, I had the class read the passage silently. Then I asked them to read it again, and this time to underline all of the specific names Thoreau uses for plants. The simple exercise prompted each student to read the paragraph at least twice and to pay attention to how Thoreau described his world.

"How would it change this passage," I asked my students, "if Thoreau had merely used words such as *bushes, plants,* or *flowers* instead of precise names?"

One student, Kevin, raised a hand. "It would be boring."

"Why?"

"You wouldn't be able to tell the difference between anything. They'd all sound the same."

"Do you know what these plants look like?" I asked.

We agreed that most people can envision strawberries, blackberries, or blueberries growing wild, but that few students have an idea of what sand-cherry would look like. Given Thoreau's description, however, most of my class thought they could draw one.

"I don't know what an umbel is," one girl said, "but I think it looks like this." She drew a cluster of blossoms on her paper.

"Why does he use the Latin names?" someone else asked.

"Good question. Does it help you to picture the plants more clearly?"

"It might if I knew Latin." A few chuckles—these students also took Latin from me, although they were only in their first year. Later, we would come back to the Latin names. For the moment, I told them to remember Thoreau's inclusion of the Latin and to be prepared to see it again.

We looked together at a couple of other passages in which Thoreau uses descriptions of specific plants and animals. Here, for instance, he includes the names of both trees and birds:

> Early in May, the oaks, hickories, maples, and other trees, just putting out amidst the pine woods around the pond, imparted a brightness like sunshine to the landscape, especially in cloudy days, as if the sun were breaking through mists and shining faintly on the hill-sides here and there. On the third or fourth day of May I saw a loon in the pond, and during the first week of the month I heard the whippoorwill, the brown-thrasher, the veery, the wood-pewee, the chewink, and other birds.

I pointed out to the students that these descriptions are more than just lists of objects. Thoreau often begins with a list, but than quickly focuses on one object or on the effect of the objects on the environment. The above passage, for instance, includes a simile, and the use of specific names serves to create a more vivid impression of the scene, to give the reader a vantage point from which to understand Thoreau's feelings and thoughts.

For a quick pre-writing exercise, I asked the students to close their eyes and recall a fairly recent time when they'd been in a natural setting.

"Call up a mental image of the place you've chosen," I said. "Catalogue the plants, animals, and other natural things that surround you. If you know a specific name for an object, think about that for a moment. If not, pick an object or two and just focus on details. What do you remember? Think of textures, sounds, shapes, colors."

My students were used to this sort of pre-writing prompt, and knew that they were free to write their thoughts down as a poem, story, or just as a string of images. The important thing is getting those first words on paper. We wrote for about ten minutes, and then those who wished to share read aloud for the class.

The fast-writes that came even from this short warm-up exercise boded well for the rest of the unit. One eighth grader dashed off this paragraph in just a few minutes:

> I'm sitting in front of the school by the peace pole on a bench. It's foggy and sprinkling. It's the middle of May, but doesn't seem like summer. All of a sudden I notice a patch of vibrant colors clashing together. It's a beautiful garden of pansies, daisies, snap dragons, poppies, and more. A whole community of many kinds of flowers. Something I walk by every day but never think to look at. Then I see it—something that stands out. It looks like a blob of orangish pink paint on a green canvas. A juicy peach is what I think of first. Or maybe a piece of fluffy cotton candy. Then I think, "I know what it is!" It's a rose. Petals surround the whole center of the flower. Many green leaves reaching out like little fingers. Thick stems with little reddish, green thorns. It's nice to look at, but I don't know if I should touch it because of the thorns. I lean over and touch it and take a deep breath in. Aaah! It smells wonderful—I'm refreshed and full of life.
>
> —*Tiana Lagemann*

My students were beginning to get the idea: close observation leads to more interesting writing.

II. Naming Details: Our Field Trip

I announced to the students that we were going on a field trip, that they should each choose a buddy so that no one got lost, and that they should bring along a pencil, paper, and something to write on. Then we walked to the front of the school and sat on the grass.

We spent a few minutes seated in a circle, enjoying being out of the classroom and looking around at the flowers that line the walkway from the road to the school offices. I pointed out a few objects I could name specifically—California poppies, digitalis, pansies, and a blossoming apple tree. Then I asked them to do the same. One student, Eric, pointed out a large oak tree. Jamie noticed that the low flowers along the walkway were different kinds of roses. Christina asked if I knew the name of one particular flower, and I handed her a book on wildflowers I'd checked out from our school library. She immediately went to work and identified it as a type of verbena.

The next step was for each student to choose a specific thing and examine it. To provide some structure, we used the following approach:

At the top of the page, each student was to write his or her name, then the name of the thing being examined. If the students didn't know whether a flower was, say, a petunia or a pansy, I had them to write a general description or even to make up a name, on the condition that they try to look it up or ask our school science teacher later on in the day.

Below the names, the students drew quick sketches of the natural thing they had chosen. This not only helped them to remember details later on, but also reinforced the physical attributes I was hoping they'd capture in their writing. Under the pictures, they wrote a physical description, adding a few sentences describing their feelings as they examined it. They also made up three metaphors or similes inspired by their observation.

Not all of the things chosen were plants. I encouraged the students to be very specific; for example, I suggested that instead of an entire plant, they might focus on a single flower, branch, or leaf. Some students chose to examine a rock, a stump, or a piece of bark. I even received one paper that the student had titled "Observations on Bird Poop."

Here's an example from David's observations, titled "Flower of a Digitalis":

Physical Description: White and purple/violet, they look like little cups, they have little hairs in them. Have dark purple spots on the bottom side of the cup and white around each spot.

Feelings: Relax and hypnotize me. They look good to eat but they have poison in them. Weird looking.

Metaphors/Similes: 1) pyramid (pointed shape); 2) explosion; 3) like a cluster of fireflies.

Later, in the classroom, the students wrote a poem based on these observations. I asked them to begin by writing a simple, physical description. If the description led them to make a personal connection to the object, that was fine, but for now it was the direct results of the observation which most interested me. Here is David's poem:

Digitalis

A cluster of bright fireflies
Colors purple, violet, and white,
The relaxing feeling of looking at
The little blossomed cups
The cups green and small at the top
Then exploding into their large colorful state
As they get closer to the bottom
Their rich purple spots glowing
This structure huge as a pyramid
Pointing itself to the sky.

—*David Endsley*

Here are a few others:

out of the wood chip flat
came a tall standing fire like a
Phoenix out of the ground

contrasted to the green
of the stem was this
plant of fire
and the harsh needles to the one
white rose.

—*Jamie Staples*

I hate it!
Thick in the forest,
Shiny as a silver spoon,
Beautiful to look at,
But don't touch
Or you'll be sorry,
That itchy, scratchy, three-leaved plant,
Known as POISON OAK!

—*Eric Howard*

III. Scientific and Common Names: Specifics in Labeling

At our next class meeting, I wrote on the board the scientific and common names of several of the flowers and plants we'd seen growing around our school:

nemophilia menziesii (Baby Blue Eyes)
trichostema lanatum (Wooly Blue Curls)
mimulus cardinalis (Scarlet Monkey Flower)
clarkus amoena (Farewell-to-Spring)

In all, I included these and about twenty other species of plants listed in a book on local flowers. As I mentioned, my English students all also took Latin from me, so in our first discussion we simply talked about how a botanist might name a flower and what Latin roots had been used for some of the plants listed on the board.

The common names (those in parentheses) were immediately interesting to my students, but the combination of the Latin and English names proved even more intriguing. The common names, we soon decided, offered vivid mental images and sometimes even suggested a story. Knowing the scientific name of a flower, however, instilled the students with a sense of ownership.

Thoreau, I reminded them, included scientific names often in his writing. He cared enough about scientific names to examine not only the attributes of the plants and animals they designated, but also the roots of the Latin words themselves:

> The ear of wheat, (in Latin *spica*, obsoletely *speca*, from *spe*, hope) should not be the only hope of the husbandman; its kernel or grain (*granum*, from *gerendo*, bearing) is not all that it bears.

As an experiment, we decided to try writing about one of the flowers or plants listed on the board without knowing what it looked like. The names themselves, we decided, were descriptive enough to create images in our minds.

"First," I instructed the class, "choose one of these scientific or common names and write out a quick physical description. It doesn't matter that you've never seen the real thing, just imagine what it might look like, based on the name."

Kate, a conscientious student in the front row, raised her hand. "Can I look up the picture first?"

"Wait until later. For now, just try writing a sentence or two to describe the flower."

Kate wrote:

> Farewell-to Spring: I think the petals droops and the flower looks limp. It's white and has green leaves around the base of the flower.

"Now," I said, "imagine that one of these names describes you, that's it's your own scientific or common name. It can be the same flower that you just described or a different one."

Perhaps because the year was approaching an end, many students also chose *clarkus amoena*. Here's how Christina explained it:

> Farewell-to-Spring (*clarkus amoena*): This describes me because I'm leaving school and graduating, saying goodbye to All Saints'.

Bryce also chose *clarkus amoena*, because, "I can't wait for spring to end, and for summer to start. It sounds happy."

Other students quickly chose various labels for themselves, and I soon discovered that before writing they wanted to share their choices and the reasons behind them; the students were excited about these names. One student explained their excitement by saying, "Names make a difference. They make you focus on certain aspects of things."

For a writing assignment, I asked the students either to describe one of the flowers on the board in a short poem, or to write about the names they'd chosen for themselves.

> The flower of the *nemophilia menziesii*
> is a gentle baby blue color
> reminding one of childhood,
> the soft color of blue as seen
> on a baby boy
>
> Iris-shaped, this flower stands
> tall among others.
> Its color brings feelings of
> joy, tranquility, happiness, longing,
> and freedom.
>
> —*Christina Hogans*

seasons

white drooping petals
hang limp.

pistils stand tall.

yellow anthers shine
like hundreds
of small suns.

farewell to spring.
farewell to spring.
Summer
has begun.

—*Kate Smith*

When they'd finished writing, we looked up pictures of the flowers and plants to compare with our mental images. Most of the time they were surprisingly close to the mark.

IV. Scientific and Common Names: Labeling Yourself

An amusing variation on the above assignment came a day later, when someone in the class suggested that we develop our own botanical names. I asked these eighth graders to give themselves both scientific names and common names, based on whatever aspects of their own personalities or physical traits they thought appropriate. Here are a few examples:

felizita—Little Happy Person
omnipotentus alexus—Alex the Omnipotent
para fantasticus aster—Fantastic Special Star
stellainternetuslibracomputeruscactus—Shannon's interests
squirlus gigantes—Giant Squirly Flower (Bryce added to this, "This plant is tall as a sunflower and comes in random, unpredictable colors. You can't plant it; it has to come to you.")

Several of the students wound up using Spanish or French to develop scientific names; in the spirit of making the assignment fun, I allowed this. I then asked them all to write brief pieces explaining the names they'd chosen for themselves. The results were generally entertaining:

Hello, my name is *omnipotentus alexus*. You can call me the all-powerful Alex, ruler of the Earth. I am a flower, invincible to man and able to rule mankind with an iron fist. I have black petals and a gray inside. Resistance is futile. Run if you can, but prepare to face slavery beneath my blossoms.

—*Alex Austin*

Felizita

If I could be a flower
I think I'd want to be
Something like an iris
Rather than a pansy.
Irises stand tall and strong,
They grow in clumps together,
This way I wouldn't get lonely
And long to have another.

—*Jessica Wasserman*

The idea that we could play with words and names and at the same time write seriously about nature was a new one for many of the students.

V. Using Your Own Name: Observing Yourself

It's a small step from creating a name for yourself to thinking about the one you already have. Our names, like those of plants and flowers, are powerful indicators of who we are. They connote stories about our past and our parents, and they determine how we think of ourselves and describe ourselves to others.

"Consider your own name," I told my students after we shared our made-up scientific names. "How'd you get it? What does it say about you? What could I tell about you if all I knew were your name? If you were a plant or animal, what would your name tell me about your features?"

I've had a lot of success with name assignments in general—drawing images inspired by names, writing family histories, making puns out of them. This assignment was no different. After the close observation exercises above, some my students were inclined to see their names as self-descriptive labels, while others simply used their own names as a starting point for writing about their interests.

Amber is a deep color
of yellow gold
a polished stone
petrified sap
I like Amber
I am Amber
an old light traveling through centuries
and in my present body young and new to this Earth
—*Amber Ray*

My name is in the upper-right hand corner
It is black on white
It is a black ferret in an Antarctic snowstorm
It is Times New Roman font, size 12
It came from my brain
To my 104-button keyboard
Serial number 0397461
Right now it is being displayed at 800 x 600 resolution
On a 14-inch SVGA monitor
In a few minutes—hopefully—
It will be on an $8^1/_2$ x 11" sheet of paper
After coming through my printer
Notorious for paper jams
Right now
All I can do
Is
Wait
Hope

Type
My name is like the L2 cache
In a Pentium II 266 MHz processor
It goes unnoticed
Until its use is required
OK
I
AM
DONE

File . . .

Print . . .

Hope . . .

—*Jason Jong*

For many of my students, this exercise demonstrated the connection between observing nature closely and writing of all kinds. Whether we were describing natural scenes or describing ourselves, the point was to be specific and detailed—as well as imaginative—in what we wrote.

VI. Conclusion: Using Nature Writing for Introspection

By this time, we had moved pretty far afield from the original assignment. But that in itself sparked an interesting discussion. What, after all, is the point of writing about nature? What's the point of close observation?

If we were all scientists, it might be simply to categorize the nature of plants of animals. But as students and writers, our task is also to use close observation as a tool for self-understanding and introspection.

Some of what my students wrote would not seem, to a casual reader, as if it had much to do with nature writing. In the poem below, Rachel reached conclusions about herself that stand alone. Yet the poem could not have happened without her examination of a single flower. Her self-description is a metaphor, as well, based on the plant she chose; she found an affinity that had escaped her notice before.

Wallflower

I like to think that I'm
outgoing,
aggressive,
even brave.
But when it comes to the

actual doing,
it's so much safer to
stand,
back to the wall,
and
wait for someone to
ask me
or
help me
or to stall until
I feel more courageous.
At the rate I'm going,
by the time I'm old I'll have
so many things left
undone
and
unsaid
piled up in my brain
that I may die of sheer
suffocation.

—*Rachel Dart*

Thoreau, too, used nature writing as a springboard for examination of himself and others. *Walden* is rarely filed under the Nature Writing category in bookstores; it's more often found in Philosophy. That's because Thoreau valued consideration not just of nature itself, but of what we look for in nature, how we look for it, and what the process of observation teaches us about who we are. "We need the tonic of wilderness," he wrote toward the end of *Walden*. "We can never have enough of Nature." Earlier, he directly linked observation of the real world to understanding of the internal one: "We are enabled to apprehend at all what is sublime and noble only by the perpetual instilling and drenching of the reality that surrounds us." As it did for Thoreau, specific, close observation of nature easily led my students to link first their feelings to the world, then their words to it.

Bibliography

Thoreau, Henry David. *Walden.* New York: Dover, 1995.

Carol F. Peck

Prayers to the Earth

Earth teach me stillness
As the grasses are stilled with light.
Earth teach me suffering
As old stones suffer with memory.
Earth teach me humility
As blossoms are humble with beginning.
Earth teach me caring
As the mother who secures her young.
Earth teach me courage
As the tree which stands all alone.
Earth teach me limitation
As the ant who crawls on the ground.
Earth teach me freedom
As the eagle who soars in the sky.
Earth teach me resignation
As the leaves which die in the fall.
Earth teach me regeneration
As the seed which rises in spring.
Earth teach me to forget myself
As melted snow forgets its life.
Earth teach me to remember kindness
As dry fields weep with rain.

　　—*Nancy Wood*

THIS POEM STOPPED ME COLD as I was browsing through *War Cry on a Prayer Feather*, a gift from my son, who had recently moved to Wyoming and had discovered "*Your* kind of book, Mom!" Like Emily Dickinson, I felt as if the top of my head had been taken off. Later, reading the jacket copy, I discovered that when Nancy Wood had been invited by the Colorado Centennial Commission to write a libretto for a symphony, she chose the Ute Indians as her subject. A skilled writer on Indian history and mores and a friend of the Utes, Wood recorded, in poems and prose, "the beliefs and ethics of a vanishing culture."

I thought of the many times I had been asked, as a poet-in-the-schools, to coordinate my writing assignments with social studies curricula, particularly Native American studies. And within a short time I had the chance to bring this poem to a third grade class and create a writing activity using it.

The students had already learned that Native Americans view all life as an interdependent circle, with everything teaching and learning from everything

else. Since these third graders especially identified with Native Americans'
respect for all forms of life, all I had to do was give each student a copy of the
poem and invite the class to read it aloud with me.

I asked if there were any words they did not know; only *limitation, regeneration,* and *resignation* needed explanation.

Next I asked which pairs of lines really reached out and grabbed them—
hands flew up, and each couplet had at least one fan. Students with outgoing
personalities loved the free, soaring eagle, while the shyer ones mentioned the
crawling ant and humble blossoms as their favorite images. Children sensitive to
sound loved repeating, "Earth teach me stillness / As the grasses are stilled with
light," whereas those fond of subtlety appreciated the image of melted snow forgetting its former life.

When it was time to write, the guidelines were simple:

"Write your own prayer to the earth about what you would like the earth to
teach *you.* Use the same pattern, 'Earth teach me _____,' and include a specific
example from nature to illustrate each quality you wish to learn. You may use the
qualities in the example poem, as long as you think of your own examples to
illustrate them. Put your best line *last.*"

These third graders were used to my asking them to write *songs* for many
things—whales, seashells, insects, even fruits and vegetables—but never had I
asked them for a *prayer.* Clearly this idea intrigued them, and they set to work
eagerly, but (for a change) nobody dashed off a quick poem and called it finished. The project challenged them, and they were proud of their results:

Earth teach me confidence
Like the birds flying in the sky.
Earth teach me beauty
Like the moon that shines all night.
Earth teach me freedom
Like the deer running in the fields.
Earth teach me cleverness
Like the foxes tricking other animals
    so they can catch them.
Earth teach me braveness
Like the rabbits being chased.

   —*Maggie Goldman, third grade*

Earth teach me hunting,
Like the panther stalking his prey.
Earth teach me inner power
Like the cat not eating the mouse.
Earth teach me medicine
Like the tiger licking his wounds.

Earth teach me toughness
Like the bear getting shot without whimpering.
Earth teach me power
Like the giant mountains that have stood there
    for hundreds of years.
Earth teach me stillness
Like the rock of hundreds of years ago.

   —Andy Morentz, third grade

Later in the year, when a combination second-third grade class wanted a writing idea to coordinate with their theme of the year, which was forests, I decided to turn prayers to the earth into prayers to the forest, with forest-related examples of the qualities prayed for. I used Nancy Wood's poem as the main model, but also shared a few of the other third graders' poems.

There were more questions about word definitions, but again, the concept and the language captured the children's imaginations, and their prayers to the forest were eloquent:

Forest teach me silence
Like the owl gliding through the night.
Forest teach me pride
Like the oak tree standing high.
Forest teach me patience
Like the wolf waiting for his prey.
Forest teach me swiftness
Like the deer running through the forest.
Forest teach me to be sly
Like the fox chasing a rabbit.
Forest teach me to be alert
Like the rabbit listening for danger.
Forest teach me light
Like the stars glowing in the night.

   —Stewart Becker, third grade

Forest teach me slyness
Like the fox when it tiptoes through the trees.
Forest teach me quiet
Like the snow when it falls.
Forest teach me fierceness
Like a thunderstorm.
Forest teach me to be slender
Like the thin crook of the moon
    on a winter night.
Forest teach me to be wise

Like the old owl.
Forest teach me to be strong
Like the beating of an eagle's wings.
Forest teach me to keep my balance
Like the squirrel keeps his balance.
Forest teach me beauty
Like the male cardinal.

    —*Anna Stumpf, second grade*

Seeing how successful this writing idea was at the elementary level, I was anxious to try it with middle schoolers. I chose a workshop of three groups of sixth graders, pulled from their classes to work with me in a large media center. We were assigned to one corner; on days when other classes were also using the center, it was sometimes hard for my young poets to concentrate. It was easier for some of them to visit with one another and generally "goof off." And frankly, not all of them were enthusiastic about the writing projects.

On "Prayers to the Earth" day, however, the media center was quiet. After presenting the writing idea, I decided to enhance the atmosphere by playing a tape I had just discovered: Carlos Nakai playing the Native American flute in a collection called "Canyon Trilogy." As the gentle music calmed the students, I could sense a new level of concentration and creative energy in the group. Some started writing immediately, while others sat with their eyes closed for several minutes. Our corner became something of a sacred space. After a long while, one girl leaned over and whispered to me, "That music even makes my handwriting better!" That day, everybody turned in a poem.

Are You Listening, Earth?

Earth teach me unselfishness
As the rivers are unselfish with their fish.
Earth teach me concern
As the foxes are concerned with winter.
Earth teach me to be carefree
As the ponies run wild with the wind.
Earth teach me to try again
Just as the flowers rise again each spring.
Earth teach me to let go
As the mother bird lets go of her nestling.
Earth teach me bravery
As a newborn kitten faces the earth.
Earth teach me to lose my anger
As eagles lose their feathers,
    sending them down to you.
Earth teach me wisdom
As the owl tells his wisdom to the animals.

    —*Joanna Sullivan, sixth grade*

E-World

Earth teach me strength
As you watch your forests burn.
Earth teach me patience
As your oceans sit.
Earth teach me to change
As the caterpillar to butterfly.
Earth teach me to be equal
As the food chain shows.
Earth teach me you
So I can learn in school.
Earth teach me to care
So I can help you.

    —Maeve Royce, sixth grade

As I began to use this writing project with other classes, I noticed that certain images reappeared—eagles, lions, deer, cheetahs, owls, flowers, trees, butterflies—but not as frequently as I might have expected. I was amazed by the fact that even very young students keep finding new examples in nature to write about. Occasionally, students stretched—*bent*—the guidelines by including man-made objects in their imagery. Cars, robots, buildings, and typewriters crept into several poems, and even Santa Claus made an appearance as an example of generosity and joy. No matter. The imagery was always in the spirit of the whole poem and reflected the poet. What more could I ask?

In the examples below, the students varied the format by using rhyme or addressing the prayer to nature rather than to Earth:

Earth Teach Me . . .

Earth teach me strength
As soil holds up to one's feet.
Earth teach me power
As lightning brings on a rush of heat.
Earth teach me mercy
As the willow leaves yield to the air.
Earth teach me readiness
Like the watchfulness of the bear.
Earth teach me silence
As the cool wind blows.
Earth teach me happiness
Like the babbling brook at my toes.
Earth teach me brightness
As the clouds reflect the sun.
Earth teach me stillness
Like my pencil when this poem is done.

    —Nichole Nicholson, seventh grade

Prayer to Nature

Nature teach me intelligence
As the snake knows where to hunt for his prey.
Nature teach me quickness
As the snake catches a mouse.
Nature teach me strength
As the snake coils around a mouse and strangles him.
Nature teach me suffering
As the mouse suffers from the agonizing pain.
Nature teach me death
As the mouse is strangled and eaten by the snake.
Nature teach me hunger
As the snake searches for another mouse.

—*Paul Brooks, eighth grade*

How would high school students respond to this exercise? My high school students loved it, and gave it their best effort.

Lessons

Earth teach me loyalty
As the wolf defends her pack all of her days.
Earth teach me faithfulness
As swans mate for life.
Earth teach me pride
As the giraffe holds her head up high.
Earth teach me trust
As baby birds know food will come.
Earth teach me peace
As the still pond never feels boredom.
Earth teach me vigor
As the running stream never tires of its course.
Earth teach me strength
As the salmon fight their way upstream to breed.
Earth teach me tenderness
As the gentle spring rain passes over the field.
Earth teach me power
As the hurricane impresses a world with its rage.
Earth teach me fortitude
As the mountain waits thousands of years for a chance to sleep.

—*Elena Jimenez, twelfth grade*

One even redid the syntax, with wonderful results:

Life Lessons

From rock I learn stubbornness
  as he sits watching his world.
From water, flow and patience
  as she wears down mountains,
    finding cracks.
From fire I learn to dream and rage
  as he dances his life away, always roaring.
From air I learn gentleness
  as she blows by, kissing my cheek.
From light and shadow I learn balance
  as one cannot exist with the other.
From life I learn death
  and how by embracing one
    I lose the other.

   —Ben Colbert, twelfth grade

The high school age students who surprised and rewarded me most, however, were those in a local detention center for juvenile offenders. I had been asked to present a series of multi-cultural poetry writing projects to this population, whose attitudes toward creative writing ranged from enthusiastic to downright hostile—"I ain't gonna write no poem!"

For the Native American segment, I decided to see how they reacted to "Prayers to the Earth." After explaining the idea, I put on the Native American flute tape to create a better atmosphere in a sterile room behind bars. Once again, the students were intrigued by the project and both calmed and energized by the music. Their poems showed deep thought and vivid imagery:

Earth teach me discipline
As the river stays within its banks.
Earth teach me patience
As the fox on the hunt.
Earth teach me pride
As the eagle on a lone branch.
Earth teach me calmness
As the midsummer breeze.
Earth teach me how to have inner strength
As the mighty waterfalls and rapids.
Earth teach me how to show compassion
As the mother bear caring for her young.

   —J.

Earth

Earth teaches me awareness
As the eagle eye hunts for prey.
Earth teaches me to trust again
As a cub would its mother.
Earth teaches me limitation
As a predator can only kill so much.
Earth teaches me to open my heart
As flowers blossom in the spring.
Earth teaches me love
As all of earth's creatures love their mother earth.
Earth teaches me to forget past pain
As the seasons change.
Earth teaches me courage
As any mother would protect its young.
Earth teaches me to be at peace with my soul
As the peace which lies deep in the heart of a forest.

　　—*D.*

But what interested me most was the way their poems reflected their current situations, their pain, their hopes.

Earth, Show Me and Make Me

Earth, make me mellow like the sounds of my alto sax,
Earth, give me the peace of mind just to relax.
Earth, teach me to let things pass like days,
Earth, teach me to see sun after it rains.
Earth, give me power like a cop,
Earth, teach me to first stop.
Earth, teach me how to live a civilized life,
Earth, you've shown me the ghetto and that life's strife.
Earth, make me bright as if I were the sun,
Earth, make me fast like a cheetah on the run.
Earth, keep me tenacious like a lion after his prey,
Earth, keep me calm like a mid-evening day.
Earth, take this on if you think you can,
Earth, keep doing your job—I'm growing from a boy to a man.

　　—*J.*

Bibliography

Nakai, R. Carlos. *Canyon Trilogy.* 1989. Distributed by Canyon Records Productions, Inc., 4143 North 16th St., Phoenix, AZ 85016.

Wood, Nancy. *War Cry on a Prayer Feather: Prose and Poetry of the Ute Indians.* New York: Doubleday, 1979.

BIBLIOGRAPHY AND RESOURCES

I reckon—When I count all—
First—Poets—Then the Sun—
Then summer—Then the Heaven of God—
And then—the list is done—

—Emily Dickinson

NONFICTION

Abbey, Edward. *The Serpents of Paradise: A Reader.* New York: Holt, 1995.

Ackerman, Diane. *A Natural History of the Senses.* New York: Random House, 1990.

———. *The Moon by Whale Light.* New York: Vintage Books, 1992.

Anderson, Lorraine, editor. *Sisters of the Earth: Women's Prose and Poetry about Nature.* New York: Vintage, 1991. Poems, essays, stories, and journal entries by a wide range of women writers, from Willa Cather to Joy Harjo, from Emily Dickinson to Adrienne Rich.

Bashō, Matsuo. *Narrow Road to the Deep North and other Travel Sketches.* New York: Viking Press, 1967.

Bass, Rick. *The Deer Pasture.* New York: Norton, 1985. Celebrates Bass's attachment to the Texas hill country.

Berry, Wendell. *What Are People For?* New York: North Point/Farrar Straus Giroux, 1990.

Beston, Henry. *The Outermost House: A Year of Life on the Great Beach of Cape Cod.* New York: Holt, 1992.

Bringing the World Alive: A Bibliography of Nature Stories for Children. New York: The Orion Society, 1995.

Carson, Rachel. *A Sense of Wonder.* New York: Harper & Row, 1991.

———. *The Edge of the Sea.* Boston: Houghton Mifflin, 1942.

———. *Silent Spring.* Boston: Houghton Mifflin, 1994.

Chatwin, Bruce. *The Songlines.* New York: Penguin, 1987.

Cobb, Edith. *The Ecology of Imagination in Childhood.* Dallas, Texas: Spring Publications, 1993.

Corbett, Jim. *Goatwalking.* New York: Penguin, 1992. A bible for anyone who wants to understand goats.

Cornell, Joseph. *Sharing Nature With Children.* Nevada City, Calif.: Dawn Publications, 1979.

Cronon, William. *Changes in the Land: Indians, Colonists, and the Ecology of New England.* New York: Hill and Wang, 1983.

Dillard, Annie. *An Annie Dillard Reader.* New York: HarperPerennial, 1995.

———. *Pilgrim at Tinker Creek.* New York NY: Harper & Row, 1974. A transcendent narrative of a year spent in Virginia's Blue Ridge mountains.

Dunn, Jon L. *National Geographic Field Guide to the Birds of North America. Revised and Updated.* Washington, D.C.: National Geographic Society, 1999.

Durrell, Gerald. *My Family and Other Animals.* New York: Penguin, 1979. A delightful narrative of a child's early fascination with natural history, and his hilarious family.

The Earthworks Group: 50 Simple Things You Can Do to Save the Earth. Berkeley, Calif.: Earthworks Press, 1990.

Elder, John, editior. *Stories in the Land: A Place-Based Environmental Anthology.* Great Barrington, Mass.: Orion Society, 1998.

Eisenberg, Evan. *The Ecology of Eden.* New York: Knopf, 1998.

Ferra, Lorraine. *A Crow Doesn't Need a Shadow: Writing Poetry from Nature.* Layton, Utah: Gibbs Smith, 1994.

Ferris, Chris. *The Darkness is Light Enough: The Field Journal of a Night Naturalist.* New York: Ecco Press, 1986.

Finch, Robert ,and John Elder, editors. *The Norton Book of Nature Writing.* New York: Norton, 1990.

Frank, Frederick. *The Zen of Seeing: Drawing as Meditation.* New York: Vintage, 1973. The drawing exercises easily translate to writing exercises.

Haines, John. *Fables and Distances: New and Selected Essays.* St. Paul, Minn.: Graywolf, 1996.

Halpern, Daniel, editor. *On Nature: Nature, Landscape and Natural History.* New York: Antaeus, 1986.

Harrison, Robert Pogue. *Forests: The Shadow of Civilization.* Chicago: University of Chicago Press, 1999. A study of wilderness in European literature.

Hay, John. *In the Company of Light.* Boston: Beacon, 1998.

———. *The Way to the Salt Marsh.* Edited and with an introduction by Christopher Merrill. Hanover, N. H.: University Press of New England, 1998.

Herman, Marina Lachecki, Joseph F. Passineau, Ann L. Schimpf, and Paul Treuer. *Teaching Kids to Love the Earth; Sharing a Sense of Wonder: 186 Outdoor Activities for Parents and Other Teachers.* Duluth, Minn.: Pfeifer-Hamilton, 1991.

Hinchman, Hannah. *A Life in Hand: Creating the Illuminated Journal.* Salt Lake City, Utah: Gibbs Smith, 1991.

———. *A Trail through Leaves: The Journal as a Path to Place.* New York: Norton, 1997.

Hogan, Linda. *Dwellings: Reflections on the Natural World.* New York: Norton, 1995.

Hughes, Ted. *Poetry in the Making.* Boston: Faber and Faber, 1970.

Hynes, H. Patricia. *A Patch of Eden: America's Inner-City Gardeners.* White River Junction, Vt.: Chelsea Green, 1996.

Johnson, Cathy. *Nature Walks: Insight and Advice for Observant Ramblers.* Harrisburg, Pa.: Stackpole Books, 1994.

———. *The Sierra Club Guide to Sketching in Nature.* San Francisco: Sierra Club Books, 1991.

Kaza, Stephanie. *The Attentive Heart: Conversation with Trees.* New York: Random House, 1993.

Kellert, Stephen R. and Edward O. Wilson, editors. *The Biophilia Hypothesis.* Washington, D.C.: Island Press, 1993.

Kieran, John. *A Natural History of New York City*. Boston: Houghton Mifflin, 1959. Detailed chapters covering all possible aspects of NYC, including history, geology, flowers, trees, shrubs, and "an ample supply of insects."

Knight, Charles. *Animal Drawing: Anatomy and Action for Artists*. New York: Dover, 1959.

Knowler, Donald. *The Falconer of Central Park*. New York: Bantam, 1986.

Kricher, John. *A Neotropical Companion: An Introduction to the Animals, Plants, and Ecosystems of the New World Tropics*. Illustrated by William E. Davis. Princeton, N.J.: Princeton University Press, 1999.

Leopold, Aldo. *A Sand County Almanac and Sketches Here and There*. Ilustrated by Charles W. Schwartz. Oxford: Oxford University Press, 1989. A classic.

Leslie, Clare Walker. *The Art of Field Sketching*. Dubuque, Iowa: Kendall Hunt, 1995.

Leslie, Clare Walker and Charles E. Roth. *Nature Journaling: Learning to Observe and Connect with the World around You*. Pownall, Vt.: Storey Books, 1998.

Logan, William Bryant. *Dirt: The Ecstatic Skin of the Earth*. New York: Riverhead Books, 1996.

Lopez, Barry. *Arctic Dreams: Imagination and Desire in a Northern Landscape*. New York: Scribners, 1986.

———. *Crossing Open Ground*. Scribner's, 1978. An excellent sampling of Lopez's writing. Of particular interest to any teacher who wants to bring children into nature is the wonderful essay "Children in the Woods."

———. *Of Wolves and Men*. New York: Scribners, 1973.

Lucretius. *On the Nature of the Universe*. Translated by R. E. Latham. New York: Penguin, 1994.

Lueders, Edward, editor. *Writing Natural History: Dialogues with Authors*. Salt Lake City: University of Utah Press, 1989. The dialogue between Gary Paul Nabhan and Ann Zwinger is especially useful for field journalists.

Lyon, Thomas. *This Incomperable Lande: A Book of American Nature Writing*. Boston: Houghton Mifflin, 1989.

MacEachern, Diane. *Save Our Planet: 750 Everyday Ways You Can Help Clean Up the Earth*. New York: Dell, 1990.

McKibben, Bill. *The End of Nature*. New York: Random House, 1989.

Matthews, John Joseph. *Talking to the Moon: Wildlife Adventure on the Plains and Prairies of Osage County, Oklahoma*. Norman: University of Oklahoma Press, 1987.

Maxwell, Gavin. *Ring of Bright Water*. New York: Penguin, 1996.

Mayer, Bernadette, and Dale Worsley. *The Art of Science Writing*. New York: Teachers & Writers Collaborative, 1988.

Milord, Susan. *The Kids' Nature Book: 265 Indoor Outdoor Activities Experiences*. Charlotte, Vt.: Williamson, 1996.

Mitchell, Joseph. *Up in the Old Hotel.* Pantheon, 1992. This collection of Mitchell's nonfiction pieces for *The New Yorker* is mostly about New York City and its citizens, but also contains exquisite descriptions of New York's flora and fauna.

Murdoch, Kath. *Ideas for Environmental Education in the Elementary Classroom.* Portsmouth, N.H.: Heinemann, 1993.

Murray, John, editor. *American Nature Writing 1998.* San Francisco: Sierra Club Books, 1998. Since 1994, Sierra Club has published five annuals, each a rich collection of new voices in nature writing.

————, editor. *American Nature Writing 1999.* Corvallis: Oregon State University Press, 1999. The first of the continuing series.

————. *The Sierra Club Nature Writing Handbook.* San Francisco: Sierra Club Books, 1995.

Nabhan, Gary Paul and Stephen Trimble. *The Geography of Childhood; Why Children Need Wild Places.* Boston: Beacon, 1994. Two fathers and naturalists combine to make sense of their children's relationship with the outside world.

Nelson, Richard. *The Island Within.* San Francisco: North Point, 1989. An exploration of an island off the Pacific Northwest coast.

————. *Heart and Blood: Living with Deer in America.* New York: Knopf, 1997.

Oliver, Mary. *Blue Pastures.* New York: Harvest Books, 1991.

Orr, David. *Earth in Mind.* Washington D.C.: Island Press, 1994.

Peterson, Roger Tory, and Virginia Marie Peterson. *A Field Guide to the Birds. A Completely New Guide to all the Birds of Eastern and Central America.* Fourth edition. Princeton, N.J.: Peterson Field Guides, 1998. Still the classic bird guide, a bible for many.

Poirier, Richard. *Robert Frost: The Work of Knowing.* New York: Oxford University Press, 1977. A close reading of Frost's poems.

Raban, Jonathan. *Bad Land: An American Romance.* New York: Vintage, 1997.

Richardson, Elwyn. *In the Early World: Discovering Art through Crafts.* New York: Random House, 1964. Out of print, but worth finding! A study of what happens when the arts are combined with close observation of the natural world.

Safina, Carl. *Song for the Blue Ocean: Encounters Along the World's Coasts and Beneath the Sea.* New York: Holt, 1997.

Sauer, Peter, editor. *Finding Home: Writing on Nature and Culture from Orion Magazine.* Boston: Beacon, 1992.

Schama, Simon. *Landscape and Memory.* New York: Knopf, 1995.

Seton, Ernest Thompson. *Wild Animals I Have Known.* Toronto: McClelland & Stewart, 1996. From previous generation of nature writers—the naturalists of the early twentieth century—Seton's portraits of animals and their ways remind us that animals are more than just "sightings" in a species count.

Shehan, Kathryn and Mary Waidner. *Earth Child: Games, Stories, Activities, Experiments & Ideas About Living Lightly on Planet Earth.* Tulsa, Okla.: Council Oak Books, 1991, 1994.

Slovic, Scott and Terrill Dixon. *Being in the World: An Environmental Reader for Writers.* New York: Macmillan, 1993.

Snyder, Gary. *A Place in Space: Ethics, Aesthetics, and Watersheds: New and Selected Prose.* Washington, D.C.: Counterpoint, 1995.

Sobel, David. *Beyond Ecophobia: Reclaiming the Heart in Nature Education.* Geat Barrington, Mass.: Orion Society, 1996.

———. *Children's Special Places: Exploring the Role of Forts, Dens, and Bush Houses in Middle Childhood.* Tucson, Az.: Zephyr Press, 1993.

Stafford, Kim. *Having Everything Right: Essays of Place.* Seattle, Wa.: Sasquatch, 1997.

Steingraber, Sandra. *Living Downstream: A Scientist's Personal Investigation of Cancer and the Environment.* New York: Random House, 1997.

Stine, Annie, editor. *The Earth at Our Doorstep: Contemporary Writers Celebrate the Landscapes of Home.* San Francisco: Sierra Club Books, 1996.

Stokes, Donald. *A Guide to Winter: Northeast and North Central America.* Boston: Little, Brown, 1979.

Sullivan, Robert. *The Meadowlands: Wilderness Adventures at the Edge of a City.* New York: Anchor Books, 1999. Part travelogue, part natural history, part social history of a place where nature has coexisted unpeacefully with the most awful industrial pollution you can imagine, for over a hundred years.

Thomashow, Mitchell. *Ecological Identity.* Cambridge, Mass.: MIT Press, 1995.

Thoreau, Henry David. *Walden.* Many editions. One of the great classics of nature writing.

Trimble, Stephen, editor. *Words from the Land: Encounters with Natural History Writing.* Reno: University of Nevada Press, 1995.

Turner, Jack. *The Abstract Wild.* Tucson: University of Arizona, 1996.

Tweit, Susan. *Seasons in the Desert: A Naturalist's Notebook.* New York: Chronicle Books, 1998. Illustrated essays about flora and fauna in the deserts of the Southwest.

Wessels, Tom. *Reading the Forested Landscape: A Natural History of New England.* Woodstock, VT: The Countryman Press, 1997.

White, Jonathan. *Talking on the Water: Conversations about Nature and Creativity.* San Francisco: Sierra Club Books, 1994.

Williams, Terry Tempest. *Refuge: An Unnatural History of Family and Place.* New York: Pantheon, 1991.

———. *An Unspoken Hunger: Stories from the Field.* New York: Vintage, 1994.

Wordsworth, Dorothy. *Grasmere Journals.* Oxford: Oxford University Press, 1933.

Zwinger, Ann, et al. *Into the Field: A Guide to Locally Focused Teaching.* Great Barrington, Mass.: Orion Society, 1999. Essays by Clare Walker Leslie, John Tallmadge, and Tom Wessels.

Zwinger, Susan, and Ann Zwinger,. editors. *Women in Wilderness.* New York: Harcourt Brace Jovanovich with Tehabi Press, 1995. A fine sampling of contemporary women's work in natural history.

POETRY

Ackerman, Diane. *Jaguar of Sweet Laughter: New and Selected Poems.* New York: Random House, 1991. Ackerman's subjects range from the Amazon rain forest to Antarctica.

Ammons, A. R. *The Really Short Poems of A. R. Ammons.* New York: Norton, 1990. Many of Ammons's poems have a quality and tone of haiku, and provide excellent models for teaching imagery, simile, and metaphor.

Arnold, Bob. *By Heart: Pages from a Lost Vermont, a Collection of Poems and Essays.* Novato, Calif.: Origin Press, 1991.

———. *Once in Vermont.* Edited by Jonathan Greene. Frankfort, Ky.: Gnomon Press, 1999.

———. *Where Rivers Meet.* Richmond: Mad River Press Press, 1999.

Berry, Wendell. *Collected Poems.* San Francisco: North Point, 1985. Berry's poems reflect his deep bond with his ancestral home, a farm on a hillside on the Kentucky River.

Bishop, Elizabeth. *The Complete Poems: 1927–1979.* New York: Noonday, 1984.

Bly, Robert, editor. *News of the Universe: Poems of Two-Fold Consciousness.* San Francisco: Sierra Club Books, 1980.

Bruchac, Joseph. *Near the Mountains.* Fredonia, N.Y.: White Pine Press, 1987.

Coleridge, Samuel Taylor. *Poems and Prose.* New York: Random House, 1997.

Daniel, John, editor. *Wild Song: Poems of the Natural World.* Athens: University of Georgia Press, 1998.

Deming, Alison Hawthorne. *The Monarchs.* Baton Rouge: Louisiana State University Press, 1997. A sixty-poem sequence inspired by the migration of the monarch butterfly.

———. *Science and Other Poems.* Baton Rouge: Louisiana State University Press, 1994.

Dickinson, Emily. *Collected Poems.* Many editions.

Dunn, Sara with Alan Scholefield, editors. *Poetry for the Earth: A Collection of Poems from around the World that Celebrate Nature.* New York: Fawcett Columbine, 1991.

Eiseley, Loren. *The Immense Journey.* New York: Random House, 1957.

————. *Notes of an Alchemist.* New York: Scribner's, 1972. One of three fine volumes of poetry that reflect Eiseley's affection for animals and sense of their (and our) place in the vaster landscape of time. Also see his books of essays.

Follett, C. B., editor. *Grrrrr: A Collection of Poems about Bears.* Sausalito, Calif.: Arctos Press, 2000.

Frost, Robert. *The Poetry of Robert Frost.* New York: Holt, Rinehart and Winston, 1987.

Gibson, Margaret. *Earth Elegy.* Baton Rouge: Louisiana State University Press, 1997.

Grennan, Eamon. *Relations: New & Selected Poems.* St. Paul, Minn.: Graywolf, 1998.

Haines, John. *The Owl in the Mask of the Dreamer: Collected Poems.* St. Paul, Minn.: Graywolf, 1996.

Harter, Penny. *Lizard Light: Poems from the Earth.* Santa Fe: Sherman Asher, 1998.

————. *Turtle Blessing.* Albuquerque, N.M.: La Alameda, 1996.

Hirshfield, Jane. *The Lives of the Heart.* New York: HarperCollins, 1997.

Hogan, Linda. *The Book of Medicines.* Minneapolis, Minn.: Coffee House, 1993.

Hopkins, Gerard Manley. *Poems of Gerard Manley Hopkins.* Oxford: Oxford University Press, 1976.

————. *Poems and Prose of Gerard Manley Hopkins.* Edited by W. H. Gardner. New York: Viking, 1990.

Hughes, Ted. *Lupercal.* Boston: Faber and Faber, 1970. Poems.

Keats, John. *The Complete Poems.* New York: Viking Press, 1977.

Kenyon, Jane. *Otherwise: New and Selected Poems.* Minneapolis, Minn.: Graywolf, 1996.

Kinnell, Galway. *Selected Poems.* Boston: Houghton Mifflin, 1982.

————. *Three Books: Body Rags/Mortal Acts, Mortal Words/The Past.* Boston: Houghton Mifflin, 1993. A volume of revised poems from three of Kinnell's earlier works.

Kunitz, Stanley. *Passing Through: The Later Poems, New and Selected.* New York: Norton, 1995. See especially "The Wellfleet Whale."

Lawrence, D. H. *The Complete Poems of D. H. Lawrence.* Edited by Vivian de Sola Pinto and Warren Roberts. New York: Viking, 1967. Excellent animal poems in the section titled "Birds, Beasts and Flowers."

Merrill, Christopher, editor. *The Forgotten Language: Contemporary Poets and Nature.* Salt Lake City: Gibbs Smith, 1991.

Merwin, W. S. *Flower & Hand: Poems 1977-1983.* Port Townsend, Wash.: Copper Canyon, 1997.

Neruda, Pablo. *The Book of Questions.* Translation by William O'Daly. Port Townsend: Copper Canyon Press, 1991.

Niatum, Duane, editor. *Carriers of the Dream Wheel: Contemporary Native American Poetry.* New York: Harper & Row, 1975.

Niedecker, Lorine. *Granite Pail: The Selected Poems of Lorine Niedecker.* San Francisco: North Point, 1985.

O'Hara, Frank. *The Selected Poems of Frank O'Hara.* New York: Random House, 1974.

Oliver, Mary. *New and Selected Poems.* Boston: Beacon, 1992.

———. *American Primitive.* Boston: Little, Brown, 1983.

Pasternak, Boris. *Selected Poems.* Translated by Jon Stallworthy and Peter France. New York: Penguin, 1990.

Piercy, Marge. *The Moon Is Always Female.* New York: Knopf, 1980.

Porter, Anne. *An Altogether Different Language: Poems 1934–1994.* Cambridge, Mass.: Zoland Books, 1994.

Rilke, Rainer Maria. *Duino Elegies.* Translated by David Young. New York: Norton, 1992.

Roberts, Elizabeth and Elias Amidon, editors. *Earth Prayers from around the World.* San Francisco: Harper San Francisco, 1991.

Roethke, Theodore. *The Collected Poems of Theodore Roethke.* New York: Anchor Books/Doubleday, 1975.

Rogers, Pattiann. *Fire-Keeper: New and Selected Poems.* Minneapolis, Minn.: Milkweed, 1994.

Schuyler, James. *The Collected Poems.* New York: Farrar, Straus & Giroux, 1993.

Stafford, William. *The Way It Is: New & Selected Poems.* Saint Paul, Minn.: Graywolf, 1998.

Stevens, Wallace. *Collected Poems.* New York: Vintage, 1990.

Snyder, Gary. *No Nature: New and Selected Poems.* New York: Pantheon, 1992.

Whitman, Walt. *The Complete Poems.* Edited by Frances Murphy. New York: Penguin, 1989.

Williams, William Carlos. *Collected Poems.* Two volumes. Edited by A. Walton Litz and Christopher MacGowan. New York: New Directions, 1986, 1988.

Wordsworth, William. *The Prelude 1799, 1805, 1850.* New York: Norton, 1979.

Wright, James. *Above the River: The Collected Poems of James Wright.* New York: Farrar, Straus & Giroux, 1990.

Young, David. *Seasoning: A Poet's Year.* Columbus: Ohio State University Press, 1999. A series of essays about the seasons, sprinkled liberally with poems (his own and others') and seasonal recipes.

FICTION

Cather, Willa. *O Pioneers!* New York: Houghton Mifflin, 1913.

Colette. *The Collected Stories of Colette.* Translated by Matthew Ward. New York: Noonday, 1984.

Elder, John and Hertha Wong, editors. *Family of Earth and Sky: Indigenous Tales of Nature around the World.* Boston: Beacon, 1994.

Hogan, Linda, Deena Metzger and Brenda Peterson, editors. *Intimate Nature: The Bond Between Women and Animals.* New York: Fawcett Columbine, 1998. Stories, essays, meditations, and poems by more than seventy contributors.

Jewett, Sarah Orne. *The Country of the Pointed Firs.* New York: Anchor, 1954.

Melville, Herman. *Moby-Dick.* Some of the liveliest passages ever written about the sea and its inhabitants (whales, sharks, men). It also contains everything known about the science of cetology at the time it was written.

Ramsay, Jarold, editor. *Coyote Was Going There: Indian Literature of the Oregon Country.* Seattle: University of Washington, 1978.

CHILDREN'S BOOKS

Asch, Frank. *Sawgrass Poems: A View of the Everglades.* Photographs by Ted Levin. New York: Harcourt Brace, 1996.

Bash, Barbara. *Urban Roosts.* Boston: Little, Brown, 1992.

Baylor, Byrd. *The Desert Is Theirs.* New York: Charles Scribner Sons, 1975.

———. *The Other Way to Listen.* New York: Charles Scribner Sons, 1978.

Bruchac, Joseph. *Between Earth and Sky: Legends of Native American Sacred Places.* Illustrated by Thomas Locker. New York: Harcourt Brace, 1996. Ten narrative poems are presented through the frame of Old Bear relating to his nephew Little Turtle, on the meaning and significance of "sacred places." A brief glossary helps children (and teachers) in the pronunciation of Indian names.

Bunting, Eve. *Flower Garden.* Illustrated by Kathryn Hewitt. New York: Bantam Doubleday Dell, 1994. For younger children. A sweet story of a girl and her father making a "garden box" to decorate the sill of their apartment building as a surprise for the girl's mother.

———. *Night Tree.* New York: Harcourt Brace, 1991.

———. *Secret Place.* Illustrated by Ted Rand. New York: Clarion Books, 1996. The portrayal of the city as something dark and forbidding may be a little heavy-handed, but the story of a "secret place" of wilderness in its center is one that city kids will find interesting and familiar.

Burnett, Frances Hodgson. *The Secret Garden.* Many editions.

Burnie, David. *Dictionary of Nature.* New York: Dorling Kindersley, 1994.

Carle, Eric. *The Very Hungry Caterpillar.* New York: Philomel Books, 1994.

———. *The Very Quiet Cricket.* New York: Philomel Books, 1990.

Cole, Joanna and Degen, Bruce. *The Magic School Bus: Inside a Beehive.* New York: Scholastic, Inc., 1996. One of many in the Magic School Bus series.

Cooney, Barbara. *Miss Rumphious.* New York: Viking, 1992.

Cherry, Lynne. *A River Ran Wild.* New York: Harcourt Brace Jovanovich, 1992.

Derby, Sally. *My Steps.* Illustrated by Adjoa J. Burrowes. New York: Lee & Low Books, 1996. A young girl's look at the passing of the seasons from the vantage point of her city stoop.

Fanelli, Sara. *My Map Book.* New York: HarperCollins, 1995.

Fleischman, Paul. *Joyful Noise: Poems for Two Voices.* New York: Harper and Row, 1988.

Frasier, Debra. *On the Day You Were Born.* New York: Harcourt Brace, 1991.

Geisel, Theodore (Dr. Seuss). *The Lorax.* New York: Random House, 1971.

Grahame, Kenneth. *The Wind in the Willows.* Many editions.

Hall, Donald. *Old Home Day.* New York: Harcourt Brace, 1996.

Hasler, Eveline. *Die Blumenstadt (The Flower City).* Translated and illustrated by Stepan Zavrel. In *The Best Children's Books in the World. A Treasury of Illustrated Stories.* Edited by Byron Press. New York: Abrams, 1996. Winner of the Bologna Children's Book Fair's Critici in Erba Prize in 1988, this colorfully illustrated story tells of a grumpy mayor's decree to get rid of all the flowers in the city so that more work might be accomplished. As the town slips into a dark gloom, two children decide they must break into the flower/dream cemetery to return color, life and happiness to their town.

Hesse, Karen. *Come On, Rain!* Illustrated by Jon J. Muth. New York: Scholastic, 1999.

MacLachlan, Patricia. *All the Places to Love.* New York: HarperCollins, 1994.

McCloskey, Robert. *Blueberries for Sal.* New York: Viking, 1976.

————. *One Morning in Maine.* New York: Viking, 1976.

————. *A Time of Wonder.* New York: Viking, 1952.

Martin, Jacqueline Briggs. *The Green Truck Garden Giveaway: A Neighborhood Story and Almanac.* Illustrated by Alec Gillman. New York: Simon and Schuster, 1997. Filled with urban gardening tips and ideas about how gardening can transform people and neighborhoods.

————. *Snowflake Bentley.* Illustrated by Mary Azarian. Boston: Houghton Mifflin, 1998. A story about perseverance and passion for an ideal, and the rewards of looking closely at any given thing.

Matthews, Andrew. *Marduk the Mighty and Other Stories of Creation.* Illustrated by Sheila Moxley. Brookfield, Conn.: The Millbrook Press, 1997. A collection of creation myths from around the world retold by the author. Some of these stories are may be scary for younger children.

Paulsen, Gary. *The Island.* New York: Bantam Doubleday Dell, 1988.

Porter, Gene Stratton. *A Girl of the Limberlost.* New York: HarperCollins, 1999.

Potter, Beatrix. *The Tale of Jemima Puddle-Duck.* Many editions.

Prelutsky, Jack, ed. *The Beauty of the Beast. Poems from the Animal Kingdom.* New York: Knopf, 1997. An anthology of poems depicting the wonders of the animal kingdom.

Pryor, Bonnie. *The House on Maple Street.* New York: Mulberry Books, 1987.

Romanova, Natalia. *Once There Was a Tree.* New York: Penguin, 1985.

Shulevitz, Uri. *Snow.* New York: Farrar, Straus & Giroux, 1998. A city is transformed by snow and a young boy's dreams.

Stafford, William. *The Animal That Drank Up Sound.* New York: Harcourt Brace, 1992.

Tamar, Erika. *The Garden of Happiness.* Illustrated by Barbara Lambase. New York: Harcourt Brace, 1996. There are numerous books about community gardens in the city bringing people together, but this is one of the better ones.

Taylor, Harriet Peck. *Two Days in May.* Illustrated by Leyla Torres. New York: Farrar, Straus & Giroux, 1999. One day a young girl wakes up to see five deer grazing in the garden behind her city apartment building. The story of how they have come to be there and how they eventually leave gives an interesting look at the sometimes uneasy relationship between the natural world and the city.

Torres, Leyla. *Subway Sparrow.* New York: Farrar, Straus & Giroux, 1993. Four strangers are drawn into working together to rescue a trapped sparrow. A good book for younger children.

White, E. B. *Charlotte's Web.* Many editions.

White, T. H. *The Once and Future King.* New York: Ace Books, 1996.

Williams, Vera B. *Cherries and Cherry Pits.* New York: Greenwillow Books, 1986. A little girl transforms a bag of cherries bought on the street into a magical tree that feeds her whole neighborhood.

Williamson, Henry. *Salar the Salmon.* Boston: Little, Brown, 1950. In this book and others (*Tarka the Otter* is another), Williamson follows the life stories of wild creatures with a devotion to immediate sensation, biological information, and vivid language unmatched by other writers.

Yolen, Jane. *Owl Moon.* New York: Philomel, 1987.

RESOURCE ORGANIZATIONS

Action for Nature, 2269 Chestnut St., Suite 263, San Francisco, CA 94123. Tel. (415) 421-2640. Email: action@dnai.com. A U.S. environmental and educational organization whose purpose is to foster respect and affection through personal action. Information on the Web: http://www.actionfornature.org/

Acorn Naturalists, 17821 East 17th St., #103, PO Box 2423, Tustin CA 92781-2423. Tel. (800) 422-8886. E-mail: EMailAcorn@aol.com. A bookseller offering over 4,000 titles on science and environmental education, nature writing, and field research. Information and catalogue on the web: http://www.acornnaturalists.com/.

The Center for Eco-Literacy, 2522 San Pablo Ave.,Berkeley, CA 94702. Tel. (510) 845-4595. Email: ecolit@ziplink.net. Dedicated to fostering children's experience and understanding of the natural world.

EE-Link. A comprehensive list of environmental education websites. http://www.eelink.net/

The Elementary Science Integration Project (ESIP), Department of Education, University of Maryland Baltimore County, 1000 Hilltop Circle, Baltimore MD 21250. Tel.: (410) 455-2373. E-mail: esip@umbc.edu. Mainly focused on teaching science to K-8 students, this organization is also involved in teaching nature writing in urban and suburban settings.
Information on the web: http://www.research.umbc.edu/~saul/

The Field Museum, 1400 South Lake Shore Drive, Chicago IL 60605-2496. Tel.: (312) 922-9410. Open 9 a.m. to 5 p.m. every day of the year except Christmas and New Year's Day. (Summer hours: 8 a.m. to 5 p.m.) One of the leading natural history museums in the United States. Their web site includes: field reports filed by working archeologists and anthropologists, research and writing activities for students, and virtual exhibitions. Information on the web: http://www.fieldmuseum.org/

The Orion Society, 195 Main St., Great Barrington, MA 01230. Tel. (413) 528-4422. The Orion Society runs a wide range of programs; it is an environmental education organization, a support network for grassroots envionmental groups, and a publisher. Of particular interest to teachers are Orion's numerous education inititives. The Stories in the Land Teaching Fellowships are annual grants to teachers developing place-based curricula. Teachers will also find the books in Orion's Nature Literacy series highly useful. *Orion Magazine* is published four times a year. The writing—by contributors such as Barry Lopez, Terry Tempest Williams, Wendell Berry, and Mary Oliver—is of exceptionally high quality, as are the photographs; each issue is junior high-plus appropriate. To join a listserv about nature writing, go to the-commons@orionsociety.org. Information on the Web: http://www.orionsociety.org/

Project Learning Tree: Environmental Education Activity Guide (Pre-K–8). The American Forest Foundation/Project Learning Tree, 1111 19th Street NW, Suite 780, Washington, DC 20036. To get this wide-ranging and enjoyable curriculum you must attend a Project Learning Tree training workshop. Workshops are held throughout the United States, and sometimes have a nominal fee of approximately $10. They're an amazing value, and well worth your time. Information on the Web: http://www.plt.org/

River of Words, 1847 Berkeley Way, Berkeley, CA 94703. Tel. (510) 433-7020. Founded by Pamela Mitchell and former Poet Laureate Robert Hass, River of Words runs an annual poetry and art contest for kids. Works must be based on watershed themes, and winners are published and flown to an awards ceremony in Washington, D.C. River of Words also publishes a Teacher's Guide, which is available for $10. Information the Web: http://www.riverofwords.org/

The Roger Tory Peterson Institute of Natural History, 311 Curtis St., Jamestown, NY 14701-9620. Tel. (716) 665-2473. Named in honor of the famous naturalist, the Peterson Institute hosts exhibitions, houses a library of work by naturalists, and runs education programs, including workshops for teachers. Information on the Web: http://www.rtpi.org/

Notes on Contributors

ELEANOR J. BADER is an activist and writer who lives in Brooklyn, N.Y. She is a regular contributor to *Library Journal, Sojourner: The Women's Forum,* and *Lilith.*

BARBARA BASH is the author and illustrator of several books on natural history for children, including *Urban Roosts: Where Birds Nest in the City* (Sierra Club Books). She has also worked for many years as a calligrapher and as a teacher of book arts and nature journaling. She now lives in the Hudson Valley of New York with her husband and son.

JOSEPH BRUCHAC is a poet, writer, and storyteller whose work often reflects his Abenaki Indian ancestry and his love of the natural world. His books include *Keepers of the Earth* (Fulcrum), *Between Earth and Sky* (Voyager), *No Borders* (Holy Cow!), *Crazy Horse's Vision* (Lee & Low), and *Lasting Echoes* (Camelot). With his wife Carol and his son James, he directs the Greenfield Review Literary Center, a non-profit organization devoted to the promotion of contemporary literature and wilderness through the Greenfield Review Press and the Ndakinna Wilderness Center (Web sites at greenfieldreview.com, nativeauthors.com, and ndakinna.com).

JACK COLLOM teaches poetry to K–12 students in Colorado schools and to B.A and M.F.A. students at Naropa University. His many books of poetry include *Dog Sonnets* (Jensen-Daniels) and *Poemics* (with Anselm Hollo and Anne Waldman, published by Autonomedia). *Red Car Goes By: Selected Poems* is forthcoming from Tuumba Press. Collom is the author of two books on teaching writing, *Poetry Everywhere: Teaching Poetry Writing in School and in the Community* (with Sheryl Noethe, Teachers & Writers Collaborative) and *Moving Windows: Evaluating the Poetry Children Write* (Teachers & Writers Collaborative).

JORDAN CLARY lives in southern California where she works as a poet-in-the-schools and as a private instructor. Having taught in prisons and continuation schools as well as in college and elementary school classes, she is a strong believer that great literature crosses all boundaries of education and social status. She has published poetry and non-fiction in a number of literary journals; some recent publications include *Red Rocks* and *Hawaii Pacific Review.*

CAROLYN DUCKWORTH writes for environmental education organizations about natural history and issues such as salmon recovery, wolf reintroduction, and bison management—subjects she has explored in essays that have appeared in *Whole Terrain* and *Northern Lights.*

MARGOT FORTUNATO GALT is the author of *The Story in History: Writing Your Way into the American Experience* (Teachers & Writers Collaborative) and four other books of poetry and nonfiction, the most recent of which is *Stop This War: Americans Protest the Vietnam Conflict* (Lerner). She teaches in the graduate school of Hamline University in St. Paul and in the Minnesota Writers-in-the-Schools program. Her work has received awards from The Loft, the Center for Art Criticism, the Jerome Foundation, the Minnesota Historical Society, and the Minnesota State Arts Board. She is currently writing a mother-daughter memoir about travels to Germany and Italy.

BARRY GILMORE teaches English and Creative Writing at Lausanne Collegiate School in Memphis, Tennessee. He is the author of *Drawing the Line: Creative Writing through the Visual and Performing Arts* (Calendar Islands), and contributed to the T&W book *Classics in the Classroom*. He is also a professional musician.

In addition to articles for teachers, CYNDE GREGORY writes adult fiction and chapter books for young readers. Her books include *Childmade: Awakening Children to Creative Writing* (Station Hill), and *Quick & Easy Learning Centers 1st–3rd: Writing* and *Twenty-five Ways to Turn Bored Writers into Brilliant Ones* (Scholastic). Her poetry, fiction, and nonfiction have appeared in many journals, magazines, and anthologies, including *North Country, The Beloit Poetry Journal,* and *Instructor.* She is currently completing *Write with Joy: A Handbook for Teachers, Parents, and Everybody Else,* from which her essay in this book was taken.

PENNY HARTER is the author of fifteen books of poems, most recently *Turtle Blessing* (La Alameda Press) and *Lizard Light: Poems from the Earth* (Sherman Asher Publishing). For many years she was a visiting poet for the New Jersey State Council on the Arts and the Geraldine R. Dodge Foundation. She has received awards from the New Jersey State Council on the Arts, the Dodge Foundation, and the Poetry Society of America. She lives in Santa Fe, New Mexico, where she teaches English at Santa Fe Preparatory School.

TERRY HERMSEN has worked with the Ohio Arts Council's Writers in the Schools program since 1973, and has published poems in many journals, including *Descant, South Dakota Review, The Journal, Outerbridge, Orion,* and *Confluence.* His two chapbooks, *36 Spokes: Bicycle Poems* and *Child Aloft in Ohio Theatre,* were published by Bottom Dog Press. With Robert Fox, he co-edited *Teaching Writing from a Writer's Point of View* (NCTE), an anthology of essays from writers and classroom teachers reflecting the lessons and experiences of poetry-in-the-schools.

WILLIAM J. HIGGINSON has made his living for many years as a visiting poet and writing consultant to schools in New Jersey and New Mexico. His work as a translator and literary historian has resulted in *The Haiku Handbook* (Kodansha), written in collaboration with his wife, the poet and teacher Penny Harter; *The Haiku Seasons* (Kodansha), which spells out the connection between haiku and nature; and *Haiku World* (Kodansha), a seasonally organized anthology of over 1,000 poems from fifty countries with commentary in the traditional Japanese manner. He writes and teaches in Santa Fe, New Mexico.

SUSAN KARWOSKA has taught writing in the classroom with Teachers & Writers Collaborative, in a drug re-hab program for mothers with young children on the Lower East Side, and at Brown University, where she received her M.F.A. in Creative Writing. She lives in Brooklyn with her husband and three children, and is at work on a novel.

CLARE WALKER LESLIE is a wildlife artist, naturalist, and educator. She is the author of six books, including *Nature Journaling* (Storey Books) and *The Art of Field Sketching* (Kendall-Hunt). She conducts workshops and classes at colleges, schools, and nature centers, including Williams College and Massachusetts College of Art. She lives in Cambridge, Mass., and Vermont.

CHRISTIAN MCEWEN was born in London and grew up in the Borders of Scotland. She teaches poetry to teachers through the Creative Arts in Learning program at Lesley College, and has worked as a writer-in-the-schools for ALPS, City Lore, and Teachers & Writers Collaborative. McEwen is the editor of *Jo's Girls: Tomboy Tales of High Adventure, True Grit, and Real Life* (Beacon) and *Naming the Waves: Contemporary Lesbian Poetry* and *Out the Other Side: Contemporary Lesbian Writing* (Crossing Press). Her poems, articles, and reviews have appeared in *Granta, The American Voice, The Nation,* and *The Voice Literary Supplement.* Christian McEwen's residencies at Central Valley were funded by ALPS (Alternative Literary Programs), which received *per capita* funding form the New York State Council on the Arts. She would like to thank Michael Rutherford for his support.

SUZANNE ROGIER MARSHALL is a language arts resource teacher at the Potomac School in McLean, Virginia. She has been teaching reading and writing since 1971 in public, private, and international schools. Drawing on her experiences as a teacher, she has published articles on poetry writing with the National Council of Teachers of English and a book, *A Falling Leaf and Other Poetry Activities* (Learning Publications).

HOLLY MASTURZO is the Field Supervisor and a Writer-in-Residence for Writers in the Schools (WITS) in Houston, Texas. She has a Ph.D. in Literature and Creative Writing from the University of Houston and teaches in those areas at the university level and in grades one through eight. She also works with several programs to foster personal and professional development for teachers of writing and literature. A native of Florida, she is completing a manuscript of prose and prose poems on the natural and cultural diversity of the Gulf Coast.

MICHAEL MORSE lives in New York City and teaches English at the Ethical Culture Fieldston School and poetry workshops for the Gotham Writers' Workshop. A nominee for Pushcart Prizes in 1994 and 1999, he has an M.F.A. in poetry from the University of Iowa. His poems have appeared in *The Colorado Review, Iowa Review, Antioch Review, Field, Spinning Jenny,* and *Fine Madness.* His essay on teaching the poetry of Margaret Walker appeared in *Sing the Sun Up: Creative Writing Ideas from African American Literature* (Teachers & Writers Collaborative). He has taught poetry in the schools for Teachers & Writers Collaborative, as well as undergraduate courses at the University of Iowa and the City University of New York.

MARY OLIVER is the author of more than fourteen books of poetry aand essays. She has won the Pulitzer Prize in Poetry and the National Book Award, and is on the Literature faculty of Bennington College. Her most recent book is *The Leaf and the Cloud,* a poem (Da Capo Press).

CAROL F. PECK was Writer-in-Residence at Sidwell Friends School in Washington, D.C., for thirteen years. She taught poetry writing at University of Maryland University College for over thirty years and still does workshops as one of Maryland's original Poets in the Schools. Currently she is specializing in writing with fringe populations: hospice patients, people in prison, and teens at risk. She has published articles, essays, children's musicals, and poetry in numerous educational and literary journals, including *Michigan Quarterly Review, New Virginia Review, Christian Science Monitor,* and *Teachers & Writers* and the anthology *Classics in the Classroom* (Teachers & Writers Collaborative). Her own books include *From Deep Within: Poetry Workshops in Nursing Homes* and *"I Ain't Gonna Write No Pome!"*

SARAH JUNIPER RABKIN teaches in the Writing Program and the Environmental Studies Department at the University of California, Santa Cruz. Her essays, articles, columns, and reviews have appeared in regional and national publications, including *Writing Nature, Interdisciplinary Studies in Literature and*

Environment, and *Storming Heaven's Gate: An Anthology of Spiritual Writings by Women.* She has led outdoor writing and illustrated journal workshops in California, Utah, Colorado, Alaska, and Wisconsin.

CHARLES E. ROTH is a science and environmental teacher and the author of twenty books. He was Director of Education for the Massachusetts Audubon Society and has received several awards for his environmental work, including the Environmental Merit Award of the EPA. He lives in Massachusetts and New Hampshire.

GARY SNYDER is an poet, essayist, mountaineer, and Buddhist ecologist. He lives in the Sierra Nevada just north of the South Yuba River. He teaches part-time at the University of California, Davis. His most recent book is *The Gary Snyder Reader* (Counterpoint).

MATTHEW SHARPE is the author of *Nothing Is Terrible* (Random House), a novel, and *Stories from the Tube* (Villard), a collection of short stories. He teaches at Columbia University, and has been teaching New York City public school students under the auspices of Teachers & Writers Collaborative for nine years.

KIM STAFFORD directs the Northwest Writing Institute at Lewis & Clark College in Portland, Oregon. He is the author of *A Thousand Friends of Rain: New & Selected Poems* (Carnegie-Mellon University Press) and *Having Everything Else Right: Essays of Place* (Sasquatch Books).

MARK STATMAN's poetry, fiction, and essays have appeared in numerous journals and collections, including *Conduit, The Village Voice,* and *The Nation.* Statman is the author of *Listener in the Snow: The Practice and Teaching of Poetry* (Teachers & Writers Collaborative), and is a recipient of fellowships from the National Endowment for the Arts and the National Writers Project. Since 1985, Statman has taught writing for Teachers & Writers Collaborative and at Eugene Lang College of New School University.

One of SAM SWOPE's children's books, *The Arboolies of Liberty Street,* is being made into an opera. Swope is a founder of Chapbooks.com, an online book publishing service for teachers, students, and others. He has taught writing for Teachers & Writers Collaborative since 1988. Swope acknowledges the Spencer Foundation, the Overbrook Foundation, and the Thomas Phillips and Jane Moore Johnson Foundation for their support of his work.

JOHN TALLMADGE is Core Professor in Literature and Environmental Studies at the Graduate School of the Union Institute. He is author of *Meeting the Tree of Life* (University of Utah), a memoir of teaching, nature writing, and wildernes travel.

MARY EDWARDS WERTSCH is author of *Military Brats: Legacies of Childhood inside the Fortress* (Aletheia). She is primarily a writer of nonfiction. Her passion for teaching poetry writing to children was born in 1994 after reading two books published by Teachers & Writers. She has been teaching ever since, primarily through St. Louis's Springboard to Learning program, which serves inner-city children, and Young Audiences.

JANINE POMMY VEGA is a poet, teacher, and performer. Her most recent books are *Mad Dogs of Trieste: New and Selected Poems* (Black Sparrow) and *Tracking the Serpent: Journeys to Four Continents* (City Lights). She is the director of Incisions/Arts, an organization that works with writers in prison.

ANN ZWINGER writes about natural history from her home place in the mountains of Colorado to the Robinson Crusoe Islands in the Pacific or Kapiti Island off New Zealand. Her latest books are *The Nearsighted Naturalist* (University of Arizona Press) and *Shaped by Wind and Water: Reflections of a Naturalist* (Milkweed). She was awarded the John Burroughs Medal for *Run, River, Run,* and recently received the John Hay Award of the Orion Society.

OTHER T&W BOOKS YOU MIGHT ENJOY

The Teachers & Writers Handbook of Poetic Forms, edited by Ron Padgett. The new revised edition of this T&W bestseller includes 76 entries on traditional and modern poetic forms by 19 poet-teachers. "A treasure"—*Kliatt*. "A small wonder!"—*Poetry Project Newsletter*. "An entertaining reference work"—*Teaching English in the Two-Year College*. "A solid beginning reference source"—*Choice*.

Poetry Everywhere: Teaching Poetry Writing in School and in the Community by Jack Collom and Sheryl Noethe. This big and "tremendously valuable resource work for teachers" (*Kliatt*) at all levels contains 60 writing exercises, extensive commentary, and 450 examples.

Listener in the Snow: The Practice and Teaching of Poetry by Mark Statman. "Filled with new ideas, a great sense of the magic of teaching writing, and inspiring encouragement to teachers to reach beyond what they've already been doing"—Herbert Kohl.

Luna, Luna: Creative Writing Ideas from Spanish, Latin American, & Latino Literature, edited by Julio Marzán. In 21 lively and practical essays, poets, fiction writers, and teachers tell how they use the work of Lorca, Neruda, Jiménez, Cisneros, and others to inspire students. *Luna, Luna* "succeeds brilliantly . . . [it] not only teaches but guides teachers on how to involve students in the act of creative writing"—*Kliatt*.

Sing the Sun Up: Creative Writing Ideas from African American Literature, edited by Lorenzo Thomas. Twenty teaching writers present exciting ways to motivate students to write imaginatively, inspired by African American poetry, fiction, essays, and drama. Essays discuss work by James Baldwin, Gwendolyn Brooks, Zora Neale Hurston, Jean Toomer, Aimé Césaire, Lucille Clifton, and others.

Classics in the Classroom: Using Great Literature to Teach Writing, edited by Christopher Edgar and Ron Padgett. 19 essays on teaching imaginative writing using Homer, Sappho, Catullus, Ovid, Shakespeare, Rumi, Bashō, Shelley, and others. "Teachers at any level will find ideas and approaches that will enliven their classes"—*Kliatt*.

The T&W Guide to Walt Whitman, edited by Ron Padgett. The first and only guide to teaching the work of Walt Whitman from K–college. "A lively, fun, illuminating book"—Ed Folsom, editor of *The Walt Whitman Quarterly*.

The Teachers & Writers Guide to William Carlos Williams, edited by Gary Lenhart. Seventeen practical and innovative essays on using Williams's short poems, fiction, nonfiction, and long poem *Paterson*. Contributors include Allen Ginsberg, Kenneth Koch, and Julia Alvarez.

Personal Fiction Writing by Meredith Sue Willis. Revised second edition. A complete and practical guide for teachers of writing from elementary through college level. Contains more than 400 writing ideas. "A terrific resource for the classroom teacher as well as the novice writer"—*Harvard Educational Review*.

Tolstoy as Teacher: Leo Tolstoy's Writings on Education, edited by Bob Blaisdell and translated by Christopher Edgar. A collection of Tolstoy's articles about the school he founded on his estate at Yasnaya Polyana. "Teachers of writing at all levels will enjoy this reading experience and all teachers should be renewed by the message"—*Language, Literature, and Literature*.

•

For a complete free T&W publications catalogue, contact
Teachers & Writers Collaborative
5 Union Square West, New York, NY 10003-3306
tel. (toll-free) 888-BOOKS-TW
Visit our World Wide Web site at http://www.twc.org/